Pro Office for iPad

How to Be Productive with Office for iPad

Guy Hart-Davis

Apress®

Pro Office for iPad: How to Be Productive with Office for iPad

ISBN-13 (pbk): 978-1-4302-4587-2

ISBN-13 (electronic): 978-1-4302-4588-9

Managing Director: Welmoed Spahr
Lead Editor: Michelle Lowman
Development Editor: Douglas Pundick
Technical Reviewer: Jennifer Kettell
Editorial Board: Steve Anglin, Mark Beckner, Ewan Buckingham, Gary Cornell, Louise Corrigan, Jim DeWolf, Jonathan Gennick, Robert Hutchinson, Michelle Lowman, James Markham, Matthew Moodie, Jeff Olson, Jeffrey Pepper, Douglas Pundick, Ben Renow-Clarke, Dominic Shakeshaft, Gwenan Spearing, Matt Wade, Steve Weiss
Coordinating Editor: Kevin Walter
Copy Editor: Mary Behr
Compositor: SPi Global
Indexer: SPi Global
Artist: SPi Global
Cover Designer: Anna Ishchenko

Distributed to the book trade worldwide by Springer Science+Business Media New York, 233 Spring Street, 6th Floor, New York, NY 10013. Phone 1-800-SPRINGER, fax (201) 348-4505, e-mail orders-ny@springer-sbm.com, or visit www.springeronline.com. Apress Media, LLC is a California LLC and the sole member (owner) is Springer Science + Business Media Finance Inc (SSBM Finance Inc). SSBM Finance Inc is a Delaware corporation.

For information on translations, please e-mail rights@apress.com, or visit www.apress.com.

Apress and friends of ED books may be purchased in bulk for academic, corporate, or promotional use. eBook versions and licenses are also available for most titles. For more information, reference our Special Bulk Sales–eBook Licensing web page at www.apress.com/bulk-sales.

Any source code or other supplementary material referenced by the author in this text is available to readers at www.apress.com. For detailed information about how to locate your book's source code, go to www.apress.com/source-code/.

This book is dedicated to Rhonda and Edward.

Contents at a Glance

Contents

About the Author

Guy Hart-Davis is the author of more than 100 computer books on subjects including Microsoft Office, iOS devices, Android devices, Macs, and Windows. His other books for Apress include *Learn Office 2011 for Mac and Beginning Office 2010*.

About the Technical Reviewer

Jennifer Ackerman Kettell has written and contributed to dozens of books about software applications, web design, and digital photography. She has worked at Microsoft and other top companies as well as doing freelance web design and online community management. Jenn has lived all over the United States but currently calls upstate New York home.

Acknowledgments

My thanks go to the many people who helped create this book:

- Michelle Lowman for signing me to write the book.

- Douglas Pundick for developing the manuscript.

- Jenn Kettell for reviewing the manuscript for technical accuracy and contributing helpful suggestions.

- Mary Behr for copyediting the manuscript with care and a light touch.

- Kevin Walter for coordinating the book project and keeping things running.

- SPi Global for laying out the chapters of the book.

- SPi Global for creating the index.

Introduction

Your iPad is a fantastic device for both work and play. By adding Microsoft's Office for iPad apps to it, you can turn it into a productivity powerhouse for creating and editing documents and spreadsheets, developing and delivering presentations, and noting down any information you want to keep.

This book shows you how to get the most out of the Office for iPad apps.

Who Is This Book For?

This book is for you—anyone who has an iPad and wants to be productive with it.

All you need to get started is your iPad and the ability to perform basic actions with it, such as navigating the Home screens and launching apps.

Some knowledge of the desktop versions of the Office apps is helpful but not essential. If you've used the desktop versions of the apps, you'll be able to apply your knowledge easily to the iPad versions. But even if you've never used the desktop versions, you'll be able to quickly become an expert with the iPad versions of the apps.

What Does This Book Cover?

This book contains 12 chapters that cover the four Office for iPad apps: Word, Excel, PowerPoint, and OneNote.

Chapter 1 will make sure you know the essentials for getting going with the Office apps on your iPad. You will download, install, and activate the apps if you haven't already done so. You will then learn essential moves such as launching apps, switching among apps, and closing apps when necessary. This chapter will also explain how to choose settings for the apps and how to reset them if problems occur.

Chapter 2 will bring you up to speed with the common tools that the apps share. You will learn to enter and format text, add graphics and shapes, use the Find and Replace tools, and print all or part of your work.

Chapter 3 will show you how to set up your OneDrive and SharePoint services on your iPad so that the Office apps can access them. You will then learn to navigate the file management screens and manage an active document from its File menu. This chapter will also explain how to share your documents with others and how to troubleshoot problems with documents.

Chapter 4 will start by giving you a short tour of the features that Word for iPad has and those it lacks compared to the desktop versions. After that, you will learn how to create new documents, how to navigate the Word interface, and how to enter and edit text in documents. Coverage will include working with tabs and line breaks, using the Paste Options feature, and displaying invisible characters, such as spaces and paragraph marks.

Chapter 5 will tell you what you need to know to format your documents effectively. You will learn how to set the page size, orientation, and margins for a document and how to apply the different types of formatting that Word provides, such as styles and direct formatting. You'll also explore Word's extra features for tables, its sections and newspaper-style columns, and its options for wrapping text around objects.

Chapter 6 will show you how to add headers, footers, and page numbers to your documents. You will also learn how to work with footnotes, endnotes, and comments; how to use the Track Changes feature to mark revisions in your documents and integrate input from multiple authors; and how to edit your documents simultaneously with your colleagues.

Chapter 7 will first make sure you understand the app's features and limitations as compared with the desktop versions. You will then learn how to create a new workbook, navigate the Excel interface, enter data in a worksheet, and customize the view to suit your preferences.

Chapter 8 will explain how to build and format worksheets quickly and efficiently on your iPad. You will start by creating the structure of your workbook by inserting, deleting, and rearranging worksheets; move on to inserting and deleting rows, columns, and cells; and then set column height and row width and hide any rows or columns you don't want people to see. After that, you will dig into formatting cells and ranges, using the Find and Replace features, and sorting and filtering your data to show the records you need. You will finish by looking at how to work with comments and how to print all or part of a workbook.

Chapter 9 will begin by making clear the difference between formulas and functions, and explaining when you use each. You will learn how to refer to cells and ranges, meet the calculation operators that Excel supports, and discover how to use them. You will also learn about common problems that occur with formulas and ways to troubleshoot them.

Chapter 10 will introduce you to Excel for iPad's wide range of chart types and subtypes, and suggest ways of finding a suitable chart to present your data clearly and persuasively. You will learn how to create a chart, change its type and subtype as needed, switch its source data or transpose its rows and columns, and give it the layout and style that will work most effectively. You will also learn how to use your Excel charts in Word documents and PowerPoint presentations.

Chapter 11 will start by covering PowerPoint's features and limitations, putting you in a good position to judge how to use the app most effectively. You will learn to navigate the PowerPoint interface, create a presentation, and add slides to it; how to add, delete, and rearrange the slides; and how to add transition effects to them. You will also find out how to give a presentation from your iPad, either on the iPad's screen or on a projector or monitor connected either via a cable or via AirPlay.

Chapter 12 will get you up to speed on using OneNote for recording, storing, and manipulating information on your iPad. You will learn to navigate OneNote's notebooks, sections, section groups, and pages; add pages and enter notes on them; and share your note pages and notebooks with others.

Chapter 1

Up and Running with Office for iPad

If you need to use Office professionally on your iPad, you're probably raring to get going. This brief chapter provides the essentials to get you up and running with the Office apps on your iPad. The chapter starts by making sure we're on the same page by recapping what Office for iPad is and what you can do with the apps. It then goes through how to download, install, and activate the apps on your iPad. The chapter then covers essential moves such as launching apps, switching among apps, and closing apps when necessary. You'll also learn how to choose settings for the apps and how to reset them when you run into problems. At the end of this chapter, I'll suggest an approach to the thorny problem of sharing an iPad with other people.

Understanding What Office for iPad Is and What You Can Do with It

Microsoft Office for iPad brings Microsoft's market-leading productivity suite to the iPad. At this writing, Office for iPad includes four apps:

- **Word:** Word is a word-processing app that enables you to create a wide range of documents—anything from a single-page letter to a fully laid-out book.

- **Excel:** Excel is a spreadsheet app that you use to record, calculate, and analyze data. Excel also includes features for creating many different types of charts.

■ **PowerPoint:** PowerPoint is an app for creating and delivering presentations. Each presentation consists of slides, to which you can add any data from straightforward text to tables, pictures, and shapes. You can also add transition effects to provide visual interest. You can deliver a presentation directly from PowerPoint for iPad.

■ **OneNote:** OneNote is an app for capturing, organizing, and sharing information. You can create a single notebook or as many notebooks as you need, add to each notebook a wide range of types of digital information (such as text, tables, and pictures), and organize that information into different tabs, sections, and folders.

Each app works similarly to the desktop versions of the Office apps, so if you're familiar with the desktop versions, you'll be able to get started with the iPad versions easily. You'll find that the iPad apps have many fewer features than the desktop versions but that they contain the essential features you need to get your work done. To access these features, use the controls on the tabbed Ribbon that appears at the top of the screen (see Figure 1-1).

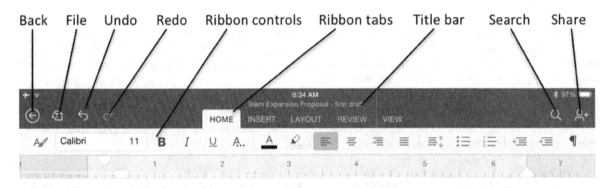

Figure 1-1. Each of the Office apps has a Ribbon that contains controls on various tabs, such as the Home tab and the Insert tab. The Ribbon area also contains essential buttons, such as the File button and the Share button

> **Note**   The chapters on the individual apps dig into the details of which features each iPad app includes and which features it is missing. See Chapter 4 for Word, Chapter 7 for Excel, Chapter 11 for PowerPoint, and Chapter 12 for OneNote.

You can use Word, Excel, and PowerPoint as standalone apps on your iPad, creating documents on the iPad and keeping them there. But the apps also integrate with Microsoft's OneDrive and OneDrive for Business online services, enabling you to store your documents online and work on them from your iPad or a computer. You can also store your documents on a SharePoint server. You can set the apps to automatically sync the changes you make on your iPad to OneDrive, so when you open a document from another computer, you see the latest version of it and can pick up work where you left off.

Unlike Word, Excel, and PowerPoint, OneNote offers online storage only. You must save your OneNote databases online, on OneDrive or SharePoint; you cannot save an OneNote database to your iPad.

Getting Office for iPad

Before you can get started with Office for iPad, you must install the apps on your iPad. You will almost certainly want to buy an Office 365 subscription to enable yourself to use all the features of the apps rather than the limited subset that you can use for free, which enable you to open and read documents but not edit them or create new ones. If you do buy an Office 365 subscription, you use the subscription to activate the apps on your iPad, unlocking the full features.

Downloading and Installing the Office Apps

You can download and install the Office apps in one or other of two ways:

- **Using your iPad:** You use the App Store app to access the App Store.
- **Using your computer:** If you sync your iPad with a computer, you can use iTunes on that computer to download the apps from the App Store. You can then sync the apps to your iPad.

Either approach works fine, so use whichever you find easier. The main advantage to using your computer comes if you sync multiple iPads with it. In this case, you can download the apps once and install them on all your iPads. Otherwise, you'll need to download the apps separately to each iPad, using more bandwidth.

Downloading and Installing the Office Apps Directly to Your iPad

Here's how to download and install the Office apps using your iPad.

1. Press the Home button to display the Home screen.

2. Tap the App Store icon to launch the App Store app.

3. Tap the Search box in the upper-right corner.

4. Type **microsoft office for ipad**. The search results appear.

5. Tap the Free button on the app you want to install first. The Install button appears in place of the Free button.

6. Tap the Install button.

7. If the Sign In to iTunes Store dialog box opens, type your password and tap the OK button.

8. After the App Store app downloads and installs the app, the app appears on the Home screen, and you can launch it by tapping it.

9. Repeat steps 5 and 6 to download and install the other Office apps that you want.

Downloading and Installing the Office Apps Using Your Computer

Here's how to download the Office apps using your computer.

1. Launch iTunes as usual. For example, in Windows, click the iTunes icon on the Start screen; on the Mac, click the iTunes icon on the Dock.

2. Open the iTunes Store by clicking the iTunes Store button in the navigation bar across the top of the window.

3. Click the Apps button in the navigation bar across the top of the window.

4. Click in the Search Store box in the upper-right corner of the iTunes window.

5. Type **microsoft office for ipad** and press Enter or Return. The search results appear.

6. Click the Free button for the app you want to install.

7. If the Sign In to iTunes Store dialog box opens, type your password and click the Sign In button. iTunes then downloads the app.

After downloading one or more of the Office apps to your computer, you can install them on your iPad as follows.

1. Connect your iPad to your computer via USB. iTunes normally opens automatically when your computer detects the iPad; if not, launch iTunes manually by clicking its icon on the Start screen or the Dock.

Note   If you have turned on wireless syncing for your iPad, you can sync it and install the apps without using USB. To start the sync manually, press the Home button, tap the Settings icon to open the Settings app, and then tap General. On the General screen, tap the iTunes Wi-Fi Sync button, and then tap the Sync Now button on the iTunes Wi-Fi Sync screen. Alternatively, you can allow your iPad to sync automatically, which occurs on a schedule when the iPad is connected to a power source.

2.   Display the contents of the iPad. How you do this depends on whether iTunes is displaying the Sidebar or not.

- **Sidebar:** In the Sidebar, first expand the Devices category if it is collapsed: move the mouse pointer over the Devices heading and then click the word Show that appears to the right of Devices. Then click the iPad's entry in the Devices list.

- **Without the sidebar:** Click the iPad button toward the right end of the navigation bar across the top of the iTunes window. If you have multiple iOS devices or iPods connected to your computer, click the Devices button, and then click the iPad's entry on the Devices pop-up menu.

3.   Click the Apps tab to display the Apps screen (see Figure 1-2).

Figure 1-2. On the Apps screen for the iPad, click the Install button for each app you want to install. The button changes to Will Install

4. In the Apps list on the left, click the Install button for each app you want to install. iTunes replaces each Install button you click with a Will Install button.

> **Note**   You can also drag an app from the Apps list to the appropriate screen in the Home Screens box. This method has the advantage of enabling you to choose which screen the app's icon lands on. You can create a new Home screen by clicking the + button in the upper-right corner of the Home Screens box.

5. Click the Apply button. iTunes syncs the apps to your iPad.

6. When the sync is complete, disconnect your iPad.

KEEPING YOUR OFFICE APPS UP TO DATE

Microsoft released the Office apps without various features that most people would regard as essential, such as printing documents. But Microsoft is continuing to develop the Office apps quickly and is adding features to them. So to get the most out of the Office apps, it's important to install updates to them.

You can download and install updates either directly on your iPad or by using the computer with which you sync your iPad. Working on the iPad is usually easier unless you need to install the updates on multiple devices, in which case you may prefer to download them to your computer and then sync them to each iPad.

On your iPad, open the App Store app and tap the Updates button on the tab bar at the bottom to display the Updates page. You can then tap the Install button to download and install an available update.

If you want your iPad to download updates automatically, open the Settings app, tap iTunes & App Store in the left column, and then set the Updates switch in the Automatic Downloads section to On. If you have a cellular iPad with a meager data plan, you may want to set the Use Cellular Data switch on the iTunes & App Store screen to Off if you set the Updates switch to On. Otherwise, large app updates can eat through your data plan quickly. The Use Cellular Data switch also controls whether your iPad uses the cellular connection for iTunes Radio and iTunes Match.

To check for updates on your computer, click the Apps button on the navigation bar in iTunes, and then click the Updates tab that appears. If updates are available, click the Update All Apps button to download the updates. You can also click an individual app to display a pop-up panel showing the details and then click the Update button to download only the update for that app.

After downloading the updates, connect your iPad to your computer and sync the updates to the iPad.

Buying an Office 365 Subscription

You can download the Office apps for free from the App Store. If you need only to be able to read existing Office documents on your iPad, you can use the apps for free. But if you want to be able to create new documents and edit existing ones, you must buy a subscription to Microsoft's Office 365 service and activate the apps to use it.

Microsoft offers enough Office 365 plans to be confusing: Office 365 Home, Office 365 Personal, Office 365 Small Business, Office 365 Small Business Premium, Office 365 Midsize Business, three Office 365 Enterprise plans, Office 365 ProPlus, and then three Office 365 Education Plans. The following list suggests a straightforward approach to this morass of versions. But because Microsoft compounds the confusion by often changing the details of the plans, make sure you check online at office.microsoft.com to find the latest information.

- If you're a home user, buy Office 365 Home ($9.99 per month or $99.99 per year). This allows you to install Office on up to five PCs or Macs, use Office on up to five iPads or Windows tablets, and gives you 20GB extra storage for each of up to five users. This is a much better deal than Office 365 Personal ($6.99 per month or $69.99 per year, which covers a single PC or Mac, a single iPad or Windows tablet, and gives 20GB extra storage for a solitary user.

Note If you have a Mac and run Windows on it using Boot Camp, you can install Office on Windows as well as on OS X. These count as separate installs even though they're on the same physical computer, so you'd normally want to buy Office 365 Home. Installing Office on a Windows or OS X virtual machine (running on top of Windows, OS X, or another operating system) also counts as a separate installation.

- If you're a small-to-medium business user, you'll need to decide between Office 365 Small Business Premium ($12.50 per user per month) and Office 365 Midsize Business ($15.00 per user per month). The main difference between the two is that Office 365 Small Business Premium is limited to a maximum of 25 users and does not have Active Directory integration, whereas Office 365 Midsize Business does have Active Directory integration and goes up to 300 users.

Caution Office 365 Small Business looks like a great bargain at $5.00 per user per month, but it doesn't include Office for iPad. You need to go up to Office 365 Small Business Premium ($12.50 per user per month) to get Office for iPad.

- If you're an enterprise user, look at the Office 365 Enterprise E3 plan and Office 365 Enterprise A4 plan, which both include Office for iPad.
- If you're in education, see if your institution has signed up for any of the Office 365 Education plans. The Office 365 Education A3 plan and Office 365 Education A4 plan include Office for iPad, whereas the Office 365 Education A2 plan does not.

Activating the Office Apps on Your iPad

Now that you have your Office 365 subscription, you're ready to activate the Office apps on your iPad. You activate the apps by linking them to your Office 365 subscription. You need perform the activation sequence on only one of the apps.

To activate the apps, follow these steps.

1. Press the Home button to display the Home screen.

2. Navigate to the Home screen that contains one of the apps.

3. Tap the icon for the app. The Office screen appears.

4. Scroll through the screens, reading the information until you reach the Sign in now screen (see Figure 1-3).

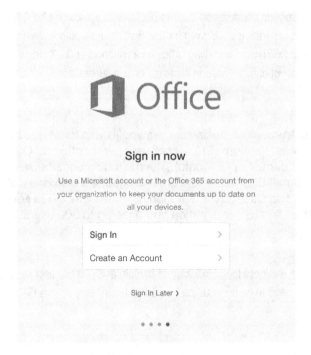

Figure 1-3. On the Sign In Now screen, tap the Sign In button to sign in to your account and activate the Office apps

Note   If you don't yet have an Office 365 account, you can tap the Create an Account button on the Sign In Now screen to take you to a page for creating one. But if you have a computer available, you may prefer to use that instead to create your account so that you can enter your information more easily. If you just want to use Office to view documents, tap the Sign In Later button.

5. Tap the Sign In button. The Sign In screen appears.

6. Type the e-mail address associated with your Office 365 subscription.

7. Tap the Next button. The OneDrive screen appears.

8. Type your password.

9. Tap the Sign In button. The Help Us Improve screen appears.

Note The error message "You need to do something extra before we can sign you in" normally indicates that the Office 365 account type you have does not include Office for iPad. The "something extra" involves signing up for an account that does include Office for iPad (and paying more). This error message may also mean that your password has expired, in which case the fix is to change the password.

---

10. Tap the Send (Recommended) button or the Don't Send button, depending on whether you want to send anonymized usage information to Microsoft.

Note The You're All Set! screen includes buttons you can tap to download the other Office apps than the one you are using. This is handy if you haven't already downloaded the other apps you want. The buttons appear even if you have already downloaded and installed the other apps.

---

11. Tap the Continue button. The You're All Set! screen appears.

12. Tap the Start Using App button (where "App" is the app's name). The app opens, and you can begin using it.

Activating the Office apps on your iPad links them to your Office 365 account and sets up the service associated with the Office 365 account, enabling you to connect to your account on the OneDrive service or the OneDrive for Business service.

Note OneDrive used to be called SkyDrive. Microsoft renamed the service to OneDrive after a trademark dispute. You can use the OneDrive app to manage files on OneDrive.

DELETING THE OFFICE APPS FROM YOUR IPAD

You can delete the Office apps from your iPad using the standard technique for any app you have installed on it. Deleting an app deletes all its data, including documents you have saved on your iPad in the app and unsynced changes to online documents. So before you delete an app, you should sync any recent changes to online documents and copy to your computer any documents saved on the iPad that you want to keep. See Chapter 2 for instructions on copying files to your computer using iTunes.

Here's how to remove an Office app from your iPad.

1. Press the Home button to display the Home screen.

2. Navigate to the Home screen that contains the app you want to remove.

3. Tap and hold the app's icon until the icons start jiggling. An X appears on the upper-left corner of each app you can remove.

4. Tap the X button on the app. The Delete dialog box opens, warning you that deleting the app will also delete all its data.

5. Tap the Delete button. iOS deletes the app and its data.

6. Press the Home button again to stop the icons from jiggling.

Opening and Closing the Apps

On your iPad, as on most computers, you open an app you want to use. You can then switch to other apps as needed. When you no longer need an app you've opened, you can close it manually.

Opening an App from the Home Screen

The most straightforward way to open is by tapping its icon on the Home screen. Follow these steps.

1. Press the Home button to display the Home screen.

2. If the app's icon doesn't appear on the first home screen that appears, scroll left or right until you find it.

> **Tip**   If your iPad is packed with apps, you can search for the app by tapping and pulling down on the Home screen to display the search box and the keyboard, and then starting to type the app's name.

3. Tap the app's icon to launch the app.

Launching an App by Opening a Document

You can also launch an app by opening a document of a type associated with the app. For example, if you receive a Word document attached to an e-mail message, you can open the document in Word like this.

1. In the Mail app, tap the message to open it.

2. Tap and hold the attachment's icon to display the Share sheet.

3. Tap the Open in Word icon on the Share sheet.

Tip   If you want to preview the document before opening it in Word, tap the attachment's icon in the message to open the attachment in the document viewer. You can then tap the Share button to display the Share sheet and tap the Open in Word icon (or the Open In icon for another app) if you want to open the document.

Switching Among Apps

You can return to a running app by pressing the Home button and then tapping the app's icon on the Home screen, but you can save time by using the app-switching feature.

1. Press the Home button twice in quick succession to display the app-switching screen.

2. Scroll left or right to find the app you want (see Figure 1-4). The Home screen appears at the left end of the list of apps on the app-switching screen, with the apps you've used most recently following it, so you can go to the Home screen by swiping right to scroll left.

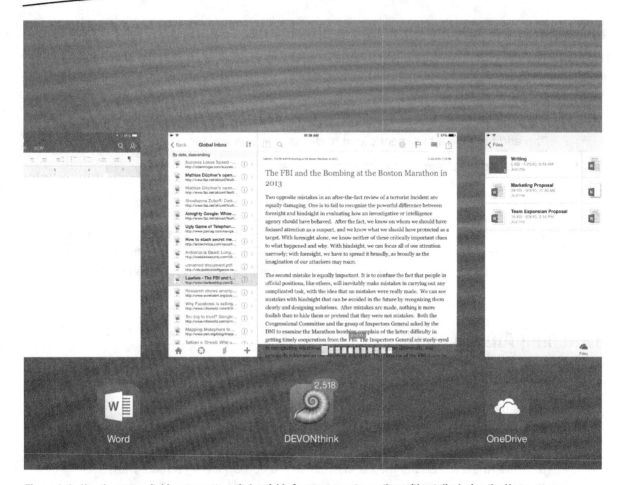

Figure 1-4. Use the app-switching screen to switch quickly from one app to another without displaying the Home screen

3. Tap the app you want to use.

Making the Office Apps' Icons Easy to Access

To make launching the Office apps easier, place them either on the first Home screen or on the favorites tray. Here are the moves you can use.

- **Unlock the Home screen for customization:** Tap and hold any icon until the icons start jiggling.

- **Move an icon:** Drag an icon to where you want it to appear. To move an icon from one screen to the previous screen, drag it to the left edge of the screen, hold it until the previous screen appears, and then continue the drag operation. To move an icon to the next screen, drag it to the right edge of the screen.

- **Create a folder:** Drag an icon onto another icon. iOS creates a folder containing the two icons. You can then rename the folder and add further apps to it.

- **Add apps to the favorites tray:** The favorites tray can contain up to six apps. To add an app, drag it to the favorites tray, wait for the other icons to make space for it, and then drop it. To remove an app, drag it off the favorites tray.

- **Add a folder to the favorites tray:** After creating a folder on a Home screen, you can drag it to the favorites tray. You can't create a folder directly on the favorites tray.

Closing an App

On the iPad, an app keeps running unless you close it. iOS manages the memory efficiently enough that, in general, you can simply leave apps open and then return to them as needed.

But if your iPad starts running more slowly, or if you find a particular app is no longer responding to the touchscreen, you can close it manually. To close the app, follow these steps.

1. Press the Home button twice in quick succession to display the app-switching screen.

2. Scroll right to find the app you want to close.

Tip   Your current app appears as the left icon on the part of the app-switching screen that appears first. To the left of this app is the Home screen; to its right are the other apps that are running, sorted from those you've used most recently to those you haven't used for longest. You can't close the Home screen.

---

3. Drag or flick the app up off the app-switching screen. iOS closes the app.

WHAT HAPPENS WHEN YOU POWER DOWN YOUR IPAD?

Apple designed your iPad to keep running iOS continuously unless a problem occurs, so you don't normally need to restart your iPad in order to keep it working well. But if your iPad starts acting oddly or running unstably, restarting it is a good troubleshooting move. A restart forces your iPad to clear all the running processes out of memory, so it can resolve various types of minor instabilities.

To restart your iPad, press and hold the Power button until the "slide to power off" prompt appears, and then drag the slider to the right. Your iPad displays a progress indicator onscreen as it powers down; when the iPad turns off, the indicator disappears, and the screen goes dark. You can then restart the iPad by pressing and holding the Power button until the Apple logo appears on the screen. When the lock screen appears, slide your finger across the screen to start unlocking it, and then enter your passcode or other unlock method.

One thing that's confusing is that when you restart your iPad like this, iOS automatically preloads all the apps that were running when you gave the power-off command. This behavior is great if you actually want to have those apps running because it means you don't have to launch each of them manually after the restart. But if the reason you're restarting your iPad is to free up memory, close all the apps before you restart it. To close the apps, press the Home button twice in quick succession to display the app-switching screen, and then swipe each app upward to close it. After you close the last app, press and hold the Power button, and then drag the "slide to power off" slider to shut down the iPad.

Choosing Settings and Resetting the Apps

Unlike the desktop versions of the Office app, each of which has hundreds of settings you can configure to make the app work the way you prefer, the Office for iPad apps have almost no settings. In fact, the main features of the Settings screen for each app are the version number and the Reset button, which you can use to reset the app if things go wrong.

Choosing Settings

To choose settings for one of the apps, open the Settings app and display the screen for the app. Follow these steps.

1. Press the Home button to display the Home screen.

2. Tap the Settings icon to open the Settings app.

3. Scroll down in the left column, and then tap the app's name in the last group to display the Settings screen.

Figure 1-5 shows the Settings screen for OneNote.

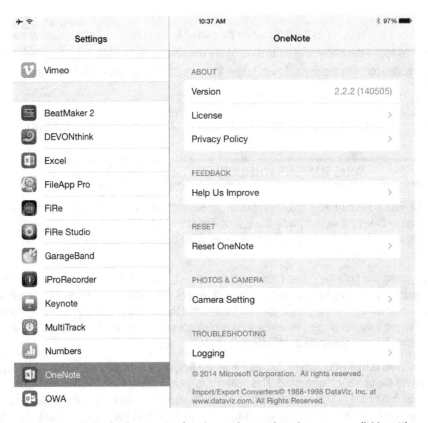

Figure 1-5. *Open an app's screen in the Settings app to view the version number, choose any available settings, or reset the app*

Here's what you can do on the Settings screen for each of the apps:

- **Version:** Look at this readout to learn the version number, which you may need to know when troubleshooting the app.

- **License:** Tap this button to display a link to the app's license.

- **Privacy Policy:** Tap this button to display a link to the app's privacy policy.

- **Help Us Improve:** Tap this button to display the Help Us Improve screen, on which you can set the Send Usage Data switch to the On position or to the Off position, as appropriate. The apps send the usage data only over Wi-Fi (so they don't use up your data plan on a cellular iPad) and anonymously, so turning this feature on is a good idea.

- **Reset:** Tap this button to display the Reset screen for the app. The next section explains how to reset an app.

These are the extra settings you can choose in OneNote and Word:

- **Camera Setting (OneNote):** Tap this button to display the Camera Setting screen, on which you can set the Use Office Lens switch to the On position or to the Off position, as needed. Office Lens is a feature for straightening out photos that you take at an angle, such as when photographing a whiteboard in a meeting.

- **Logging (OneNote):** Tap this button to display the Logging screen, on which you can set the Enable Logging switch to the On position or to the Off position. Keep logging turned off unless you are working with Microsoft Support to resolve an issue.

- **AutoFormat As You Type (Word):** Set the AutoFormat As You Type switch to the On position if you want Word to automatically apply formatting as you type (see Chapter 4 for the details). If you prefer not to use automatic formatting, set this switch to the Off position.

Resetting an Office App

If things go wrong with one of the Office apps, you may need to reset the app to get it working again properly. These are the two things that are most likely to go wrong:

- **The documents in your document cache become corrupted:** The Office apps store documents you download from OneDrive or SharePoint in an area called the *document cache*. If problems occur when you are syncing documents, the copies in the document cache may become corrupted. The solution to this problem is to clear the document cache and download the files again. You can clear the document cache for each app separately, so clearing the document cache for Excel doesn't affect the document cache for Word.

> **Caution**   Before clearing the document cache, it is a good idea to back up the files it contains to your computer. You may also need to download the recovered files to your computer after clearing the cache. I'll explain how to perform both these moves in Chapter 3.

- **The apps start refusing your login credentials:** After you activate your Office account, your iPad caches your credentials, so you don't normally need to enter them again when the apps check that you're authorized to use them. But sometimes the apps will refuse your login credentials. When this happens, you need to delete the credentials and then sign in again, making your iPad cache the credentials once more.

> **Note**   If you had OneNote installed on your iPad before you installed the other Office apps, you may get an error saying that you have no subscription. This occurs because the iPad is using the credential it has cached for OneNote for the other apps, but the credential is not valid for these apps. To resolve this problem, delete your login credentials for Word, Excel, or PowerPoint, and then sign in again.

Here's how to reset an Office app on your iPad.

1. If the app is running, close it.
   a. Double-press the Home button to display the app-switching screen.
   b. Swipe the app up off the list.
2. Press the Home button to display the Home screen.
3. Tap the Settings icon to open the Settings app.
4. Scroll the left column down to the bottom.
5. Tap the app you want to reset. This example uses Word. The app's screen appears. Tap the Reset button; for example, tap the Reset Word button. The Reset screen for the app appears (see Figure 1-6).

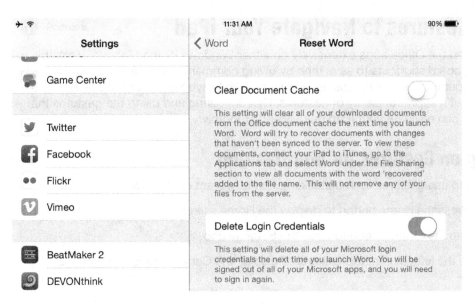

Figure 1-6. *On the Reset screen for the app, set the Clear Document Cache switch, the Delete Login Credentials switch, or both to the On position*

6. Set the Clear Document Cache switch to the On position if you want to clear your document cache.

7. Set the Delete Login Credentials switch to the On position if you want to delete your login credentials.

8. Press the Home button to display the Home screen.

9. Tap the app's icon to launch the app. For example, tap the Word icon.

> **Note**   If you set the Clear Document Cache switch to the On position, you'll see the message "Clearing document cache" briefly as the app clears the document cache. The file-management screen appears as usual, and you can open a document.

If you set the Delete Login Credentials switch to the On position, the app deletes your login credentials and displays the introductory screens. Scroll through these as before until you reach the Sign In Now screen, tap the Sign In button, and sign in to your account.

> **Note**   After clearing the cache, deleting your login credentials, or both, the app automatically sets the relevant switch or switches in the Settings app to the Off position. You don't need to reset the switches manually.

Using Gestures to Navigate Your iPad

If you've used the Office apps extensively on either Windows or the Mac, you probably use a dozen or more keyboard shortcuts to save time by giving commands accurately using the keyboard instead of moving your hand to the mouse. Lacking a physical keyboard, your iPad doesn't offer keyboard shortcuts, but it supports plenty of gestures. By configuring and using the gestures that you find the best fit, you can navigate your iPad quickly and smoothly.

Turning on Gestures for Multitasking

If you want to use gestures for multitasking, first turn them on. Follow these steps.

1. Press the Home button to display the Home screen.

2. Tap the Settings icon to open the Settings app.

3. In the left column, tap General to display the General screen (see Figure 1-7).

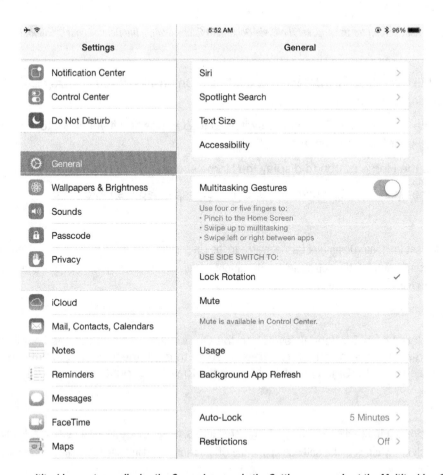

Figure 1-7. To use multitasking gestures, display the General screen in the Settings app and set the Multitasking Gestures switch to the On position

4. Tap the Multitasking Gestures switch and set it to the On position.

Tip   While you're on the General screen in the Settings app, you might want to make sure you've chosen a suitable setting in the Use Side Switch To box. Tap the Lock Rotation button, placing a check mark on it, if you want to be able to use your iPad's side switch to lock the screen rotation. Tap the Mute button if you want to use the switch for muting the sound instead. If you choose Lock Rotation, the Mute button appears in Control Center; if you choose Mute, the Lock Rotation button appears in Control Center, so you can easily access both.

Using Gestures for Multitasking

After setting the Multitasking Gestures switch to the On position, you can use these three gestures to multitask:

- **Display the Home screen:** Pinch inward with four or five fingers (whichever you find easier).

- **Display the app-switching screen:** Swipe up with four or five fingers.

- **Switch from app to app:** Swipe left or right with four or five fingers.

Locking the Screen Orientation

Your iPad automatically rotates the screen to display the content in the appropriate orientation for the way you're holding the device, so if you are holding the iPad in portrait orientation (taller than wide) and turn it to landscape orientation (wider than tall), the screen changes to landscape to match. This normally works well, but if you are holding the iPad very flat, you may find the orientation changing when you don't want it to.

When you need to prevent the orientation changing, you can lock it. You can lock and unlock the orientation in two ways:

- **Side switch:** If you've selected the Lock Rotation button in the Use Side Switch To box on the General screen in the Settings app, move the side switch to turn rotation locking on or off.

- **Control Center:** If you've selected the Mute button in the Use Side Switch To box on the General screen in the Settings app, swipe up from the bottom of the screen to open Control Center, and then tap the Rotation Lock button.

SHARING AN IPAD WITH OTHER PEOPLE

Normally, an iPad is a single-user device, like an iPhone and most other smart phones. iOS provides no mechanism for multiple users, unlike the Android operating system, which enables you to set up multiple user accounts on a single tablet, giving each user a separate area for their own content and settings.

Arguably, it's best to have an iPad of your own rather than sharing one with other people, but you may not always have the choice. So if you need to share your iPad with other people, you will need to find a way to work around the limitations. For example, if your company provides a pool of iPads to workers as needed, you will want to make sure that your accounts and data are no longer on the iPad when you hand it back in to the pool for the next person to use.

If time permits, you can erase all the content and settings on the iPad, enabling the next user to set it up from scratch. This approach is useful if each user has the iPad for a substantial period of time—say, at least several days—rather than just for an hour or two.

Here's how to erase all the content and settings.

1. Press the Home button to display the Home screen.

2. Tap the Settings icon to open the Settings app.

3. Tap the General button in the left column to display the General screen.

4. Tap the Reset button to display the Reset screen.

5. Tap the Erase All Content and Settings button.

6. Tap the Erase button in the first Erase iPad dialog box.

7. Tap the Erase button in the second Erase iPad dialog box.

Setting the iPad up again after erasing all content and settings takes a while, especially the time needed to install all the apps on it. For shorter usage terms, you may be content to take a faster and less robust approach to removing one user's settings and data and replacing them with the next user's settings and data. For example,

- Use the iCloud screen in the Settings app to add or remove the user's iCloud account from the iPad. Adding the iCloud account makes the account's mail, contacts, calendars, reminders, Safari bookmarks, notes, and other items available to the iPad; removing the account removes these items.

- Use the Mail, Contacts, Calendars screen in the Settings app to add or remove other Internet accounts. Adding an account makes its various items available, such as an Exchange account can include mail, contacts, calendars, reminders (tasks), and notes. Removing the account removes these items.

- Use one of the Office app's screens in the Settings app to delete a user's credentials and document cache, as discussed earlier in this chapter. The next user can then log into her own Office 365 account and access her documents.

> **Note**   If you're sharing an iPad in a situation where you administer the iPad, such as sharing the device with other members of your family, use the Restrictions feature to prevent other people from using features that you don't want them to use. For example, you can turn off the Facebook and Twitter apps if you need to clamp down on social networking.

Summary

In this chapter, you learned the basics of the Office for iPad apps: what they are, what you can do with them, and how to get them up and running on your iPad. You know how to launch apps and switch among them, and how to choose settings for the apps and reset them when necessary.

In the next chapter, I'll cover how to use common tools in the Office apps—everything from text to pictures, shapes, and printing.

Chapter 2

Using Common Tools in the Office Apps

The four Office apps for iPad have very different purposes and capabilities, but they share a set of common tools. For example, in each app, you can enter and format text, add graphics and shapes, use the Find and Replace tools, and print all or part of your work. There are minor differences in implementation among the apps, but it makes sense to cover the tools together in a single chapter rather than cover them separately for each app.

This chapter uses Word for the examples, because it's arguably the most accessible of the apps. You'll start by creating a new document to work in.

Launching Word and Creating a New Document

To give yourself somewhere to work, launch Word and open a blank document. Follow these steps.

1. Press the Home button to display the Home screen.

2. Tap the Word icon to launch Word.

3. If Word displays a document, tap the New tab button in the tab bar to display the New screen. Otherwise, Word should display the New screen automatically.

4. Tap the New Blank Document icon to create a new blank document.

Note The Office apps come with templates that enable you to create various kinds of documents. You'll dig into the details of using templates in the chapters on the individual apps.

Using the Ribbon

As in the desktop versions, each Office app displays the Ribbon control bar at the top of the screen. Figure 2-1 shows the Ribbon in Word for iPad.

Figure 2-1. The Ribbon includes multiple tabs plus buttons for essential commands

As you can see in the figure, the Ribbon has multiple tabs, each of which contains a separate set of controls. Some of the tabs are static, meaning that they appear on the Ribbon all the time the app is open. Other tabs are context-sensitive, meaning that they appear when you select items that require them. For example, when you insert a table, the Table tab appears on the Ribbon, providing controls for working with the table. When you tap outside the table, the Table tab disappears from the Ribbon again.

Each app has a Home tab, which is displayed at first, and an Insert tab. Beyond those two, the tabs are tailored to the apps. Here is the full list of static tabs:

- **Word:** Home, Insert, Layout, Review, View
- **Excel:** Home, Insert, Formulas, Review, View
- **PowerPoint:** Home, Insert, Transitions, Slide Show, Review
- **OneNote:** Home, Insert, View

> **Note**   You can't customize the Ribbon on the iPad. But given how straightforward the Ribbon is to use, you may not even want to customize it.

As with the static tabs, the selection of context-sensitive tabs varies depending on the app's features. For example, Excel's context-sensitive tabs include the Chart tab (see Figure 2-2), the Picture tab, and the Shape tab.

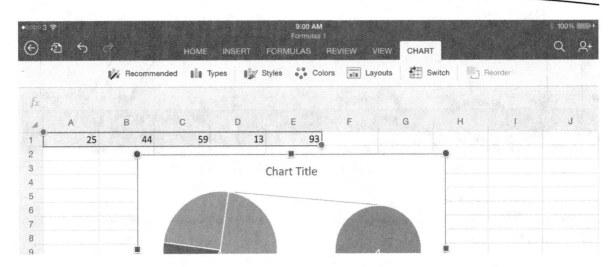

Figure 2-2. The Ribbon displays context-sensitive tabs, such as the Chart tab shown here, when you select the appropriate object

As well as the tabs, the Ribbon contains a set of buttons that is largely standardized across the apps. Figure 2-3 shows OneNote, which has the most extensive set of buttons. Here's what the buttons do:

- **Back:** Tap this button to display the file-management screen.

- **File:** Tap this button to display the File pop-up panel.

- **Undo:** Tap this button to undo the last action.

- **Redo:** Tap this button to redo the last action you have undone.

- **Search:** (Not on PowerPoint). Tap this button to display the Search field, which enables you to search your document for specific text. On Word and Excel, you can replace text as well.

- **Share:** Tap this button to display the Share pop-up panel, which contains buttons for sharing the document with others.

- **Play Slideshow:** (PowerPoint only). Tap this button to start playing the slideshow from the current slide.

- **Full Screen:** (OneNote only). Tap this button to switch to full-screen mode, enabling you to see more of the document.

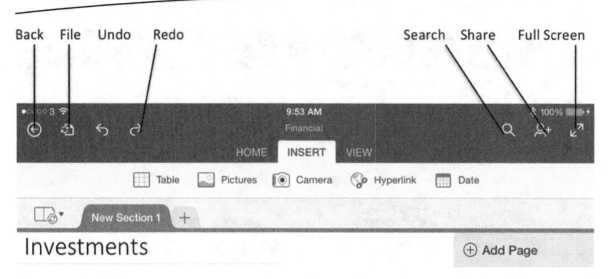

Figure 2-3. *The buttons on the Ribbon give you instant access to essential commands*

To give a command using the Ribbon tabs, you tap the appropriate tab to display its controls, and then tap the control you need. Some of the controls, such as the Bold button or Italic button, give the command directly. Others display pop-up panels from which you choose the appropriate option.

Tip When you need more space on screen, tap the currently active Ribbon tab to collapse the Ribbon, hiding the part that contains the controls. When you need the Ribbon again, tap the tab you want to use.

Naming and Saving a Document

After creating a document, you'll normally want to give it a name that's descriptive or easily identifiable. Like the desktop apps, Word, Excel, and PowerPoint for iPad give each new document you create a default name, such as Document 1 (Word), Workbook 1 (Excel), or Presentation 1 (PowerPoint). OneNote makes you name a new notebook as soon as you create it instead of assigning a default name.

To name a document and choose where to save it, follow these steps.

1. Tap the File button to display the File pop-up panel (see Figure 2-4).

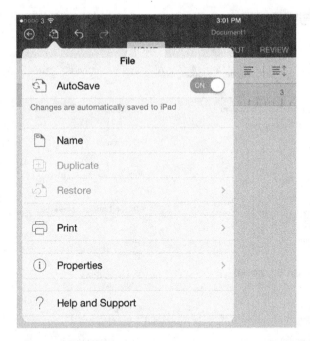

Figure 2-4. Open the File pop-up panel and tap the Name button to start naming and saving a file

2.   Tap the Name button to display the Save As dialog box (see Figure 2-5).

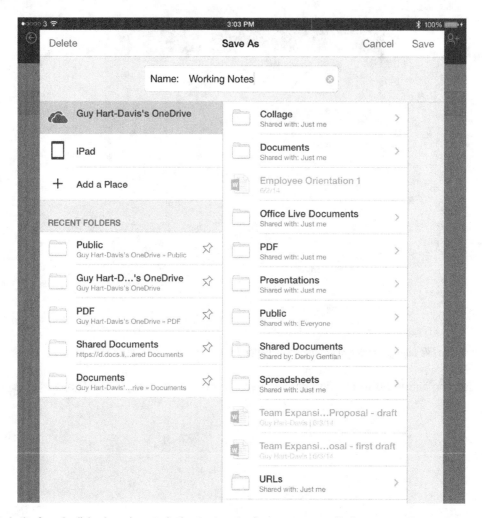

Figure 2-5. In the Save As dialog box, choose whether to store the document on your iPad or on an online service

3. Tap the X button at the right end of the name box to clear the default name.

4. Type the name in the Name box.

5. Choose where to store the document:

   a. In the upper-left corner of the Save As dialog box, tap the button for the appropriate online service (such as OneDrive) or tap the iPad button.

   b. In the list of folders, tap the folder to use.

   c. Alternatively, tap a folder in the Recent Folders list.

6. Tap the Save button. The app saves the document using the name and location you chose.

Note   Each app saves a new document using that app's latest file format. You can't save a document in an older format, such as the Word 97–2003 format (which people still use to ensure compatibility with older versions of Word or with other apps). You can open and view documents in older formats, but you need to convert them to the latest formats in order to edit them.

Now that you've named and saved the document, you can either let the app's AutoSave feature save it automatically after you make changes or turn off AutoSave so that you can save it manually whenever you want. The apps turn on AutoSave by default for each new document, so they automatically save your documents unless you explicitly turn it off.

Tip   When AutoSave is on, the File button shows two curving arrows on the page icon; when AutoSave is off, the page icon appears without the arrows. So you can see at a glance whether you need to save a document manually.

If you prefer to save your documents manually, turn AutoSave off by tapping the File button near the left end of the Ribbon and then setting the AutoSave switch to the Off position. The Save button then appears on the File pop-up panel (see Figure 2-6), and you can save the document at any time by clicking it.

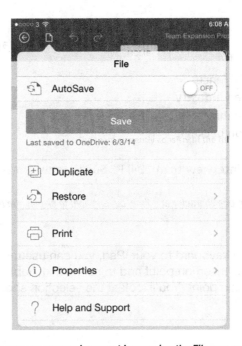

Figure 2-6. After turning off AutoSave, you can save a document by opening the File pop-up panel and tapping the Save button

Working with Text

Chances are that you'll need to work extensively with text in at least some of your documents. This section shows you how to place the insertion point, enter text quickly, and select and manipulate text.

As on the desktop apps, the techniques for working with text vary somewhat depending on the app. For example, in Excel, you can tap a cell to select it, and then type text into it, deleting any existing content without needing to select it. This section shows Word, which has the most straightforward implementation of text. You'll look at the differences in working with text in Excel, PowerPoint, and OneNote in the chapters on those apps.

Placing and Moving the Insertion Point

To make text land in the right place in the document, you need to position the insertion point between the appropriate characters.

If you need to place the insertion point at the end of a paragraph or between words, you can simply tap that point in the document. The insertion point appears as a blue line, and you can start typing.

To position the insertion point more precisely, or to move it into a word, tap and hold as near as possible to the right place. When the magnifying circle appears (see Figure 2-7), move your finger to move the insertion point one character at a time. You can move up or down from one line or paragraph to the next as needed.

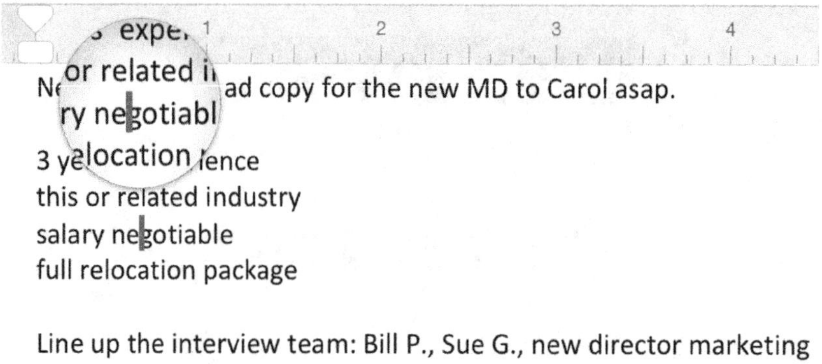

Figure 2-7. *To move the insertion point one character at a time, tap and hold to display the magnifying glass, and then drag your finger to move the insertion point*

If you've connected a hardware keyboard to your iPad, you can use the keyboard's arrow keys and keyboard shortcuts to move the insertion point and to select text. Table 2-1 explains the keyboard shortcuts for moving the insertion point. You'll look at the selection shortcuts later in this chapter.

Table 2-1. Navigation Shortcuts Using a Hardware Keyboard

Keyboard Shortcut	Effect
Left arrow	Move the insertion point one character to the left.
Right arrow	Move the insertion point one character to the right.
Up arrow	Move the insertion point up one line.
Down arrow	Move the insertion point down one line.
Command+Down arrow	Move the insertion point to the end of the document.
Command+Up arrow	Move the insertion point to the start of the document.
Command+Left arrow	Move the insertion point to the start of the line.
Command+Right arrow	Move the insertion point to the end of the line.
Option+Down arrow	Move the insertion point to the start of the next paragraph.
Option+Up arrow	Move the insertion point to the start of the current paragraph (if it is in a paragraph) or to the start of the previous paragraph (if it is at the beginning of a paragraph).
Option+Left arrow	Move the insertion point to the start of the current word (if it is within a word) or to the start of the previous word (if it is between words).
Option+Right arrow	Move the insertion point to the start of the next word.

Entering Text Quickly with the Onscreen Keyboard's Hidden Features

The onscreen keyboard is largely straightforward to use, but it has several hidden features that you will want to exploit to make the most of it. This section tells you what you need to know about the obvious and less-obvious features.

Displaying the Onscreen Keyboard

To display the onscreen keyboard, tap an area of a document or of the user interface that can accept text input. The keyboard at first displays the letters keyboard (see Figure 2-8) unless the insertion point is in an area that accepts only a different kind of input. For example, if the insertion point is in a field that requires numeric input (such as a telephone number), the numbers keyboard appears.

Figure 2-8. *The onscreen keyboard normally displays the letters keyboard at first. You can tap the .?123 button to display the numbers keyboard*

Note   When a hardware keyboard is connected, the iPad doesn't display the onscreen keyboard when you tap an area that can accept text input. You can display the onscreen keyboard by pressing the Eject key on some hardware keyboards.

With the keyboard displayed, you can start typing text by tapping the keys. To type a capital letter, tap the Shift key once and then tap the key. To turn on Caps Lock, tap the Shift key twice in quick succession.

Turning Off Auto-Capitalization

iOS's Auto-Capitalization feature automatically turns Shift on for the first letter of a paragraph or sentence. If you prefer not to have Shift automatically applied like this, you can turn it off on the Keyboard screen in the Settings app. Auto-Capitalization is a systemwide setting; you can't change it for just a single app. Follow these steps.

1.   Press the Home button to display the Home screen.

2.   Tap the Settings icon to open the Settings app.

3.   Tap the General button on the left to display the General screen.

4.   Tap the Keyboard button (scroll down if necessary) to display the Keyboard screen.

5.   Set the Auto-Capitalization switch to the Off position.

While you've got the Keyboard screen displayed, you may want to check your settings for these other options:

- **Auto-Correction:** Set this switch to On or Off to enable or disable automatic correction of apparent spelling mistakes that iOS detects.

- **Check Spelling:** Set this switch to On or Off to enable or disable spell checking.

- **Enable Caps Lock:** Set this switch to On if you want to use Caps Lock or to Off if you don't. Caps Lock is usually helpful, but switch it off if you find yourself triggering it by accident—for example, when using your iPad on public transit.

- **"." Shortcut:** Set this switch to On if you want to be able to type a period by tapping the spacebar twice in quick succession. This shortcut is usually helpful, but you can switch it off if you keep typing periods by mistake.

- **Split Keyboard:** Set this switch to On if you want to be able to use the split keyboard (discussed later in this chapter) or to Off if you don't.

On the Keyboard screen, you can also create and edit your text shortcuts. You'll look at how to use this feature later in this chapter.

Switching Among the Letters Keyboard, Numbers Keyboard, and Symbols Keyboard

The onscreen keyboard has three main layouts: letters, numbers, and symbols. From the letters keyboard, you can tap the .?123 button to switch to the numbers keyboard (see Figure 2-9). You can then tap the #+= button to switch to the symbols keyboard (see Figure 2-10).

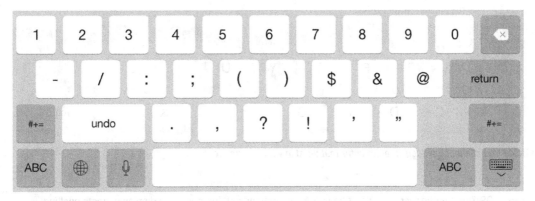

Figure 2-9. From the numbers keyboard, you can tap the #+= button to display the symbols keyboard or tap the ABC button to display the letters keyboard

Figure 2-10. From the symbols keyboard, you can tap the 123 button to display the numbers keyboard or tap the ABC button to display the letters keyboard

Note Excel provides a special numbers keyboard to help you enter data, formulas, and functions easily in your worksheets. You'll meet this keyboard in Chapter 7.

Working with Suggestions

In iOS 8, suggestions for completing the current word or phrase you're typing appear automatically on a bar above the keyboard (see Figure 2-11). You can accept a suggestion by tapping it. If none of the suggestions is what you want, keep typing.

Figure 2-11. You can touch a suggestion to enter that word in your document

Note iOS 7 and earlier versions don't have the suggestions bar. Instead, they display a single spelling correction or completion suggestion in a pop-up bubble. You can accept the correction or suggestion by typing a space or another punctuation character, such as a period or comma, or reject it by touching the X button on the bubble.

Entering Punctuation Quickly

The letters keyboard includes keys for the two most frequently used punctuation marks, the comma and the period. You can also type an exclamation point by tapping Shift and then tapping the comma key, or type a question mark by tapping Shift and then tapping the period key.

To access other punctuation, you normally tap the .?123 key, tap the relevant key (such as the semicolon key), and then tap the ABC key to return to the letters keyboard. But you can also type a punctuation character and return to the letters more quickly by tapping and holding the .?123 key and then sliding your finger to the character you want. When you lift your finger, iOS inserts the character and displays the letters keyboard again.

Entering Variant Characters

When you need to enter a variant character, such as an accented character or a related character, tap and hold the base character to display a pop-up panel of the characters available (see Figure 2-12). Slide your finger to the character you want, and then lift your finger from the screen.

Figure 2-12. You can enter variant characters from the pop-up panel that appears when you tap and hold the base character

Tip   Characters that have variants include the vowels (a, e, i, o, and u), S, C, N, Y, Z, comma, period, hyphen, forward slash (/), question mark, exclamation point, single quote, double quote, ampersand (&), $, 0 (zero), and %. The period, question mark, and exclamation point have different variants on the numbers keyboard than on the letters keyboard.

If you need to type in a foreign language on your iPad, you can add a software keyboard for that language. Open the Settings app, tap General, tap Keyboard, tap Keyboards, and then tap Add New Keyboard. The software keyboard for a language may lay out the characters differently and may make other variant characters available.

Undocking and Splitting the Onscreen Keyboard

By default, the onscreen keyboard appears at the bottom of the screen in whichever orientation you're holding your iPad. When the iPad is in landscape orientation, the keys appear at a larger size, but you can see less of the document; when the iPad is in portrait orientation, you can see more of the document, but the keyboard is correspondingly smaller.

The keyboard's position at the bottom of the screen is called having the keyboard *docked*. You can undock the keyboard so that you can move it up the screen to wherever you find more convenient. And you can split the keyboard into left and right halves so that you can type with your thumbs while holding the iPad with both hands.

To undock or split the keyboard, tap and hold the button in its lower-right corner, the same button you tap to hide the keyboard. When the pop-up menu opens (see Figure 2-13), tap the Undock button to undock the keyboard, leaving it in a single piece, or tap the Split button to split the keyboard into halves.

Figure 2-13. To undock or split the onscreen keyboard, tap and hold the button in the lower-right corner, and then tap the Undock button or the Split button on the pop-up menu

Whether you undock the keyboard or split it (as shown in Figure 2-14), you can move it up or down the screen by dragging the button in the lower-right corner.

Need to get the ad copy for the new MD to Carol asap.

Call Bill to get a quote.

People for the interview committee: Ann, Phil F., Frankie + someone from Marketing?

Check the web rates and click-through percentage for last 2 weeks.

Figure 2-14. You can move the split keyboard up or down the screen to the position you find most comfortable

Tip   After splitting the onscreen keyboard, you can type some of the letters in the middle by touching "ghost" keys. Tap just to the right of the T key to type Y, or tap just to the left of the Y key to type T; tap to the right of the G key to type H, or tap to the left of the H key to type G; tap to the right of the V key to type B, or tap to the left of the B key to type V. This move also works on the numeric and symbol keyboards.

When you want to merge the split keyboard back together, dock the floating keyboard, or both, tap and hold the button in the lower-right corner, and then tap the Dock button or the Dock and Merge button on the pop-up menu.

Tip   To merge and dock the keyboard, you can also simply drag the button in the lower-right corner until the keyboard reaches the bottom of the screen; at that point, iOS merges and docks it automatically.

Entering Text via Dictation

You can enter text in the Office apps by tapping the microphone button to the left of the spacebar on the onscreen keyboard, dictating the text, and then tapping the Done button. Dictation can be a great way of entering text quickly and accurately, provided that you're somewhere you can speak to your iPad without sharing secrets or disturbing others.

The iPad's built-in microphone does a fair job of capturing audio, but you'll normally get more accurate results by using a headset microphone.

Note   Dictation requires an Internet connection to pass your spoken input to Apple's servers and to return their interpretation of it. It's best to dictate only a sentence or two at a time, but you'll soon notice if you're trying to dictate too much. Review your dictation closely, because while there won't be any typos, whole words and phrases can easily come out wrong and change your meaning disastrously.

Entering Text Quickly by Using Shortcuts

iOS includes a feature called shortcuts for enabling you to enter text quickly. Shortcuts are somewhat like the AutoCorrect feature in the desktop versions of the Microsoft Office apps, but shortcuts are systemwide, not restricted to a particular app or set of apps. So once you create a shortcut, you can use it in any app equally easily.

Tip   In iOS, shortcuts are text only, unlike the formatted AutoCorrect entries you can create in the desktop version of Microsoft Word, and cannot contain paragraph marks. If you have an iCloud account, you can sync your shortcuts by turning on the Documents & Data option in iCloud settings. iCloud then automatically syncs your shortcuts across your iOS devices and any Macs that you sync with the same account.

Here's how to create and manage shortcuts.

1. Press the Home button to display the Home screen.

2. Tap the Settings icon to open the Settings app.

3. Tap the General button on the left to display the General screen.

4. Tap the Keyboard button (scroll down if necessary) to display the Keyboard screen.

5. Tap the Shortcuts button to display the Shortcuts screen (see Figure 2-15).

Figure 2-15. On the Shortcut screen in the Settings app, you can create shortcuts to enable yourself to enter text more quickly and accurately

Note   On some versions of iOS, the Add New Shortcut command appears directly on the Keyboard screen, so you don't need to tap the Shortcuts button.

6. Tap the Add (+) button to display the Shortcut screen (see Figure 2-16).

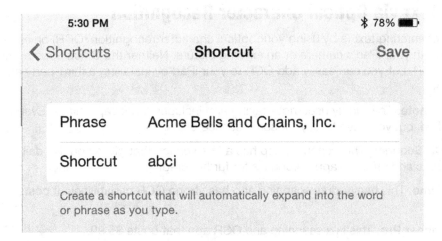

Figure 2-16. On the Shortcut screen, type the phrase for the shortcut and the shortcut that will trigger it

7. Type the replacement text—the text you want the shortcut to enter—in the Phrase box. You can also paste in the text if you've copied it from a document.

8. Type the shortcut text in the Shortcut box.

9. Tap the Save button. The Shortcuts screen or the Keyboard screen appears again, and you can create other shortcuts as needed.

> **Note** On the Shortcut screen, you'll notice that the Shortcut field is marked "Optional" before you enter text in it. You can add the replacement text on its own, and iOS will suggest the full word when you type enough characters to identify it. Adding a shortcut like this also prevents iOS from checking the spelling of the word.

To use a shortcut, you simply type its shortcut text. In iOS 8, the replacement text (or that part of it that will fit) appears on the suggestions bar (see Figure 2-17); tap the button to insert the text. In iOS 7, a pop-up bubble appears showing the replacement text for the shortcut. Tap the spacebar or type a punctuation character to enter the replacement text. If you trigger a shortcut by accident, tap the X button at the right end of the pop-up bubble to prevent iOS from entering the replacement text.

Figure 2-17. You can enter a shortcut in any app that accepts text input by typing the shortcut text and then tapping the button showing replacement text on the suggestions bar

Entering Text via Optical Character Recognition

Another way of entering text is by using your optical character recognition (OCR) on either a photo that you take with your iPad's camera or an existing picture. Neither the Office apps nor the iPad have built-in OCR, but you can easily add OCR to your iPad by installing a third-party app. Here are four examples:

- **Evernote.** The widely used note-taking app includes OCR capabilities. Evernote is free, but you have to pay for some service plans.
- **OCR Scanner.** This scanning app has a free version that gives you five daily credits and offers in-app purchases for further credits.
- **Prizmo**. This heavy-duty scanning app has strong OCR capabilities. It costs $9.99.
- **Scanner Pro.** This is a scanning and OCR app that costs $6.99.

After using OCR to get the text from a picture, you can copy the text and paste it into a document.

Selecting Text

To select text, double-tap a word to select it. iOS displays selection handles at the beginning and end of the selection and displays the Edit menu, a pop-up toolbar containing buttons such as Cut, Copy, Paste, and Delete (see Figure 2-18). You can then drag the selection handles to the appropriate points in the text. You can drag the selection handles up and down as well as left and right, but you cannot make them pass each other.

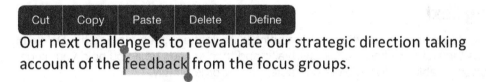

Figure 2-18. To make a selection, double-tap a word, and then drag the selection handles to the appropriate points

If you connect a hardware keyboard, you can select text by using standard keyboard shortcuts. Table 2-2 shows the most widely useful selection shortcuts.

Table 2-2. Selection Shortcuts Using a Hardware Keyboard

Keyboard Shortcut	Effect
Shift+Left arrow	Extend the selection one character to the left.
Shift+Right arrow	Extend the selection one character to the right.
Shift+Up arrow	Extend the selection up one line.
Shift+Down arrow	Extend the selection down one line.
Shift+Command+Down arrow	Extend the selection to the end of the document.
Shift+Command+Up arrow	Extend the selection to the start of the document.
Shift+Command+Left arrow	Move the end of the selection to the end of the previous line.
Shift+Command+Right arrow	Extend the selection to the end of the line.
Shift+Option+Down arrow	Extend the selection to the start of the next paragraph.
Shift+Option+Up arrow	Extend the selection to the start of the current paragraph (if it is in a paragraph) or to the start of the previous paragraph (if it is at the beginning of a paragraph).
Shift+Option+Left arrow	Extend the selection to the start of the current word (if the left end of the selection is within a word) or to the start of the previous word (if it is between words).
Shift+Option+Right arrow	Extend the selection to the start of the next word.
Command+A	Select all the content of the document or the current container, such as a text box.

Using Cut, Copy, and Paste

To use Cut, Copy, and Paste, first select the text as described in the previous section, and then tap the Cut button or the Copy button on the Edit menu. Both cutting and copying place the text on the clipboard, a shared memory area for transferring data between apps; cutting removes the text from the document, whereas copying does not.

To paste in the item you've cut or copied, tap to place the insertion point in the appropriate place in the document; if necessary, tap and hold to display the magnifying glass, and then drag the insertion point to where you want the pasted item to land. You can then tap the Paste button on the Edit menu to paste in the text.

Deleting Text

You can delete text by placing the insertion point to its right and then tapping the Delete button. The app deletes the first few characters individually, and then speeds up if you hold your finger on the Delete button, enabling you to delete characters and words rapidly.

You can also delete text by selecting it and then tapping the Delete button. Or if you want to replace some text with other text, select the existing text, and then start typing the new text over it.

Another option is to select text and then tap the Cut button to cut it from the document. Cutting the text like this places the text on the Clipboard, from which you can insert it in a document. Or you can just leave the text there until you copy or cut something else, at which point the text gets deleted.

Connecting a Hardware Keyboard

The iPad's on-screen keyboard is as good as Apple has been able to make it, but it still can't compare with a physical keyboard, especially if you are a touch-typist. So when you need to work extensively—or rapidly—with text, you may want to connect a physical keyboard to your iPad.

You can connect a physical keyboard to your iPad either via Bluetooth or via the Lightning port. If you have an older iPad, you can connect a keyboard via the Dock Connector port.

> **Tip**   After connecting a hardware keyboard, you can press any key to wake up your iPad. At the lock screen, you can type your passcode or password using the keyboard to unlock the iPad. If it's a password rather than a passcode, press Enter to tell iOS you've finished typing the password.

Connecting a Keyboard via Bluetooth

Bluetooth can be a great choice for an iPad keyboard because its wireless nature means you don't have to connect a cable to the iPad's Lightning port or Dock Connector port. You can choose from a wide variety of Bluetooth keyboards designed for use with iPads, including keyboards built into an iPad case or iPad cover and keyboards that include iPad stands. Or you can simply connect a general-purpose Bluetooth keyboard to your iPad.

> **Note**   When evaluating hardware keyboards for use with your iPad, see which dedicated keys each keyboard offers. For example, some hardware keyboards include dedicated keys for controlling media playback and for actions such as Cut, Copy, Paste, Undo, and Redo, which can help you produce accurate work more quickly.

Here's how to connect a keyboard via Bluetooth.

1. Press the Home button to display the Home screen.

2. Tap the Settings icon to open the Settings app.

3. Tap Bluetooth in the left column to display the Bluetooth screen.

4. If the Bluetooth switch is set to the Off position, tap it and set it to the On position.

5. Turn on the Bluetooth keyboard.

6. Make the Bluetooth keyboard discoverable. Usually, you press a button to do this. The keyboard then appears in the Devices list on your iPad, listed as Not Paired (see Figure 2-19).

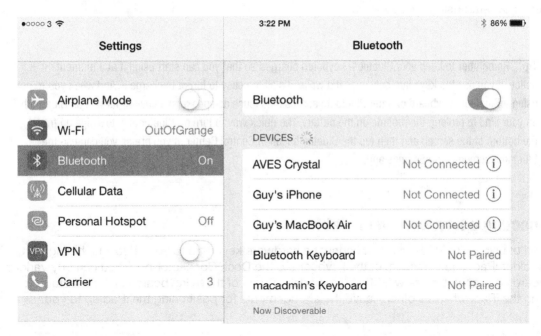

Figure 2-19. On the Bluetooth screen in the Settings app, set the Bluetooth switch to On, and then tap the button for the keyboard you want to pair

7. In the Devices list, tap the button for the keyboard. The Bluetooth Pairing Request dialog box opens (see Figure 2-20), showing the code you must enter to confirm the pairing request.

Bluetooth Pairing Request
Enter the code "6251" on "Bluetooth
Keyboard", followed by the return or
enter key.

Cancel

Figure 2-20. *When the Bluetooth Pairing Request dialog box opens, type the code on the keyboard to confirm the pairing request, and then press Return or Enter*

8. Type the code on the keyboard and press Return or Enter. The keyboard then appears as Connected in the Devices list.

You can now start using the keyboard.

Tip   Remember to keep your Bluetooth keyboard charged so that you can start using it at a moment's notice. If you use the keyboard only once it a while, it's all too easy to forget to charge it. And when you're not using a Bluetooth keyboard or other Bluetooth accessories (such as speakers), consider turning off Bluetooth on your iPad to prolong the runtime on the battery. The quick way to turn off Bluetooth is to swipe up from the bottom of the screen and then tap the Bluetooth icon in Control Center; if you prefer, you can use the Bluetooth screen in the Settings app.

Connecting a Keyboard via a Cable

Instead of using Bluetooth, you can connect a hardware keyboard to your iPad's Lightning port; on an older iPad, you can connect the keyboard to the Dock Connector port. You can buy various keyboards designed for use with the iPad models. Some of these keyboards include a stand for holding the iPad, whereas others leave the arrangements for positioning the iPad up to you.

Tip   You can connect most USB keyboards to a Lightning-equipped iPad by using the Apple Lightning to USB Camera Adapter. For an older iPad with the Dock Connector port, use the Camera Connector that comes in the Apple iPad Camera Connection Kit. You can buy these items from the Apple Store (http://store.apple.com) or other online stores. USB keyboards that require extra power, such as those with backlit keys, may not work.

Changing the Keyboard Layout for a Hardware Keyboard

After connecting a hardware keyboard, you can change the layout the iPad uses for it. For example, if you prefer the Dvorak keyboard layout, you can set the iPad to interpret the hardware keyboard's input as Dvorak.

Follow these steps to change the keyboard layout.

1. Press the Home button to display the Home screen.

2. Tap Settings to open the Settings app.

3. Tap General to display the General screen.

4. Tap International to display the International screen.

5. Tap Keyboards to display the Keyboards screen.

6. Tap the button for your language—for example, the English button. A screen with the same name as the button appears.

7. In the Choose a Hardware Keyboard Layout section, tap the layout you want, such as Dvorak.

Positioning Graphics, Shapes, and Other Objects

The Office apps enable you to insert tables, pictures, shapes, and text boxes in your documents. These objects have different contents and properties, but you position and resize them in largely the same way.

Understanding How You Position Graphical Objects

Even though an Office document appears to be flat, it actually consists of multiple separate layers. Until you add objects to a layer, the layer is transparent, so you see right through it to whatever is underneath. One layer contains the text; the other layers contain graphical objects. Having these multiple layers enables you to position graphical objects either in front of the text layer or behind the text layer. You can also position a graphical object in front of another graphical object—for example, to superimpose one graphical object on another.

Each of the Office apps lets you position graphical objects in the graphics layers, where you can move them freely. Word also lets you position graphical objects as inline characters in the text layer. When you do this, Word places the graphical object just like a character in the document's text. If you then insert text before the graphical object, it moves further down the document.

Arranging Graphical Objects to Control Which Is Visible

When you have placed multiple graphical objects in the same area of a document (as discussed a little later in this chapter), you may need to arrange the order in which they appear in the document's layers to control how they appear in relation to each other. For example, you may need to move a particular object to the front of the stack of document layers so that it appears on top of the other objects, or move another object back so that it appears behind one of its companion objects.

To change where an object appears in the layers, follow these steps.

1. Tap the object you want to move up or down the stack of layers.

2. Tap the Reorder button to display the Reorder pop-up panel (see Figure 2-21).

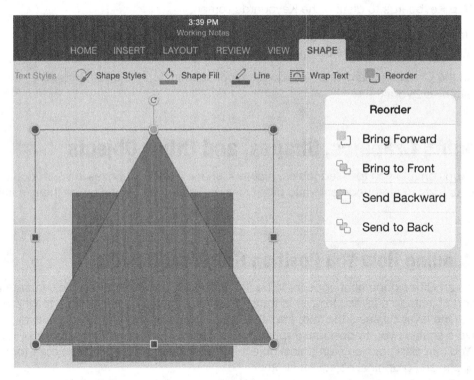

Figure 2-21. Use the buttons on the Reorder pop-up panel to move the selected object up or down the stack of layers in the document

3. Tap the appropriate button:

    ▓ **Bring Forward:** Tap this button to bring the object forward by one layer.

    ▓ **Bring to Front:** Tap this button to bring the object all the way to the front.

    ▓ **Send Backward:** Tap this button to send the object backward by one layer.

    ▓ **Send to Back:** Tap this button to send the object all the way to the back.

4. When you finish reordering the objects, tap outside them and make sure the result looks the way you want.

Working with Graphics

The Office apps make it easy to insert pictures in your documents from the Photos collection on your iPad or from your photo stream. After inserting a picture, you can resize it, reposition it, and format it to look the way you want.

Inserting a Picture

Here's how to insert a picture in a document.

1. Tap the Insert tab of the Ribbon to display its controls.

2. Tap the Pictures button to display the Photos pop-up panel (see Figure 2-22).

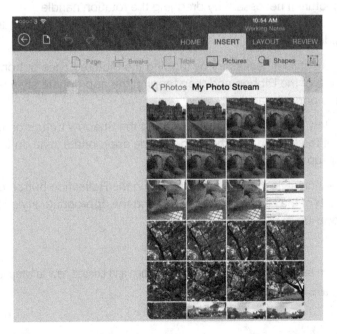

Figure 2-22. Tap the Pictures button on the Insert tab of the Ribbon to display the Photos pop-up panel, tap the button for the collection that contains the photo you want to use, and then tap the picture

3. Tap the button for the photo collection you want to use. For example, tap the Camera Roll button to display the Camera Roll panel.

4. Tap the photo you want to insert. The app adds the photo to the document, displays selection handles around it, and displays the Picture tab of the Ribbon. This tab appears when a picture is selected. It provides tools for formatting to the picture.

Resizing and Formatting a Picture

After inserting a picture, you can resize it and format it so that it looks the way you want. Follow these steps.

1. If the picture isn't currently selected, tap it to select it. Selection handles appear around the picture, and the Picture tab appears on the Ribbon, displaying its controls.

2. Resize the picture as needed by dragging the selection handles:

    ▪ **Resize proportionally:** Drag a corner handle to resize the picture proportionally, keeping it undistorted.

    ▪ **Resize in one dimension only:** Drag a side handle. The picture becomes distorted in that dimension.

3. Move the picture as needed by dragging it.

4. Rotate the picture if necessary by dragging the rotation handle (the round button with the curling arrow above the handle in the middle of the upper side).

5. Apply a picture style if necessary by tapping the Picture Styles button on the Picture tab of the Ribbon and then tapping the appropriate style on the Picture Styles pop-up panel.

6. Apply a shadow style if necessary by tapping the Shadow button on the Picture tab of the Ribbon and then tapping the appropriate style on the Shadow pop-up panel.

7. Apply a reflection style if necessary by tapping the Reflection button on the Picture tab of the Ribbon and then tapping the appropriate style on the Reflection pop-up panel.

Note   In Word, you can tap the Wrap Text button on the Ribbon and choose how to wrap text around the object. Chapter 5 explains the wrapping options.

When you finish formatting the picture, tap outside the picture to deselect it. You can then see the full effect of the formatting changes you've made.

GIVING THE OFFICE APPS ACCESS TO YOUR PHOTOS

The first time you tap the Pictures button on the Insert tab of the Ribbon in any of the Office apps, iOS displays a dialog box prompting you to give the app access to your photos. Normally, you'll want to tap the OK button in this dialog box so that you can use the photos. If you do this, iOS allows the app to access the photos, and the Photos pop-up panel appears, showing a list of the available photo collections, such as Camera Roll and My Photo Stream.

But if you tap the Don't Allow button in the "App" Would Like to Access Your Photos dialog box, iOS denies the app access. If you later want to give the app access to the photos, you need to take the following steps.

1. Press the Home button to display the Home screen.

2. Tap the Settings icon to open the Settings app.

3. Tap the Privacy button in the left column to display the Privacy screen.

4. Tap the Photos button to display the Photos screen.

5. Set the switch for the app to the On position instead of the Off position.

Similarly, if you decide you no longer want an app to be able to access your photos, go to the Photos screen and set its switch to the Off position.

Working with Shapes

Word, Excel, and PowerPoint provide a selection of shapes you can use to illustrate and decorate your documents. The apps break down the shapes into eight categories—Lines, Rectangles, Basic Shapes, Block Arrows, Equation Shapes, Flowchart Shapes, Stars and Banners, and Callout—to help you find the shape you need. After inserting a shape, you can reposition it, resize it, and format it as needed.

Note   OneNote doesn't have shapes at this writing.

Here's how to insert a shape in a document.

1. Tap the Insert tab of the Ribbon to display its controls.

2. Tap the Shape button to display the Shapes pop-up panel.

3. Scroll the Shape pop-up panel down as needed to reach the appropriate category of shape (see Figure 2-23).

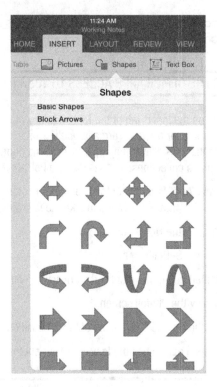

Figure 2-23. Word, Excel, and PowerPoint provide a wide variety of shapes

4. Tap the shape you want to insert. The shape appears in your document and the Shape tab appears on the Ribbon (see Figure 2-24).

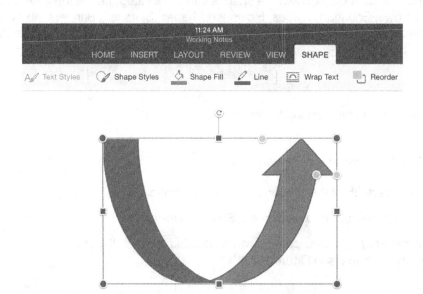

Figure 2-24. Use the controls on the Shape tab of the Ribbon to format the selected shape

5. Reposition the shape as needed by dragging it.

6. Resize the shape as needed by dragging the selection handles:

    ■ **Resize proportionally:** Drag a corner handle.

    ■ **Resize in one dimension only:** Drag a side handle.

    ■ **Change the shape:** Drag a yellow handle. For example, on the curving arrow shown in Figure 2-24, you can adjust the width of the arrow, the arrow head, and the space between the left and right sides.

7. Tap the Shape Styles button to open the Shape Styles pop-up panel, and then tap the style you want.

8. Tap the Shape Fill button to display the Shape Fill pop-up panel, and then tap the fill color to use.

9. Tap the Line button to open the Line pop-up panel, and then tap the color to use for the outline.

When you finish formatting the shape, tap outside the shape to deselect it.

Working with Text Boxes

In Word, Excel, and PowerPoint, you can insert text boxes to position text exactly where you need it. Text boxes work in a similar way to shapes. You can format them with shape styles, shape fills, and lines, but you can also apply text styles to them.

> **Note**   In the desktop versions of Word, you can link two or more text boxes so that text flows from one to another. When the text reaches the end of the first text box, the next word appears in the second text box, and so on. At this writing, Word for iPad doesn't let you link text boxes like this. But you can open a document that already contains linked text boxes in Word for iPad and edit the text as needed.

Here's how to insert a text box, position and format it, and add contents.

1. Tap the Insert tab of the Ribbon to display its controls.

2. Tap the Text Box button to insert a standard-size text box in the middle of the screen.

3. Drag the text box to where you want it.

4. Resize the text box as needed by dragging its side handles or corner handles.

5. To format the text box, tap the Shape tab of the Ribbon. You can then apply formatting by tapping the Text Styles button, the Shape Styles button, the Shape Fill button, or the Line button and making your choice on the resulting pop-up panel.

6. Tap the text box to display the Edit menu (see Figure 2-25).

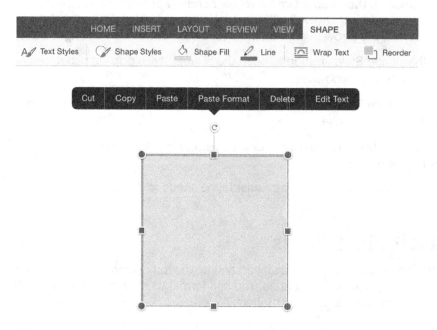

Figure 2-25. After inserting a text box, use the controls on the Shape tab of the Ribbon to format it. Then tap the text box and tap the Edit Text button on the pop-up control bar to enter the text

7. Tap the Edit Text button to open the text box for editing.

8. Type or paste the text into the text box.

When you finish working with the text box, tap elsewhere in the document to deselect the text box.

Printing from Your iPad

Given that the decades-long dream of the paperless office seems finally to have died, you will likely want to print some of your Office documents. You can print directly from your iPad provided that your printer supports Apple's AirPrint protocol.

Tip   If you don't have an AirPrint-compatible printer, you can print to a regular printer by installing Printer Pro ($7.99) on your iPad. Alternatively, if you have a Mac, you can install handyPrint (www.netputing.com; donationware) to make printers attached to your Mac available to your iPad and other iOS devices.

Here's how to print the current document.

1. Tap the File button on the Ribbon to display the File pop-up panel.

2. Tap the Print button to display the Printer Options panel (see Figure 2-26).

Figure 2-26. Use the Printer Options panel to set the printer, range, and number of copies. Then tap the Print button

3. If the Printer button doesn't show the printer you want to use, tap the button to display the Printer panel, and then tap the right printer. The Printer Options panel appears again.

4. To change the range, tap the Range button, and then use the controls on the Page Range panel to specify the range. For example, you may want to print just the first page of a document.

5. If necessary, tap the + button or the – button to adjust the number of copies.

6. Tap the Print button to print the document.

Summary

In this chapter, you learned how to use common tools in the Office apps. After launching an app (Word) and creating an new document, you looked at how to use the Ribbon; how to name and save a document, and choose whether to use the AutoSave feature; and how to work with text. You learned how to insert pictures, shapes, and text boxes; position them where you want them; and format them to look good. You also learned how to print from your iPad to an AirPrint-enabled printer or to a computer running AirPrint-compatible software.

Chapter 3

Managing Your Office Documents

In this chapter, you will learn how to manage your Office documents. First, you will set up your OneDrive and SharePoint services on your iPad so that the Office apps can access them. You will then learn to navigate the file management screens and manage an active document from its File menu. After that, this chapter will explain how to share your documents with others and how to troubleshoot problems with documents.

Setting Up Your Services

As you saw in Chapter 1, you need to activate the Office apps before you can get anything done in them. By this point, your iPad should have the Office account that you used for activation configured for use. This is your primary account.

You can add other accounts and services as needed. If you no longer need an account or service other than your primary account, you can remove it.

Adding a Service

To add an account or service, follow these steps.

1. Open one of the Office apps by tapping its icon on the Home screen.

2. If the app opens the document you were using last, tap the Back button to close the document and display the file management screens.

3. Tap the Open icon in the left column to display the Open screen.

> **Note**   You can also tap the Account icon at the top of the left column and then tap the Add a Service button in the Add a Service dialog box. But because the Add a Service dialog box lets you add only OneDrive or OneDrive for Business at this writing, not SharePoint, it is usually easier to display the Open screen and tap the Add a Place button.

4.   Tap the Add a Place button. The Add a Place dialog box opens (see Figure 3-1).

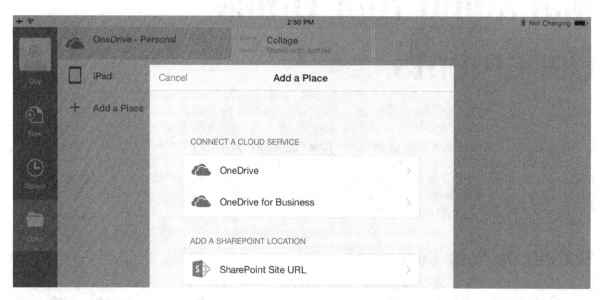

Figure 3-1. *To start adding an account, tap the Add a Place button on the file management screens in one of the Office apps, and then tap the account type in the Add a Place dialog box*

5.   Tap the appropriate button.

OneDrive: Tap this button to add a personal OneDrive account. This is the standard type of OneDrive account, so unless you know you have a OneDrive for Business account, choose this type. In the OneDrive dialog box (see Figure 3-2), type your account name and password, and then tap the Sign In button.

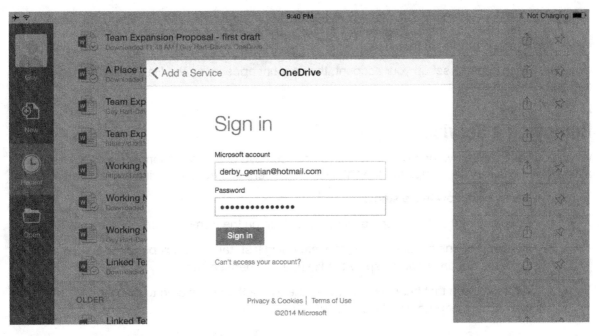

Figure 3-2. In the Sign In dialog box for OneDrive, type your account name and password, and then tap the Sign In button

OneDrive for Business: Tap this button to add an OneDrive for Business account, such as one provided by your company or your school. In the OneDrive for Business dialog box, type your account name and password, and then tap the Sign In button.

Tip   For a OneDrive for Business account, you can select the Keep Me Signed In check box to have the Office app keep you signed in to the service. This is helpful as long as you keep your iPad protected against others using it.

Note   If OneDrive prompts you for an e-mail address to which Microsoft can send a security code if you get locked out of your account, select the appropriate e-mail account in the Where Should We Send Your Code? pop-up menu, and tap the Next button. In the next dialog box, type the code you received via e-mail and tap the Next button.

> *SharePoint Site URL*: Tap this button to add a SharePoint site by specifying its URL, the Internet address. Provide your SharePoint credentials when the app prompts for them.

Once the Office app has set up your account, the account appears on the file management screens, and you can start using it.

Removing a Service

When you have set up two or more services, you can remove ones you no longer need. You must always have one service set up, and the Office apps prevent you from removing the last service.

To remove a service, follow these steps:

1. Open one of the Office apps by tapping its icon on the Home screen.

2. If the app opens the document you were using last, tap the Back button to close the document and display the file management screens.

3. Tap the button that bears your name at the top of the left column to display the Account pop-up panel (see Figure 3-3).

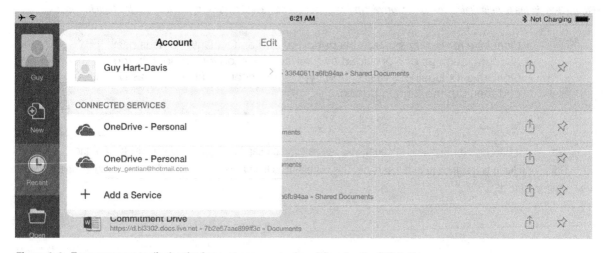

Figure 3-3. Tap your name to display the Account pop-up panel, and then tap the Edit button

4. Tap the Edit button to turn on editing mode (see Figure 3-4). A red Remove icon appears to the left of each service you can delete.

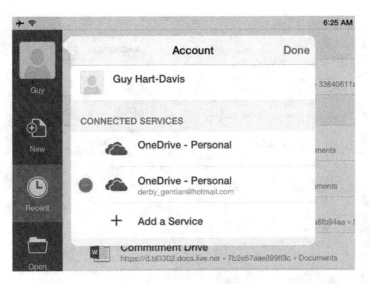

Figure 3-4. In editing mode, tap the Remove icon to the left of the service you want to remove

Note   The Edit button doesn't appear if you have only one service set up.

5. Tap the Remove icon for the appropriate service. A red Remove button (with "Remove" in white text) appears on the right of the button.

6. Tap the Remove icon for the appropriate service. A red Remove button (with "Remove" in white text) appears on the right of the button.

7. Tap the red Remove button. The Are you sure you want to remove this service? dialog box opens (see Figure 3-5).

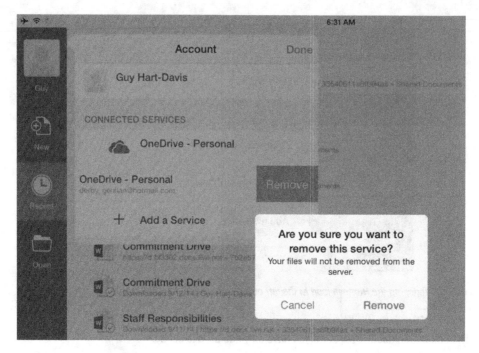

Figure 3-5. Tap the Remove button in the Are you sure you want to remove this service? dialog box to remove the service

8. Tap the Remove button in the dialog box. The app removes the service.

9. Tap the button with your name at the top of the left column to hide the Account pop-up panel.

Signing Out from Your Account

Normally, you'll want to stay signed in to your Office account so that you can use the apps and access your documents quickly on your iPad. But if you use multiple accounts for Office, such as a work account and a personal account, you will need to sign out of one account so that you can sign in to the other account, because you can be signed in to only one account at a time.

Here's how to sign out of your account.

1. Open one of the Office apps by tapping its icon on the Home screen.

2. If the app opens the document you were using last, tap the Back button to close the document and display the file-management screen.

3. Tap the button that bears your name at the top of the left column to display the Account pop-up panel.

4. Tap the button with your name and e-mail address in the Account section to display the Account dialog box (see Figure 3-6).

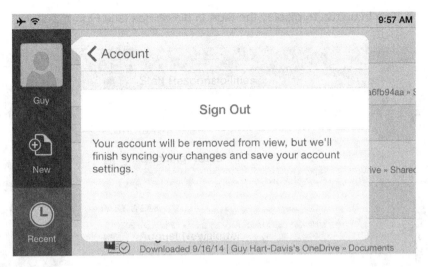

Figure 3-6. *To sign out from your account, open the Account dialog box and then tap the Sign Out button*

5.   Tap the Sign Out button. The Sign Out dialog box opens (see Figure 3-7).

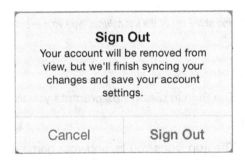

Figure 3-7. *Tap the Sign Out button in the Sign Out dialog box to confirm that you want to sign out*

6.   Tap the Sign Out button. The app signs you out.

Signing In to an Account

After you sign out, the Sign In button appears in place of the account button (the button showing your name) in the left column on the file management screens. You can sign in to a different account (or the same account, if you like) by following these steps.

1. Tap the Sign In button to display the Sign In dialog box (see Figure 3-8).

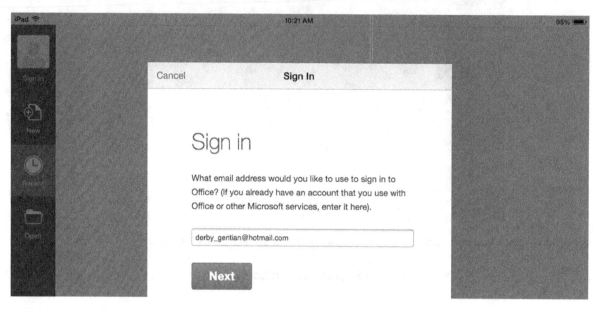

Figure 3-8. *To sign in, tap the Sign In button at the top of the left column, type your username in the Sign In dialog box, and then tap the Next button*

2. Type your username.

3. Tap the Next button. The Sign In dialog box prompts you for your password.

4. Type your password.

5. Tap the Next button. The app signs you in, and your name appears on the account button at the top of the left column on the file management screens.

Caution   Any local documents—documents you store on your iPad rather than on an online drive—are not tied to the account that creates them. This means that you can work on local documents no matter which account you are currently signed in to. You can also work on local documents while you are not signed in.

Navigating the File Management Screens

Once you've got your account and services set up, you're ready to create new documents and open existing documents. As in the desktop versions of the apps, you perform these tasks from within the appropriate app. For example, you create a new spreadsheet workbook from within Excel or a new presentation from within PowerPoint.

Because the iPad doesn't have a file management app, you also perform file management tasks with documents, such as renaming a document or deleting a document, from inside the relevant apps. This is different from the desktop version of the apps.

> **Note**   You can perform some file management tasks by using the OneDrive app, which you can download for free from the App Store.

Displaying the File Management Screens

To start exploring the file management screens, open the Office app you want to use by tapping its icon on the Home screen.

Depending on what you last did in the app, it may display the last document you opened. If it does so, tap the Back button to close the document and display the file management screens.

The file management screens have four buttons on the left: a button with your first name, the New button, the Recent button, and the Open button. As you saw earlier in this chapter, tapping the button that bears your name displays the Account dialog box, in which you can add or remove service. The following sections explain how to work with the screens that the other three buttons display.

Creating New Documents from the New Screen

To create a new document, tap the New button, and then tap the appropriate button on the New screen. Figure 3-9 shows the New screen in Word.

Figure 3-9. To create a new document, tap the appropriate template or design on the New screen

Your choices on the New screen vary greatly by app.

- *Word*: Word provides templates loaded with content and formatting to help you quickly create specific types of documents, such as business letters, school newsletters, and resumes.

- *Excel*: Excel provides templates that give you a jump-start on creating a wide range of workbook types, from household budgets and inventory lists all the way to annual financial reports and Gantt project planners.

- *PowerPoint*: PowerPoint provides a wide range of design themes but not (at this writing) content templates.

Note   OneNote doesn't have a New screen. To create a new notebook, tap the Notebooks button in the left column, and then tap the Create Notebook button on the Notebooks pane. There are no choices for you to make about the notebook's design or content.

Working on the Recent Screen

To work with documents you've used recently in this app, tap the Recent button in the left column. The Recent screen appears (see Figure 3-10), showing your recent documents organized in descending date order, so the most recent documents appear at the top. The Recent screen breaks up the list of documents into sections with names such as Today, Yesterday, Past Week, and Past Month. The Pinned section appears at the top of the list if you have "pinned" documents to the list (see the nearby sidebar for details on pinning).

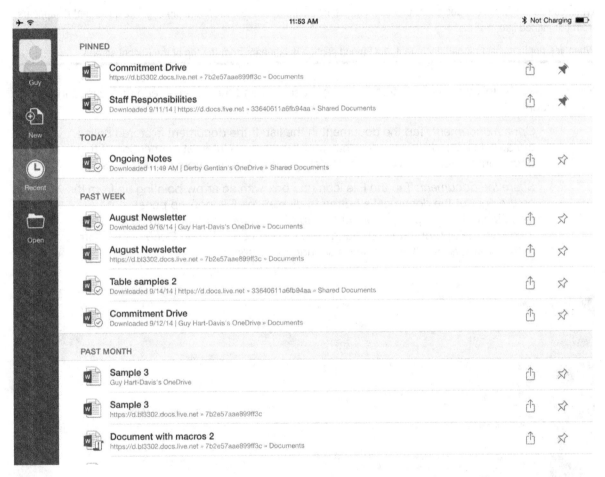

Figure 3-10. On the Recent screen, you can open a document, pin a document to the list, or display the File pop-up panel

---

PINNING A DOCUMENT TO THE RECENT SCREEN FOR INSTANT ACCESS

To keep your important documents immediately to hand, you can pin them to the Recent screen. The pinned documents appear in a section called Pinned at the top of the Recent screen. This section appears only when you have pinned documents.

To pin a document, tap the pushpin icon on the right of a document's button. The pushpin changes from an outline to solid color, and the document moves to the Pinned section.

When you no longer need a document to be pinned, tap its pushpin icon to remove the pinning. The document disappears from the Pinned list.

When you unpin the last pinned document, the Pinned section disappears from the top of the Recent screen.

You can take the following actions from the Recent screen and the Open screen (discussed in the next section):

- *Open a document*: Tap the document in the list. If the document is stored online, the app downloads it, provided that your iPad has an Internet connection. If the document is stored on your iPad, the app opens it rather more quickly.

- *Share the document*: Tap the File icon (the box with an arrow pointing up from it) on the right of the document's button to display the File pop-up panel (see Figure 3-11), tap the Share button to display the Share pop-up panel, and then give the appropriate command. See the section "Sharing Documents," later in this chapter, for full coverage on sharing documents.

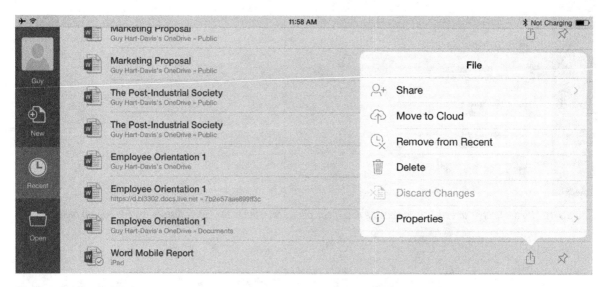

Figure 3-11. Tap the File icon on the document's button on the Recent screen to display the File pop-up panel

- *Move the document from your iPad to OneDrive*: Tap the File icon on the document's button to display the File pop-up panel, and then tap the Move to Cloud button. In the Choose Name and Location dialog box (see Figure 3-12), change the name if necessary, select the folder in which you want to store the document, and then tap the Save button. As you'd imagine, this command is available only for documents saved on your iPad.

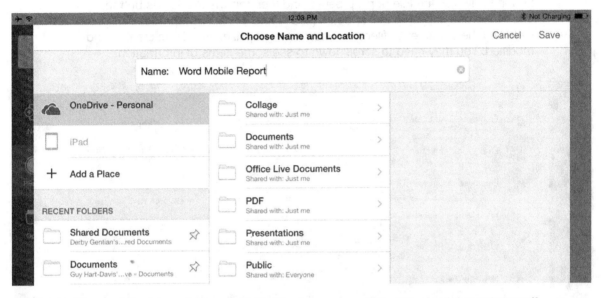

Figure 3-12. When moving a document from your iPad to iCloud, you can specify the folder—and change the name if necessary—in the Choose Name and Location dialog box

- *Remove the document from the Recent list*: Tap the File icon on the document's button to display the File pop-up panel, and then tap the Remove from Recent button.

- *Delete the document*: Tap the File icon on the document's button to display the File pop-up panel, and then tap the Delete button. In the confirmation dialog box that opens (see Figure 3-13), tap the Delete button.

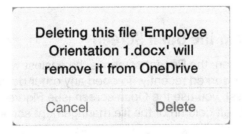

Figure 3-13. Tap the Delete button in the confirmation dialog box to finish deleting a document

- *Discard changes you have made to the document*: Tap the File icon on the document's button to display the File pop-up panel, and then tap the Discard Changes button. This button is available only if the document contains changes that have not been synced with the online service on which the document is stored.

- *View the properties for the document*: Tap the File icon on the document's button to display the File pop-up panel, and then tap the Properties button. The Properties pop-up panel appears (see Figure 3-14), showing details including the document's filename, location, type, size, and dates created and modified. You may need to scroll down to see some items of information.

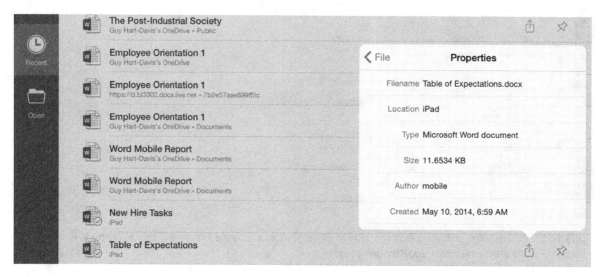

Figure 3-14. The Properties pop-up panel includes the document's filename, location, type, and date last modified

---

Tip Look at the Type readout in the Properties pop-up panel if you need to determine a document's type. This readout enables you to distinguish regular documents, workbooks, and presentations from macro-enabled ones and from templates.

Opening a Document from the Open Screen

As you saw in the previous section, the Recent screen is the easiest way to open an existing document with which you have worked recently. To open any other document (or indeed any document your iPad can access), you use the Open screen (see Figure 3-15), which you display by tapping the Open button in the left column of the file management screens.

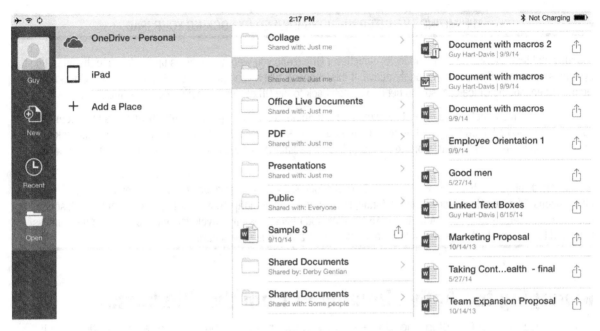

Figure 3-15. Tap the Open button in the left column to display the Open screen, navigate to the document you want to open, and then tap its button

---

Note   You can add a place to the first column by tapping the Add a Place button and then work in the Add a Place dialog box that opens.

You can navigate the Open screen easily by following these steps.

1. In the first column, tap the location, such as your OneDrive account or your iPad. The documents and folders in that location appear in the second column.

2. In the second column, tap the folder that contains the document you want to open. (If the document is in the top level of the location, simply tap the document's button to open it.)

3. Navigate further through the folder structure as necessary.

4. Tap the document you want to open.

Note   Instead of opening a document, you can tap the File button to display the File menu, and then use the commands explained in the previous section. For example, you can move a document from your iPad to the cloud, share a document with others, or rename a document.

MINIMIZING THE INTERRUPTIONS CAUSED BY LOCKING YOUR IPAD

You may find that, every time your iPad locks, whichever Office app you were using gives up the focus to the operating system, so that the Office app is no longer active. If this happens, when you unlock your iPad, your iPad displays the Home screen, not the Office app, so you need to switch back to the Office app so that you can resume work.

This takes a moment, but it would be okay except for one thing: the Office app momentarily displays the document you were working on, then goes back to the file management screens while it reloads the document. This makes for enough of an interruption to your work to be disruptive, especially if the document is large, your Internet connection is slow, or both.

If your iPad displays this behavior, you may want to set a long Auto-Lock interval on your iPad to minimize the interruptions. From the Home screen, tap Settings, tap General, and then tap Auto-Lock to reach the Auto-Lock screen, and then tap a button such as 10 Minutes or 15 Minutes. You may also want to avoid locking the iPad manually unless you need to conserve battery power or leaving it unlocked is a threat to your security.

Managing the Active Document from the File Menu

After you open a document in one of the apps, you can perform some management actions on it from the File menu within the app. Tap the File button near the left end of the Ribbon to display the File menu (see Figure 3-16). You can then take the following actions:

- *Toggle AutoSave on or off*: Set the AutoSave switch to the On position or to the Off position, as needed.

- *Save the document*: When AutoSave is off, tap the Save button to save the document.

- *Name*: If this button appears and is available, tap it to display the Save As dialog box. You can then enter the document's name, choose the folder in which to save it, and tap the Save button.

- *Duplicate*: Tap this button to create a copy of the document. The app displays the Choose Name and Location dialog box (shown earlier in Figure 3-12), in which you can give the file a different name, save it in a different location, or both.

- *Restore*: Tap this button to display the Restore pop-up panel (see Figure 3-17). From here, you can tap the Restore to Last Opened button to restore the document to how it was when you last opened it, or tap the View Version History Online button to switch to your browser and display other versions available online.

- *Print*: Tap this button to display the Print pop-up panel, from which you can print the document, as discussed in Chapter 2.

- *Properties*: Tap this button to display the Properties pop-up panel, which displays information ranging from the filename, location, and type to when it was created, last modified, and who last modified it.

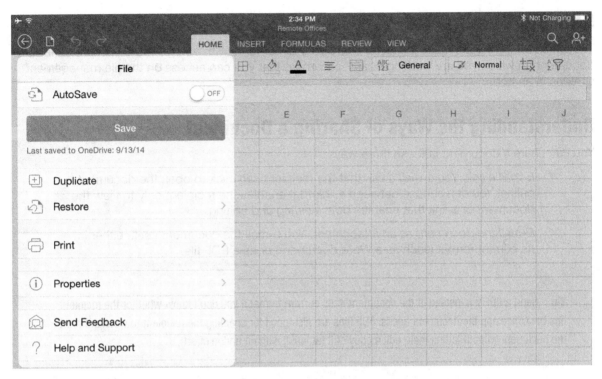

Figure 3-16. You can perform several file management actions from the File menu for the open document

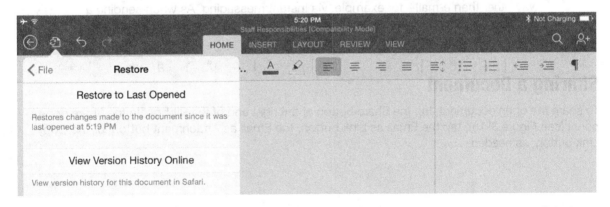

Figure 3-17. On the Restore pop-up panel, you can tap the Restore to Last Opened button to restore the document to its state when you last opened it

Note   The File menu in OneNote is more limited than the File menu in the other apps. The only management command it offers is the Sync Your Notebook command, which does just what its name says.

Sharing Documents

The Office for iPad apps make it easy to share your documents with others. You can share either the document on which you are working or any document that you can access on the file management screens in an app.

Understanding the Ways of Sharing a Document

You can share a document in these three ways:

- *E-mail a link*: You e-mail a link that the recipient can click to open the document online. You can choose between a link that enables the recipient only to view the document or a link that enables both viewing and editing.

- *E-mail the document as an attachment*: You e-mail the document itself, either in its current format (such as a Word document) or as a PDF file.

> **Tip**   Send a PDF file instead of the document in its current format if you don't know whether the recipient has the Office app the document needs. PDF files are also good for enabling the recipient to view and print the document without letting them edit a copy of it (at least, without undue effort).

- *Copy a link*: You can copy a link to the document so that you can share it in a way other than e-mail—for example, via instant messaging. As when sending a link, you can choose between a link for viewing only and a link for both viewing and editing.

Sharing a Document

To share the open document, tap the Share button at the right end of the Ribbon. In the Share pop-up panel (see Figure 3-18), tap the Email as Link button, the Email as Attachment button, or the Copy Link button, as needed.

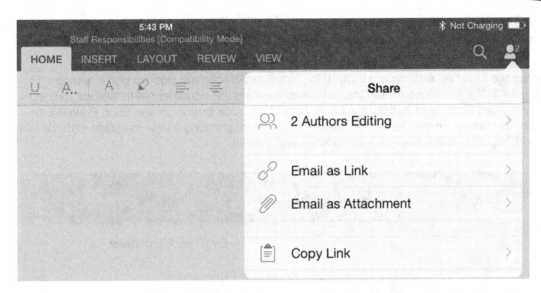

Figure 3-18. *To share the current notebook or e-mail the current page, open the Share pop-up panel and tap the appropriate button*

If you tap the Email as Link button or the Copy as Link button, the Email as Link pop-up panel (see Figure 3-19) or the Copy as Link pop-up panel appears. Tap the View Only button or the View and Edit button, as needed.

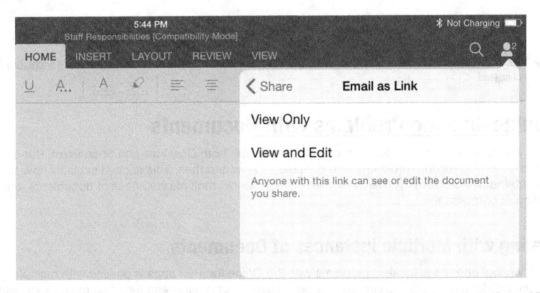

Figure 3-19. *On the Email as Link pop-up panel or the Copy as Link pop-up panel, tap the View Only button or the View and Edit button to specify the type of link to create*

After you tap the View Only button or the View and Edit button on the Email as Link pop-up panel, Mail opens with the skeleton of an e-mail message created. Fill in the recipient, add any text needed, and then tap the Send button.

If you tap the Email as Attachment button, the Email as Attachment pop-up panel appears (see Figure 3-20). You can then tap the button for sending the document in its current format (the Send Word Document button, the Send Excel Workbook button, or the Send PowerPoint Presentation button) or the Send PDF button. Mail opens, showing a new message with the file attached. You can then complete the message and send it.

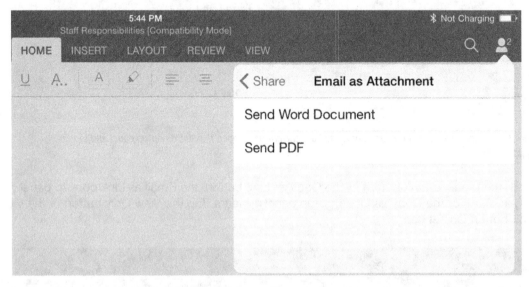

Figure 3-20. *From the Email as Attachment pop-up panel, you can either send the document in its current format or create a PDF file to send instead*

Troubleshooting Problems with Documents

At this writing, Office for iPad works impressively well with both OneDrive and SharePoint. But even so, you're likely to run into problems with documents now and then. This section explains how to deal with the two problems you're most likely to experience: multiple instances of documents, and puzzling error messages.

Dealing with Multiple Instances of Documents

At this writing, one of the trickiest problems with the Office for iPad apps is dealing with multiple instances of documents. You create a document, save it as normal—and then find multiple instances of it. For example, in Figure 3-21, Word shows three instances of the document called "Team Expansion Proposal – first draft" and three instances of the document called Working Notes. This happens both with documents that you edit simultaneously with colleagues (which can cause extra instances to accommodate unresolved conflicts) and on documents that you don't share.

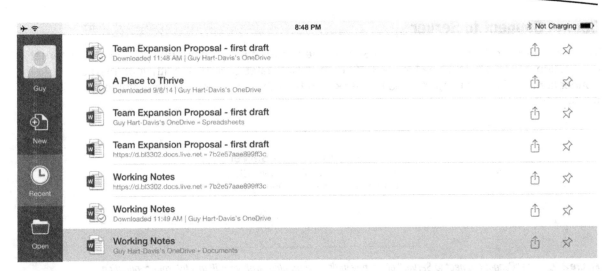

Figure 3-21. *You may find multiple instance of a document in your online locations even though you have created only one instance*

At this writing, there's no clear solution to this problem, so you need to proceed cautiously, especially if the documents are in a shared location and other people may be editing them.

Usually—as you'd hope—the most recent instance of the document has the latest changes. But don't assume that it's safe to go with the most recent instance and delete the others—at least check the other instances of a document and make sure that you've chosen the most promising of them to keep. For a quick check, you can look at the details in the Properties pop-up panel from the Recent screen or the Open screen; but to be certain that you're dealing with the right instance of the document, you'll need to open the different instances and look at them.

> **Tip**   The Properties pop-up panel that you can display from the Recent screen or the Open screen in the file management screens often displays less information than the Properties pop-up panel that you can display when you have a document open. So if you really need to see the details about a document, open it in the app, tap the File button to open the File menu, and then tap the Properties button.

If you run into the errors described in the next section when you try to open an instance of a document, you'll be on surer ground for deleting it.

Dealing with Errors

This section introduces you to three errors you may run into when using the Office for iPad apps:

- Cannot Connect to Server
- Cannot Connect to Site
- File Unavailable

Cannot Connect to Server

The error message "Cannot Connect to Server: The server may be unavailable. Check your internet connection and try again." (see Figure 3-22) typically indicates a problem with your Internet connection. So the first thing to do is to check whether other apps are having a problem accessing the Internet.

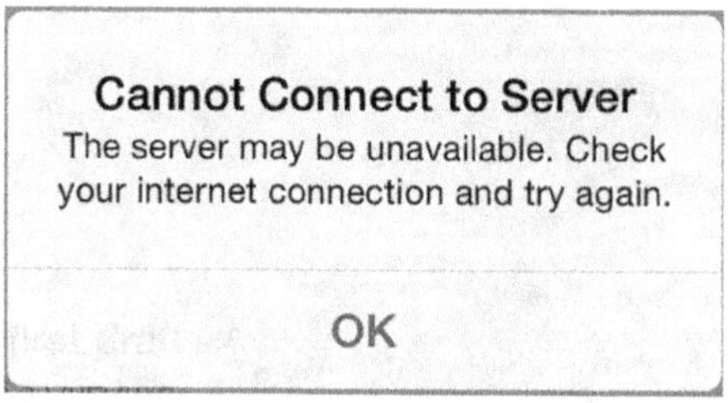

Cannot Connect to Server

The server may be unavailable. Check
your internet connection and try again.

OK

Figure 3-22. The "Cannot Connect to Server" error may indicate a problem with your iPad's Internet connection

Open Safari and see if it can reach web sites. If so, your Internet connection is fine, and you'll probably want to restart the Office app.

> **Tip**   Once the Mail app has used the Domain Name Service (DNS) to establish the IP address for each mail server you use, it typically retains that IP address until you close the app. This means that Mail may be able to send and receive mail even when your iPad has lost DNS functionality. For this reason, use Safari or another app to test your Internet connectivity rather than using Mail.

If Safari can't reach web sites, troubleshoot your iPad's Internet connection as usual. For example,

- Restart your Internet router if other devices are unable to connect to the Internet.
- Turn Airplane Mode on and then off again. This forces your iPad to reconnect to your cellular carrier (if it is a cellular iPad) and to Wi-Fi networks.
- Connect to a different Wi-Fi network if one is available.
- Turn your iPad off and then restart it.

Cannot Connect to Site

The error message "Cannot Connect to Site: The site doesn't have a valid security certificate." (see Figure 3-23) appears to be a bug, because the sites that typically produce it have valid security certificates before and afterward.

Figure 3-23. *The "Cannot Connect to Site" error is usually a bug*

To deal with this error, press the Home button twice to display the app switcher, and then swipe the app that raised the error up off the list of apps to close it. Open the app again and try opening the document again.

File Unavailable

The error "File Unavailable: The file has either been moved or deleted." (see Figure 3-24) occurs when you try to open a ghost instance of a document—an instance of the document that still appears on the file management screens but is no longer present on the server.

Figure 3-24. *The "File Unavailable" error occurs when you try to open a ghost instance of a document*

At this writing, the only way to deal with this error is to leave the ghost instance of the document alone until OneDrive or SharePoint gets rid of it. You may be able to clear the ghost instance from the list on the file management screens by restarting the app, but this works only sometimes. If you try to delete the ghost instance, the app typically displays the Cannot Delete File dialog box (see Figure 3-25), telling you that the file is currently in use.

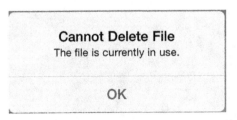

Figure 3-25. *The Office app may claim that the ghost instance of the document is in use when you try to delete it*

Summary

In this chapter, you learned how to manage your Office documents. You now know how to set up your OneDrive and SharePoint services on your iPad, manipulate documents from the file management screens and from the File menu within the active document, and how to share your documents with others. You also know how to troubleshoot some of the awkward problems that occur with documents on OneDrive and SharePoint.

Chapter 4

Getting Up to Speed with Word for iPad

In this chapter, you will get up to speed with Word for iPad. This chapter will first dig into the app's features and limitations so that you know what to expect and what will be missing. You will then learn how to create new documents, how to navigate the Word interface, and how to enter and edit text in the document. Along the way, you will find out how to work with tabs and line breaks, use the Paste Options feature to control what you paste, and display invisible characters when you need to see them.

Understanding Word for iPad's Features and Limitations

You probably wouldn't expect Word for iPad to offer the 1,500-odd features that Word for Windows does—and you'd be right. Microsoft has sensibly concentrated on implementing the essential features and has omitted specialized features that few people use.

> **Note** Microsoft is gradually adding features to Word, so the details in this section may no longer be accurate by the time you read it. For example, Microsoft added printing and the ability to create new comments to Word for iPad soon after releasing the app. So you should update Word on your iPad to the latest version, either by running the App Store app on your iPad and looking on the Updates tab or by using iTunes on your computer.

This chapter starts by digging into the features that Word does have and those it lacks. It then looks at what happens to document content that Word for iPad doesn't support.

Which Features Does Word for iPad Have and Lack?

Word for iPad enables you to perform standard actions with documents, as discussed in Chapter 2. You can create a new document and save it either on your iPad or on a supported cloud service, such as OneDrive or SharePoint; you can open and close existing documents; you can print a document; you can duplicate an existing document; and you can restore a document to an earlier version.

At this writing, Word for iPad lacks or has only partial implementations of several important features that the desktop versions of Word offer:

- *Templates*: Word for iPad enables you to create documents based on a selection of templates included with the app. But there is no straightforward way to create a document based on a template of your own. Nor can you create your own templates on Word for iPad.

- *Views*: Whereas the desktop versions of Word give you a handful of different views, ranging from the everyday Draft view and Print Layout view to the more specialized Master Document view, Word for iPad has a single view. This view is a layout view in which objects appear on screen as they will appear in the final document.

- *Outlines and master documents*: Given that Word for iPad doesn't have the Outline view or Master Document view, it'll be no surprise that the app lacks the desktop versions' features for manipulating outlines quickly and easily. You can still change the structure of a document by applying Heading styles, but you cannot view just the headings. If you create long documents, you'll feel this loss more acutely than if you mostly work with short documents.

- *Fields*: Word for iPad has partial support for fields. You can view and update existing fields, but you cannot enter new fields (except for page numbers). Similarly, you cannot create cross-references, indexes, or content tables (such as tables of contents or tables of figures).

- *Endnotes*: Word for iPad offers partial support for endnotes too. You can view and edit existing endnotes—you can even delete them—but you cannot create new endnotes.

- *Tables*: Word for iPad enables you to create and edit tables, but it doesn't have as extensive table features as the desktop versions.

- *Spelling and grammar checking*: Word for iPad enables you to check the spelling in your documents, but it doesn't have grammar-checking features.

- *Mail merge*: Word for iPad doesn't have features for creating merged documents, such as form letters, labels or envelopes, or catalogs.

- *WordArt, equations, SmartArt*: Word for iPad doesn't have advanced features such as WordArt (text-based illustrations you can create in the desktop versions of Word), equations, or SmartArt diagrams (such as flow charts or hierarchical diagrams).

- *Macros and VBA*: Word for iPad doesn't have the Visual Basic for Applications (VBA) programming language, which enables you to automate tasks using macros and user forms (custom dialog boxes).

What Happens to Content That Word for iPad Does Not Support?

When you open a document that includes content that Word for iPad doesn't fully support, the app displays as much of the content as possible so that you can view it even if you cannot edit it. For example, if you open a document that contains WordArt items, Word displays them correctly and even enables you to edit their text. Similarly, equations appear correctly in Word for iPad, and you can format them, but you cannot edit their contents.

Note   When you open a document that contains VBA, Word for iPad displays a message saying that it cannot run macros but will preserve them. When you tap the Convert and Edit button, Word converts the document from its older format (such as the Word 97–2003/Word 98–2004 format, which can contain VBA code) to the .docm format, the new file format that can contain VBA (whereas the .docx format cannot). After you save the document, the File Upgraded dialog box appears, telling you that the document "has been upgraded, and may include minor layout changes."

Creating a New Document on Your iPad

Here's how to create a new document in Word on your iPad.

1. Open Word if it's not already running. If Word displays the document you were using last, tap the Back button to display the file management screen.

2. Tap the New button in the left column to display the list of available templates (see Figure 4-1).

Figure 4-1. Tap the New button to display the available templates, and then tap the template on which you want to base the new document

3.   Tap the template you want to use. Word creates a new document based on that template. You can add content to the document using the methods discussed later in this chapter.

> **Note**   Use the New Blank Document to create a default document with a minimalist design and no contents.

4.   If you want to name the document immediately, tap the File button and then tap Name. The Save As dialog box opens, and you can enter the filename, choose the location, and then tap the Save button to save the document.

Navigating the Word Interface

Once you've opened a document, you'll see the Word interface. As you can see in Figure 4-2, Word has the following five static tabs on the Ribbon:

- *Home*: This tab contains essential formatting commands, such as styles, fonts and font sizes, and alignment.

- *Insert*: This tab enables you to insert pages, breaks, footnotes, and Office-standard items such as tables, pictures, shapes, and text boxes.

- *Layout*: This tab provides controls for setting the page size, orientation, and margins; changing the text direction; creating newspaper-style columns of text; and setting up headers, footers, and page numbers.

- *Review*: This tab allows you to work with comments and with Track Changes, the revision-marking feature. You can also block authors from editing particular parts of a document and set the language for the proofing tools to use.

- *View*: This tab enables you to turn the spelling checker on and off, toggle the display of the ruler, and open the Word Count pop-up panel.

Figure 4-2. Word has five static tabs on the Ribbon, plus context-sensitive tabs such as the Table tab (shown here with shading beneath it). The Home tab provides essential formatting commands

Word also has various context-sensitive Ribbon tabs, such as the Table tab shown in Figure 4-2. These tabs appear only when an object that requires them is active. (This document layout includes a table, but this is hard to see in the figure.)

Entering and Editing Text in a Document

After creating a new document, you'll likely want to add text to it. This section makes sure you have the skills you need to enter and edit text in documents.

MAKING THE MOST OF AUTOFORMAT AS YOU TYPE

Like the desktop versions, Word for iPad includes a feature called AutoFormat As You Type that automatically reformats your text as you work. AutoFormat As You Type can save you time and effort, so it's well worth spending a few minutes learning what it can do—especially as some of its actions can come as a surprise if you don't know about them.

You can turn AutoFormat As You Type on or off by opening the Settings app, tapping the Word button in the left column, and then setting the AutoFormat As You Type switch to the On position or to the Off position, as appropriate. Unlike the desktop apps, which enable you to choose which actions AutoFormat As You Type should perform, AutoFormat As You Type in Word for iPad gives you only an on/off choice for the feature as a whole.

AutoFormat As You Type on the iPad performs the following actions:

- Replaces straight quotes ("") with smart quotes ("").
- Replaces typed fractions (such as 1/4) with fraction characters (such as ¼).
- Formats a word preceded and followed by an asterisk (such as *emphasis*) with boldface (removing the asterisks).
- Formats a word preceded and followed by an underscore (such as _necessary_) with italics (removing the underscores).
- Replaces typed ordinal numbers (such as 1st) with superscript ordinals (such as 1st).
- Replaces a hyphen preceded and follow by a space as an en dash (a short dash), and replaces two hyphens in succession with an em dash (a longer dash).
- Replaces Internet paths (such as http://www.apress.com or mailto:info@apress.com) with hyperlinks.
- Applies bulleted-list formatting when you start a paragraph with an asterisk, a hyphen, or a greater-than sign followed by a space or tab.
- Applies numbered-list formatting when you start a paragraph with a number or letter followed by a period or closing parenthesis, and then type a space or tab.
- Adds a decorative border when you type three or more hyphens, underscores, asterisks, tildes, equal signs, or hash marks at the beginning of a paragraph and then press the Enter key. Try these out to see the types of lines they produce.
- Creates a table when you type a series of plus signs and hyphens indicating how many columns you want and their relative widths. Each plus sign indicates a column border, so +--+--+--+ produces a three-column table. The number of hyphens indicates the relative width of the columns, so here the columns are equal width.

These actions are similar to those in the desktop versions, which have several actions that Word for iPad doesn't have at this writing: applying heading styles by using combinations of Enter and Tab keypresses; using tabs and backspaces to set the left indent and first-line indent; formatting the beginning of a list item like the item before it; and defining styles based on your formatting.

Entering Text with the Onscreen Keyboard

Like many iPad apps, Word for iPad provides an onscreen keyboard for entering text in your documents. You can display the keyboard by tapping in a part of the document that can accept text (this means that in a typical document, you can tap almost anywhere). When you don't need the keyboard for now, you can hide it by tapping the Hide Keyboard button in the lower-right corner of the keyboard.

With the keyboard displayed, move the insertion point to the appropriate point if necessary, and then tap the keys. If the Suggestions bar displays the word you're typing (see Figure 4-3), tap the word to insert it.

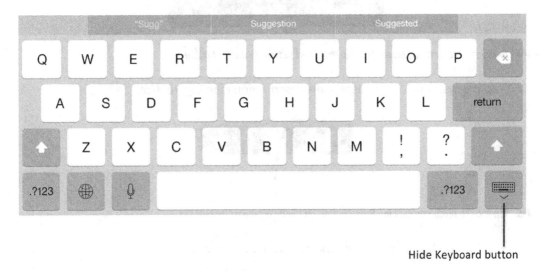

Hide Keyboard button

Figure 4-3. You can enter text by tapping the keys on the onscreen keyboard and accepting any suitable suggestions from the Suggestions bar

Note   Unlike Excel, which has custom keyboards to help you enter data and calculations more easily, Word uses standard iPad keyboards.

Inserting Tabs and Line Breaks

To lay out text the way you want, you may need to use tabs and line breaks. Tabs are useful for laying out columns of text when you don't want to use tables.

Tip   A line break is different from a paragraph character. You use a line break to end the current line and make the text continue on the next line. If the paragraph style of the current paragraph has a different style set for the Style for Following Paragraph setting, inserting a line break instead of a paragraph enables you to continue the current style on a new line. For example, the Heading 1 style may have Body Text set for the Style for Following Paragraph settings, so when you tap Return at the end of a Heading 1 paragraph, Word applies the Body Text style to the next paragraph. By inserting a line break instead of a paragraph, you can make the next line have the Heading 1 style as well. You might want to do this for a multiline heading.

Here's how to insert a tab or a line break.

1. Tap the appropriate point in the text to display the Edit menu (see Figure 4-4).

Figure 4-4. To insert a tab or a line break, first tap the Insert button on the Edit menu

2. Tap the Insert button to display the Insert menu (see Figure 4-5).

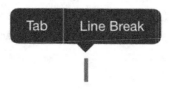

Figure 4-5. Tap the Tab button or the Line Break button on the Insert menu, as nedeed

3. Tap the Tab button or the Line Break button, as needed.

THREE TIMES NOT TO USE A TAB

Tabs are great when you need to line up multiple short text items in paragraphs, but there are three times when you shouldn't use tabs because Word offers the following better alternatives:

- *Indenting a whole paragraph:* To indent a whole paragraph, don't put a tab at the beginning of each line and a line break at the end. Instead, tap the Indent button near the right end of the Home tab of the Ribbon to indent the whole paragraph in a single move; tap again to indent it further. If you need to decrease or remove the indent, tap the Unindent button, the button to the left of the Indent button.

- *Creating multi-line columns of text:* To lay out multi-line or multi-paragraph blocks of text in columns, use a table instead of tabs.

- *Creating newspaper-style columns:* To create columns where the text runs all the way down the first column and then continues at the top of the second column (and so on), use the Columns feature. See Chapter 5 for details.

Setting Tabs

Here's how to set tabs in a document.

1. Tap in the paragraph for which you want to set tabs. If you want to set tabs for multiple paragraphs, select them.

2. If the ruler isn't displayed across the top of the screen below the Ribbon, tap the View tab and then set the Ruler switch to the On position.

3. Tap the point on the ruler where you want to place the tab. A tab marker appears bearing an L, indicating that it is a left-aligned tab.

4. If you need to reposition the tab, tap it and drag it to the right place. Word displays a readout showing the exact position (see Figure 4-6).

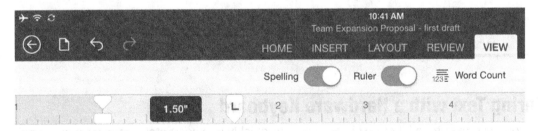

Figure 4-6. Tap the ruler to place the tab. You can then position the tab more exactly by using the readout that appears when you tap and hold the tab

5. If you need to change the tab's type, double-tap the tab marker. Double-tap once to change it to a center tab, double-tap again for a right tab, double-tap again for a decimal tab, or double-tap a fourth time for a bar tab. Figure 4-7 shows the symbol for each tab type. See the nearby sidebar for an explanation of the tab types and their uses.

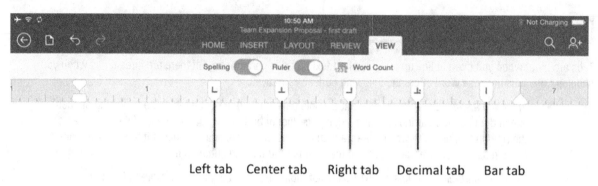

Figure 4-7. *Each tab type has a distinctive marker on the ruler*

> **Note**   To remove a tab, tap it and drag it off the ruler into the document.

USING WORD'S FIVE TYPES OF TABS

To enable you to create exact text layouts, Word gives you five types of tabs:

- *Left tab:* This is the normal type of tab. Text appears left-aligned after a block of white space.

- *Center tab:* Word aligns the center of the text on the position of the tab. Center tabs are useful for headings and similar display text.

- *Right tab:* Text appears right-aligned at the position of the tab. As you type more text, it moves back to the left. Right tabs are useful for laying out headers and footers.

- *Decimal tab:* Text appears aligned on the decimal point (the period) in the text. You normally use decimal tabs to align columns of numbers on the decimal point; this is especially useful when the numbers have different numbers of decimal places.

- *Bar tab:* A vertical bar character (|) appears at the position of the tab. This is a way of drawing a vertical line down the screen using characters rather than lines. Bar tabs are outmoded, but there's nothing to stop you from using them if you find them useful.

Entering Text with a Hardware Keyboard

When you need to enter a lot of text in a document quickly and accurately, connect a hardware keyboard to your iPad as discussed in Chapter 2. The hardware keyboard not only makes it easier to type but also enables you to see much more on screen because the onscreen keyboard isn't taking up a large proportion of the space.

Tip   You can use the keyboard shortcuts explained in Chapter 2 for navigating around your documents and selecting text. If your keyboard has a Command key, you can use standard keyboard shortcuts such as Copy (Command+C), Cut (Command+X), Paste (Command+V), Undo (Command+Z), and Undo (Shift+Command+Z).

If you need to make the onscreen keyboard available temporarily without disconnecting the Bluetooth keyboard in Settings (or by turning off Bluetooth in Control Center), try pressing the Eject key on the keyboard. Only some keyboards have the eject key, and this trick works on only some of them, but it's handy if it works on yours.

Copying and Pasting Text

You can copy text in Word as usual by selecting what you want to copy and then tapping the Copy button on the Edit menu. You can then paste the text wherever you need it.

Note   You can also copy other objects by using the same method: tap to select the object, and then tap the Copy button on the Edit menu.

When you paste text into a document, Word displays a Paste Options button below and to the right of the pasted material. You can tap this button to display the Paste Options menu (see Figure 4-8), and then tap the appropriate button:

- *Keep Source Formatting*: Tap this button to make the pasted material keep its original formatting.

- *Match Destination Formatting*: Tap this button to make the pasted material pick up the formatting of the paragraph into which you pasted it.

- *Keep Text Only*: Tap this button to remove any formatting from the pasted material, leaving only the text.

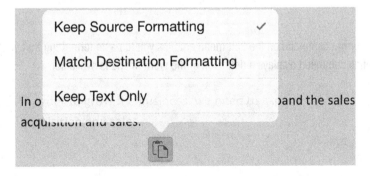

Figure 4-8. After pasting text, you can tap the Paste Options button and change the formatting of the pasted material

> **Tip**   In some cases, you get the same result from using the Match Destination Formatting option as from using the Keep Text Only option. This is normal.

Editing Text

Word for iPad makes it as easy as possible to enter text using the touchscreen. When you want to add to the existing text, tap to position the insertion point. You can then type text or tap the Delete key to delete the character to the left of the insertion point.

> **Note**   When you tap in existing text, Word positions the insertion point between words by default. To position the insertion point precisely, tap and hold to display the pop-up magnifier, and then move your finger to drag the insertion point to where you need it.

To change an existing word (or multiple words), it's usually easiest to select the text and then type over it (replacing it with what you type) than to delete it one character at a time. Double-tap a word to select it, and then drag the selection handles to enlarge or reduce the selection as needed. You can then either type in the correction or give a command from the Edit menu for text (see Figure 4-9). For example, tap the Cut button to cut the text from its current position to the Clipboard so that you can then paste it in somewhere else, or tap the Delete button to delete the text without placing it on the Clipboard.

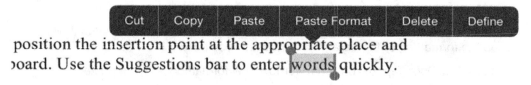

Figure 4-9. The Edit menu for text includes the Cut, Copy, Paste, and Delete commands

> **Note**   The Paste Format command on the Edit menu enables you to paste formatting that you've copied from other text. The Define command displays a definition of the word (if one is available).

> **Tip**   If you're used to using a hardware keyboard to edit text in the desktop versions of Word, you'll probably be able to edit much more quickly in Word for iPad if you connect a hardware keyboard.

Displaying Invisible Characters

Word normally doesn't display invisible characters such as spaces, tabs, paragraph marks, and breaks (page breaks and other breaks). But when you need to see them, you can display them by tapping the Show/Hide button at the right end of the Home tab of the Ribbon. As you can see in Figure 4-10, a line break appears as a blue arrow going down and to the left, a paragraph mark appears as a blue paragraph symbol (or pilcrow, ¶), a tab appears as a blue arrow pointing to the right, and a page break appears as a blue line with the words "Page Break" in it. Spaces also appear as blue dots, but you'll need good eyes to see these in the figure.

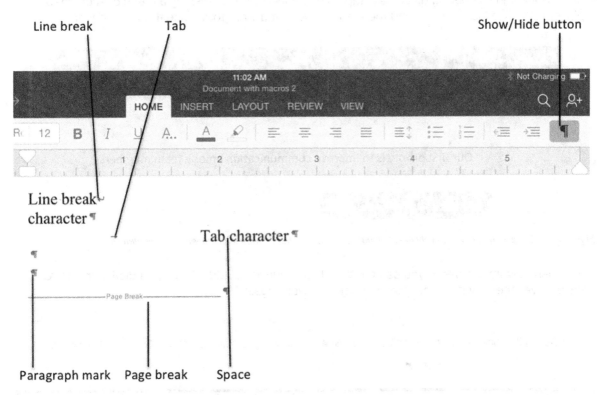

Figure 4-10. *Tap the Show/Hide button on the Home tab of the Ribbon when you need to see spaces, tabs, and paragraph marks*

Checking the Spelling

Word includes a spelling checker that you can use to check text automatically as you write. The spelling checker is normally turned on by default to help you avoid mistakes. You can turn the spell checker on or off as needed by tapping the View tab of the Ribbon and then setting the Spelling switch to the On position or to the Off position.

> **Tip**   If you find the spelling checker distracting when you're focusing on composing text, set the Spelling switch on the View tab of the Ribbon to the Off position until you finish writing. You can then turn the spelling checker on and deal with all the queries at once.

When the spelling checker is on, Word displays a wavy red underline under each word that doesn't appear in its spelling dictionary. Tap an underlined word to display a menu of suggested replacements (see Figure 4-11), and then tap the word you want to replace the queried word.

Figure 4-11. *Tap a word the spelling checker has queried, and then tap the replacement word on the menu*

If the queried word is correct, you can tap the +Learn button to add it to Word's dictionary. Word then removes the underline and doesn't query the word again.

> **Note**   If the spelling checker doesn't suggest the word you want, you can simply type the correction needed.

SETTING THE PROOFING TOOLS LANGUAGE

To control which language Word is using for the spelling checker, tap the Review tab and then tap the Set Proofing Tools Language button, the button to the right of the Block Authors button at the right end. In the Set Proofing Tools Language pop-up panel that opens, tap the language you want to use.

Checking the Word Count of a Document

Tap the Word count button on the View tab to display the Word Count pop-up panel (see Figure 4-12), which shows you the numbers of pages, words, characters with spaces, and characters without spaces in the document. Set the Include Additional Text switch to the On position if you want to include any text in text boxes, footnotes, and endnotes in the count; set this switch to the Off position if you want to count only the main text.

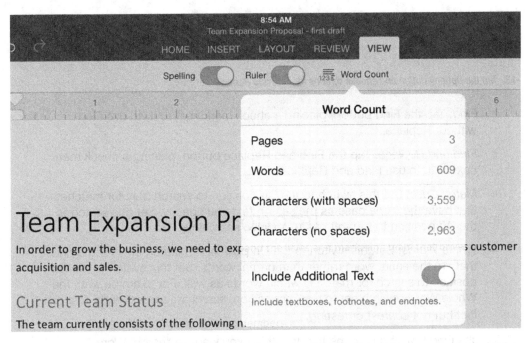

Figure 4-12. Open the Word Count pop-up panel to see how many pages, words, and characters your document contains

Using Find and Replace

Word provides a straightforward Find and Replace feature that enables you to search your documents for specific text and, optionally, replace it. Compared to the Find and Replace features in Word for Windows or Word for the Mac, the Find and Replace features on the iPad are limited, but they still have enough power to save you time and effort.

Here's how to use Find and Replace.

1. Tap in the document at the point where you want to start searching.

2. Tap the Search icon (the magnifying glass) near the right end of the Ribbon to display the Find and Replace bar.

3. Tap the Options button (the cog icon) at the left end of the Find and Replace bar to display the Options panel (see Figure 4-13), and then choose the options you want.

Figure 4-13. Tap the Options button and choose options for Find and Replace

- *Find*: Tap the Find button, placing a check mark next to it, to use Find without Replace.

- *Find and Replace*: Tap the Find and Replace button, placing a check mark next to it, to use Find and Replace.

- *Match Case*: Set this switch to the On position to search only for matches that have the same case as the search text you specify. Set this switch to the Off position to turn off case-sensitive searching.

- *Whole Words*: Set this switch to the On position to search only for matches that are the entire word rather than partial words. Set this switch to the Off position to search for matches within words as well. For example, with the Whole Words switch set to the On position, searching for *test* finds *Test* or *test* but not *contest* or *testing*.

4. Tap the Find box and type the text for which you want to search. Word searches automatically as you type the search text and selects the first match (if there is one). The number of matches appears at the right side of the Find box.

> **Tip**   To find text that appears at the beginning of a word, include a space before the text. Similarly, to find text that appears at the end of a word, put a space after it. These searches are often effective, but beware of quotes or punctuation making them miss some instances.

5. If you're using Find and Replace, tap in the Replace With box and type the replacement text. Figure 4-14 shows the Find and Replace bar in use.

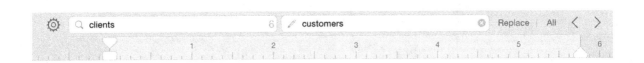

clients
6
customers
Replace
All
We need to give our clients a higher-appeal value proposition.

***Figure 4-14.** The Find and Replace bar in action*

6. Control the Find operation or the Find and Replace operation by tapping the appropriate command buttons.
   - >: Tap this button to find the next instance of the search term.
   - <: Tap this button to find the previous instance of the search term.
   - *Replace*: (Find and Replace only.) Tap this button to replace the current instance of the search term with the replacement text.
   - *All*: (Find and Replace only.) Tap this button to replace all instances of the search text with the replacement text.
7. When you finish using the Find feature or the Find and Replace feature, tap anywhere in the document to hide the Find and Replace bar.

Summary

In this chapter, you learned how to get started with Word for iPad. The chapter first examined the app's features and limitations, then showed you how to create new documents, navigate the Word interface, and enter and edit text. You now know the essentials of creating documents, including how to enter characters that don't appear on the keyboard; how to display invisible characters; and how to use the Spelling, Word Count, and Find and Replace features.

Chapter 5

Formatting and Laying Out Your Documents

As you saw in the previous chapter, Word for iPad makes entering text in your documents easy, especially if you connect a hardware keyboard. Once you've put the text in place, you'll likely want to format the text of your documents and lay out the pages so that they have the desired look.

This chapter will tell you what you need to know to format your documents effectively. The chapter will start by showing you how to set the page size, orientation, and margins for a document. You will then learn about the different types of formatting that Word provides, how to use styles to apply formatting swiftly and consistently, and how to add direct formatting for special effects when needed. You will then explore Word's extra features for tables, investigate how to use sections and create columns of text, and learn your options for wrapping text around objects.

Setting the Page Size, Orientation, and Margins

Each new document you create is based on a template, including the New Blank Document type of document. The document receives a wide range of settings from the template, including its page size, orientation, and margins. If necessary, you can change the page size, orientation, and margins at any point by using the controls on the Layout tab of the Ribbon.

To change the page size, tap the Layout tab of the Ribbon, tap the Size button, and then tap the appropriate button on the Size pop-up panel (see Figure 5-1).

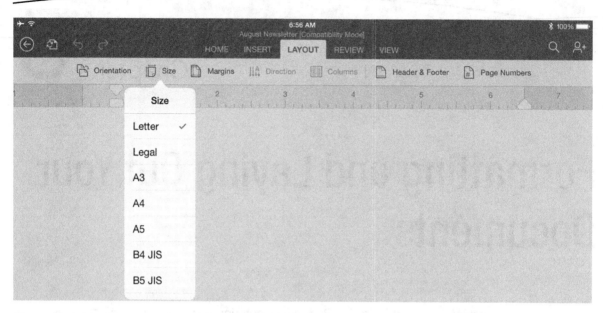

Figure 5-1. *Use the Size pop-up panel to set the page size for the document*

Note   If you need different page sizes for different pages in the document, create a separate section for each page that needs a different size from its predecessor. See the "Using Sections to Create Complex Documents" section for coverage of sections.

To change the page orientation, tap the Orientation button on the Layout tab, and then tap the Portrait button or the Landscape button on the Orientation pop-up panel (see Figure 5-2).

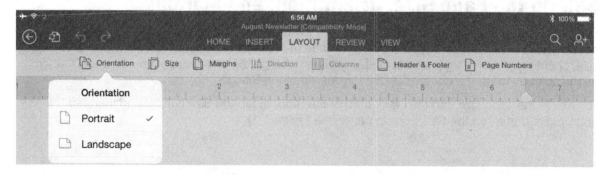

Figure 5-2. *You can change the orientation quickly between portrait and landscape by displaying the Orientation pop-up panel on the Layout tab and tapping the appropriate button*

To change the margins, tap the Margins button on the Layout tab, and then tap the appropriate button on the Margins pop-up panel (see Figure 5-3). These are your choices:

- *Normal*: Tap this button to set standard-width margins for the page size, such as 1.25-inch margins on 8.5×11-inch paper.

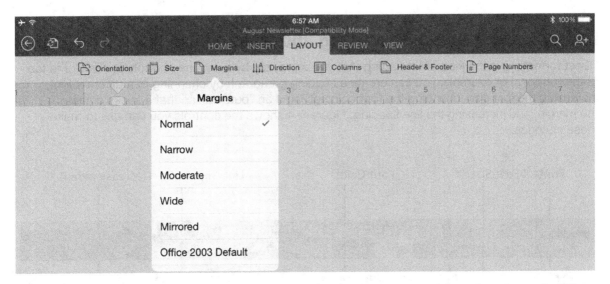

Figure 5-3. Use the Margins pop-up panel to quickly set the margin width. Alternatively, drag the margin markers on the Ribbon to the appropriate positions

Note   You can also set exact margins by dragging the margin markers on the ruler. If the ruler is hidden, tap the View tab of the Ribbon and set the Ruler switch to the On position.

- *Narrow*: Tap this button to set the margins to a narrow but printable width, such as 0.5-inch margins on 8.5×11-inch paper.

- *Moderate*: Tap this button to set the margins between the Narrow setting and the Normal setting, such as 1.0-inch margins on 8.5×11-inch paper.

- *Wide*: Tap this button to set wide margins, such as 2-inch margins on 8.5×11-inch paper.

- *Mirrored*: Tap this button to create mirrored margins for facing pages. With mirrored margins, the two outside margins (the left margin on the left page and the right margin on the right page) are the same width as each other, and the two inside margins (the right margin on the left page and the left margin on the right page) are the same width as each other.

- *Office 2003 Default*: Tap this button to set the margins to their default settings for Office 2003. This setting can be useful if your company or organization is still using Office 2003 as a standard. If not, you're usually better off choosing one of the other width settings.

Understanding the Different Types of Formatting

Word gives you such a wide variety of formatting that it's easy to waste time by using the wrong ones for your needs. This section explains the different types of formatting and shows you the best and fastest way to use them.

Understanding Direct Formatting and When to Use It

Direct formatting is the kind of formatting that you can apply by using the controls on the Home tab of the Ribbon. For example, you can create a heading paragraph by changing to a different font, increasing the font size, changing the font color, giving it an "outdent" so that it sticks out into the margin, and increasing the line spacing. Figure 5-4 shows the controls you can use to make these changes.

Figure 5-4. You can apply direct formatting by using the controls on the Home tab of the Ribbon

Each part of this formatting is easy enough to apply—tap this button, tap that button, and then tap the other button—but it takes time. And if you need to create another heading of the same type, you need to do it all over again. Or you can copy and paste the formatted text and type the new heading over it (as many people do) or use the Paste Format feature to paste the formatting that you've copied from one heading onto the text for a new heading you've typed.

Because direct formatting takes extra time and effort, you'll do best to apply it only when you have formatted your documents almost completely using styles, which are discussed next.

Understanding Styles and When to Use Them

To save you from having to apply large amounts of formatting manually, Word includes a feature called styles. A *style* is a collection of formatting that you can apply all at once. On the iPad, you apply a style by tapping the Styles button on the Home tab of the Ribbon and then tapping the appropriate style on the Styles pop-up panel (see Figure 5-5).

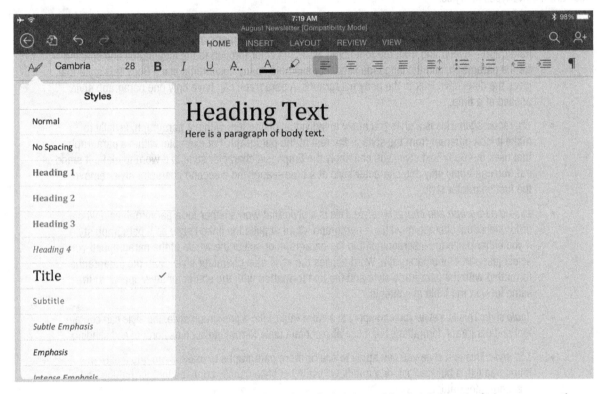

Figure 5-5. You can format text or an object more quickly and consistently by applying a style from the Styles pop-up panel on the Home tab of the Ribbon

Word's templates come with styles built in and ready for you to use. If you use a desktop version of Word, you can edit the styles in a template or document, or create new styles of your own, to make them suit your needs better. On Word for iPad, you can't edit the existing styles or create new styles.

> **Note**   In the desktop versions of Word, styles enable you not only to apply formatting quickly and easily but also to change it quickly. You can switch among different sets of styles called Quick Styles to change the look of each paragraph to which you've applied one of the styles in the Quick Styles set. You can modify a style (for example, by changing the font or the indentation) and see Word implement the change immediately on each paragraph that uses the style. And you can use the Find and Replace feature to search for one style and replace it with another style. These capabilities are not available on Word for iPad at this writing.

UNDERSTANDING THE FIVE TYPES OF STYLES

Word uses five different types of styles. Word for iPad blurs the distinctions among the different types, but knowing about the different types can be helpful when you're troubleshooting formatting issues, especially in the desktop versions of Word.

These are the five types of styles:

- *Paragraph style*: This is a style you apply to a whole paragraph at a time; you can't apply it to just part of a paragraph. A paragraph style contains a full range of formatting for that paragraph—everything from the font name, size, and color through to the indentation and spacing for the paragraph, and the language used. For example, many documents use a Body Text style that gives the distinctive look to the body paragraphs. A paragraph can have only one paragraph style applied at a time.

- *Character style*: This is a style you apply to individual characters within a paragraph, usually to make it look different from the style of the rest of the paragraph. For example, within a paragraph that uses the Body Text style, you can apply the Emphasis character style to a word to make it stand out. You can apply only one character style at a time—applying a second character style removes the first character style.

- *Linked paragraph and character style*: This is a style that works either for a paragraph as a whole or for individual characters within a paragraph. Word applies the linked style as a paragraph style if you either place the insertion point in the paragraph or select the whole of the paragraph. If you select just part of the paragraph, Word applies the style as a character style. Both the paragraphs formatted with the paragraph style and the text formatted with the character style appear at the same level in the table of contents.

- *Table style*: This is a style you can apply to a Word table. Like a paragraph style, the style can contain font and paragraph formatting, but it can also contain table formatting such as borders and shading.

- *List style*: This is a style you can apply to one or more paragraphs to make them into a list—a numbered list, a bulleted list, or a multilevel list. A list style usually contains font formatting and numbering formatting.

Formatting Your Documents the Best Way

The best way to format your documents is by applying styles first and then applying direct formatting afterward as needed for tweaks. For a straightforward document, you may not need to apply any direct formatting.

Start by applying a paragraph style to each paragraph. You can then apply a character style to any text within the paragraphs that needs special treatment. For example, you can apply the Book Title style to the name of a book title or other work to make it stand out from the text.

The selection of styles available in a document varies depending on the template, and in some cases on the document itself. Word for iPad enables you to use the styles saved in either the document itself or in the template attached to the document. Most documents include styles for titles, headings, and different types of emphasis. As an example, Table 5-1 explains the styles available in the New Blank Document template.

Table 5-1. Styles in the New Blank Document Template

Style Name	Style Type	Use This Style For
Normal	Paragraph	Any paragraph that doesn't need another paragraph style. In templates that have no Body Text styles, such as this template, use Normal for body text.
No Spacing	Paragraph	A paragraph that needs no space above it or below it, and no extra indents.
Heading 1–9	Paragraph	Top-level headings, second-level headings, third-level headings, and so on.
Title	Paragraph	The title at the top of the document.
Subtitle	Paragraph	The document's subtitle, if it has one.
Subtle Emphasis, Emphasis, Intense Emphasis	Character	Adding differing degrees of emphasis to words or phrases. Typically, the Emphasis style is the equivalent of applying italics with direct formatting. The Intense Emphasis style typically involves a change of color as well.
Strong	Character	Making words or phrases stand out. Typically, the Strong style is the equivalent of applying boldface with direct formatting.
Quote	Paragraph	Quotations that you need to have stand out from the main text.
Intense Quote	Paragraph	Quotations that you want to pop out from the main text.
Subtle Reference, Intense Reference	Paragraph	References that you want to make clear (Subtle Reference) or emphasize (Intense Reference). Intense Reference usually changes the color as well.
Book Title	Character	Making the title of a book, movie, or other work stand out. Typically, the Book Title style is the equivalent of applying italics and boldface with direct formatting.

Note At first, the Styles pop-up panel displays the heading styles Heading 1 through Heading 4. Once you use the Heading 4 style, Word adds the Heading 5 style to the Styles pop-up panel. When you use Heading 5, Word adds Heading 6, and so on up to Heading 9.

Applying Styles

Here's how to apply a style.

1. Select the text to which you want to apply the style.

    ■ If you're applying a paragraph style to a single paragraph, you can tap to place the insertion point in the paragraph. You don't need to select the whole paragraph, because Word applies to style to the whole paragraph.

    ■ If you're applying a paragraph style to multiple paragraphs, select those paragraphs. You don't need to select the beginning of the first paragraph and the end of the last paragraph, so you can make a "messy" selection if that's easier.

    ■ If you're applying a character style to a single word, you can place the insertion point in the word. But you may find it easier to double-tap the word to select it than to move the insertion point so that it is inside the word.

2. Tap the Home tab of the Ribbon to display its controls.

3. Tap the Styles button to display the Styles pop-up panel.

4. Tap the style you want to apply.

Applying Direct Formatting

After applying styles—or if you decide not to use styles for whatever reason—you can apply direct formatting to it. The Home tab of the Ribbon gives you instant access to font formatting, paragraph formatting, and bulleted and numbered lists.

Applying Font Formatting

To apply font formatting, select the text you want to format, and then use the controls on the left side of the Home tab of the Ribbon (see Figure 5-6).

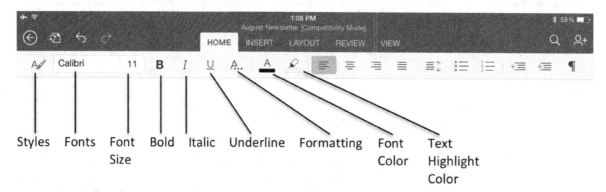

Figure 5-6. The font-formatting controls appear on the left side of the Home tab of the Ribbon

> **Tip**   If you want to format the word in which the insertion point is currently positioned, you don't need to select the word. This works only if the insertion point is within the letters of the word, not before the word or after it.

To change the font, tap the Fonts button to display the Fonts pop-up panel (shown on the left in Figure 5-7). You can then tap the font you want to use. To pick a particular font weight and style, tap the i button to the right of the font's name, and then tap the appropriate button on the font's pop-up panel (shown on the right in Figure 5-7).

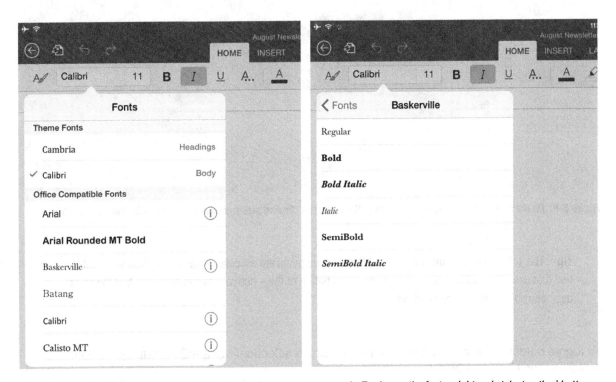

Figure 5-7. *On the Fonts pop-up panel (left), tap the font you want to apply. To choose the font weight and style, tap the i button, and then tap the appropriate option on the font's pop-up panel (right)*

To change the font size, tap the Font Size button to display the Font Size pop-up panel (see Figure 5-8). You can then either tap the font size you want or tap the + button and – button to adjust the font size one point at a time.

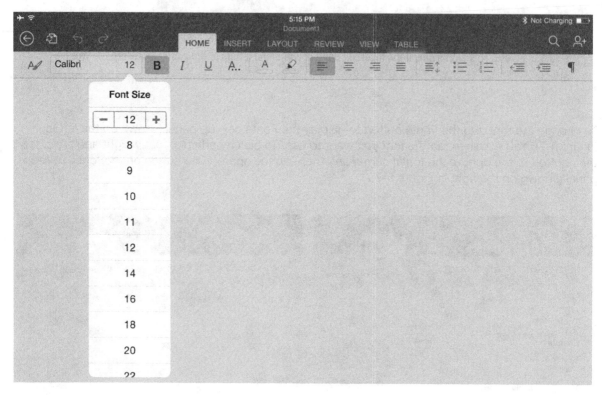

Figure 5-8. *On the Font Size pop-up panel, either tap the button for the font size you want or tap the + button and – button*

> **Tip**   The + button and – button in the Font Size pop-up panel are especially useful when you've selected text that uses different font sizes. By tapping the + button or the – button, you can make each of the sizes used one point larger or one point smaller.

To toggle boldface, italic, or underline on or off for the selection, tap the Bold button, the Italic button, or the Underline button.

> **Tip**   If you've connected a hardware keyboard that has a Command key, you can use keyboard shortcuts to toggle bold (press Command+B), italics (press Command+I), or underline (press Command+U).

To apply strikethrough, subscript, or superscript, or text effects, tap the Formatting button to display the Formatting pop-up panel (see Figure 5-9). You can then tap the Strikethrough button, the Subscript button, or the Superscript button to apply one of those types of formatting. To apply a text effect, tap the Text Effects button to display the Text Effects pop-up panel (see Figure 5-10), and then tap the effect you want.

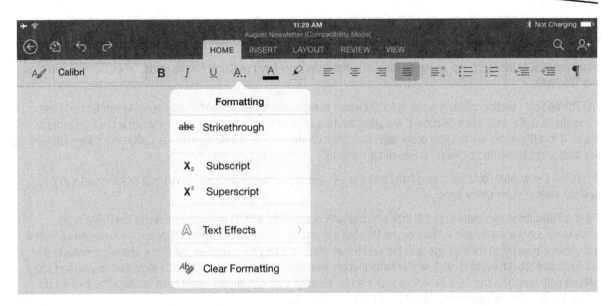

Figure 5-9. From the Formatting pop-up panel, you can apply strikethrough, superscript, subscript, or text effects. You can also clear existing direct formatting from the selection

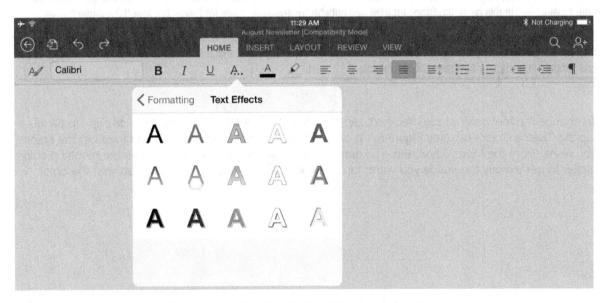

Figure 5-10. You can apply text effects to selected text from the Text Effects pop-up panel

Note   Tap the Clear Formatting button on the Formatting pop-up panel to remove any existing direct formatting from what you've selected. This move is helpful both for standardizing formatting and for troubleshooting formatting problems caused by direct formatting that you can't see (or can't easily see).

UNDERSTANDING HOW OFFICE FOR IPAD SUBSTITUTES FONTS

When you look at the Fonts pop-up panel, you'll see that it contains three sections: Theme Fonts, Office Compatible Fonts, and iOS Fonts.

The Theme Fonts section contains a pair of fonts chosen to work well together, one for headings and one for body text. For example, in the New Blank Document template, the Headings font is Cambria and the Body font is Calibri. Cambria is a serif font (the serifs are the little projections that finish off the strokes of letters), whereas Calibri is a sans-serif font, one that doesn't have serifs ("sans" is French for "without").

The Office Compatible Fonts list shows fonts that you can use in your documents and have them look the same in a desktop version of the Office apps.

The iOS Fonts list shows fonts from iOS that aren't directly compatible with all desktop versions of the Office apps. Many of the fonts are available in Word on the Mac but not usually available in Word on Windows. If you use these fonts in a document in an Office for iPad app, and then open that document on your computer, the Office app will substitute any iOS fonts that are not available with similar fonts that are available. If using the exact fonts is important to you, and you will use both Windows and OS X as well as your iPad for creating your documents, you'll need to check the font list on each platform to make sure Word doesn't have to substitute fonts.

You may also run into font substitutions the other way. When you open a document on your iPad that has been created in a desktop version of the Office app, you may see the message "Text may look different, because this file use fonts that aren't available." In this case, the Office for iPad app substitutes available fonts for those that aren't available.

Font substitutions change the look of text and may alter the layout, but unless the document is very precisely laid out, they're not usually a big problem. If a substitution results in text using a font that's unreadable or that you don't like, you can simply apply another font from those available.

To change the font color of selected text, tap the Font Color button. In the Font Color pop-up panel, tap the Theme Colors tab (see Figure 5-11) or the More Colors tab as needed, and then tap the color you want. From the More Colors tab, you can tap the Custom Color button and use the resulting color picker to get exactly the shade you want; tap the Apply button when you're satisfied with the color.

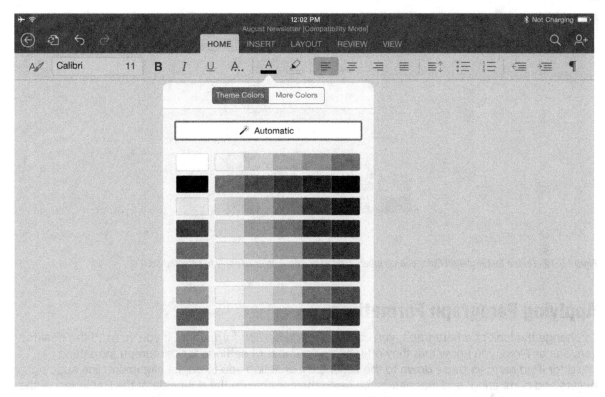

Figure 5-11. On the Font Color pop-up panel, tap the Theme Colors tab or the More Colors tab, and then tap the color you want

Note   Tap the Automatic button on the Theme Colors tab of the Font Color pop-up panel to apply the automatic theme color. This makes Word apply a color that contrasts with the background, such as black font on a white background. If you change the background to a dark color, Word changes the font color to keep the text readable.

If you need to highlight selected text, tap the Text Highlight Color button, and then tap the color to apply on the Text Highlight Color pop-up panel (see Figure 5-12). Tap the No Color button to remove an existing highlight.

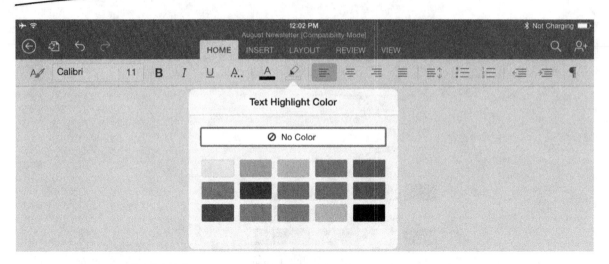

Figure 5-12. *On the Text Highlight Color pop-up panel, tap the highlight color to apply to selected text*

Applying Paragraph Formatting

To change the look of a paragraph, you can alter its paragraph formatting. If you've used the desktop versions of Word, you know that they offer a large number of settings for paragraph formatting. Word for iPad narrows these down to the essentials, enabling you to adjust alignment, line spacing, bullets and numbering, and indentation by using the controls on the right side of the Home tab of the Ribbon and (for first-line indents) the ruler.

Selecting the Paragraphs to Format

As usual, you first select the paragraphs you want to affect. If you want to affect only a single paragraph, tap to place the insertion point in it. Because the paragraph formatting applies to entire paragraphs, you don't need to select the beginning of the first paragraph in the selection or the end of the last paragraph—as long as you've selected part of the paragraph, that's fine.

Setting Paragraph Alignment and Indents

To change the alignment, tap the appropriate button on the Home tab of the Ribbon (see Figure 5-13): Align Left, Center, Align Right, or Justify. Justify aligns the text on both margins, so it can create uneven amounts of space between words. For lines with few words, justified text may appear awkwardly spaced.

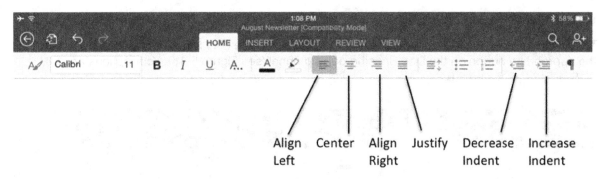

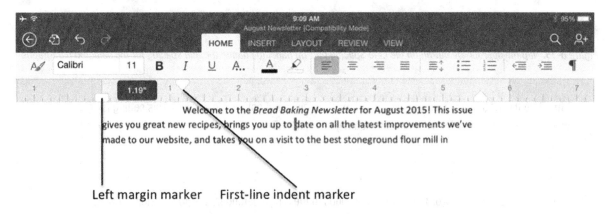

Figure 5-13. Tap the appropriate alignment button to align the selected paragraphs. Tap the Increase Indent button or the Decrease Indent button to alter the indentation

Tap the Increase Indent button or the Decrease Indent button to set the indentation of the selected paragraphs. You can decrease the indent only up to the position of the left margin marker. To "outdent" the paragraph further, drag the left margin marker on the Ribbon to the left.

To set a first-line indent, drag the first-line indent marker on the Ribbon to the appropriate position. A pop-up readout shows you the exact position, such as 0.94" (see Figure 5-14).

Figure 5-14. Drag the first-line indent marker on the Ribbon to set the first-line indent. Drag the left margin marker to set the left margin

Tip   You can drag the first-line indent marker to the left past the left margin marker to create a hanging indent, an indent in which the first line sticks out to the left of the rest of the paragraph.

Changing the Line Spacing

To change the line spacing for the selected paragraphs, tap the Line Spacing button and then tap the appropriate button on the Line Spacing pop-up panel (see Figure 5-15). Your options are 1.0, 1.15, 1.5, 2.0, 2.5, and 3.0.

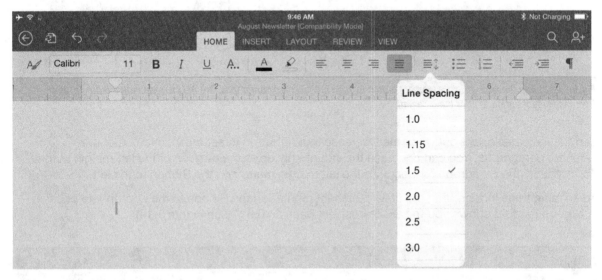

Figure 5-15. Tap the appropriate button on the Line Spacing pop-up panel to change the line spacing for the selected paragraphs

Tip   Use the 1.15-line spacing to give a paragraph a "close but not too close look." This setting is useful where single spacing looks too tightly packed together and 1.5-line spacing looks looser than you want.

Note   The 1.0 setting in Word for iPad corresponds to the Single setting in desktop versions of Word. Similarly, the 1.5 setting corresponds to the 1.5 Lines setting and the 2.0 setting corresponds to the Double setting. The 1.15 setting, 2.5 setting, and 3.0 setting on the iPad correspond to the Multiple setting in desktop versions with the appropriate number (1.15, 2.5, and 3.0) specified. Word for iPad offers no way to set other line spacings, such as Exactly and At Least, that the desktop versions provide. Word for iPad also does not enable you to adjust the Before setting and After setting for a paragraph. (You use these settings in the desktop versions to increase or decrease the amount of space after a paragraph. For example, you might add 6 points after a body text paragraph to create a small gap between paragraphs without changing the line spacing.)

Applying Bullets and Numbering

Word for iPad enables you to apply standard bullets and numbering quickly from the Home tab of the Ribbon.

Caution   Word for iPad doesn't offer custom bullets and numbering as the desktop versions of Word do. Nor does Word for iPad provide multilevel lists, such as numbered lists with subnumbered items. But if you set custom bullets or custom numbering in a document using a desktop version of Word, the bullets or numbering will appear correctly when you open the document on Word for iPad. You can add items to the existing levels of the list, but changing list paragraphs to different levels (for example, promoting a subnumbered item to a main numbered item) tends to wreck the formatting of the whole list. The list's formatting may not change until you save the document, so try making minor changes, then close the document and reopen it to see if the formatting remains stable, before you devote time and effort to changing the list.

To apply bullets, tap the Bullets button to display the Bullets pop-up panel (shown on the left in Figure 5-16), and then tap the button for the style of bullet you want. To apply numbering, tap the Numbering button to display the Numbering pop-up panel (shown on the right in Figure 5-16), and then tap the button for the numbering style to use.

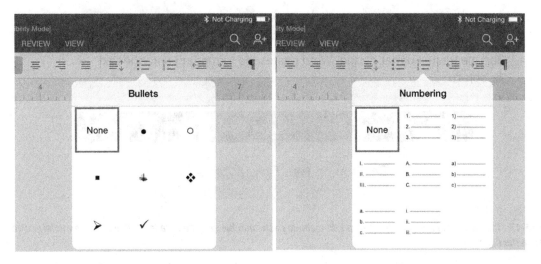

Figure 5-16. You can apply bullets quickly from the Bullets pop-up panel (left) or numbering from the Numbering pop-up panel (right)

Tip   You can start a bulleted list by typing a frequently used bullet character, such as an asterisk (*), followed by a tab or space, at the beginning of a line. Similarly, you can start a numbered list by typing any of several numbering formats (such as **1**, **1)**, or **1.**) at the beginning of a line and then typing a tab or a space.

Note   Bullets and numbering you apply by using the Bullets pop-up panel and the Numbering pop-up panel are paragraph formatting rather than characters typed in the document. To remove bullets or numbering, select the paragraph or paragraphs, open the Bullets pop-up panel or the Numbering pop-up panel, and then tap the None button.

Tip   To enter an actual bullet character in text, tap and hold the − (hyphen) key on the onscreen keyboard until the pop-up panel of alternate characters appears, and then tap the bullet button.

Pasting Formatting

When you've applied exactly the direct formatting that you need to some text or to an object, you can use the Paste Format feature to apply that formatting to other objects that need it. Follow these steps.

1. Select the text (or the object) that has the formatting you want to copy. The Edit menu appears automatically when you make the selection.

2. Tap the Copy button on the Edit menu. This copies both the text (or object) and its formatting to the Clipboard.

3. Select the text (or object) to which you want to apply the formatting. Again, the Edit menu appears automatically (see Figure 5-17).

4. Tap the Paste Format button. Word pastes the formatting onto the text or object.

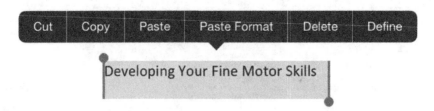

Figure 5-17. Tap the Paste Format button on the Edit menu to paste onto the selection the formatting of the material you've copied to the Clipboard

Tip   The copied material and formatting remains on the Clipboard until you copy or cut something else, so you can paste the formatting onto other text or objects until then.

Using Word's Extra Table Features

Tables in Word can be a great way of laying out text in rows and columns in order to make the information easy to read. Word for iPad includes several extra table features over those included in the other Office for iPad apps, including converting existing text to a table and making header rows repeat on each page that a multipage table covers.

Converting Existing Text to a Table

When creating a document, you may find that you need to turn some text you've written into a table. For example, you may have started to create a list separated by tabs but then found that some items require multiple lines, which makes using tabs a nightmare.

Word for iPad enables you to create tables from existing text separated with either tabs or commas. Tabs are usually easier unless you happen to have comma-separated text to work with.

CONVERTING TAB- OR COMMA-SEPARATED MATERIAL INTO A TABLE SUCCESSFULLY

When converting tabbed material into a table, you must make sure of three things:

- *Each paragraph contains the same number of tabs or commas:* If the paragraphs you convert contain different numbers of tabs or commas, Word creates enough columns for the paragraph with the most tabs or commas. You'll then need to move cell contents around and get rid of the surplus cells.

- *Each item is separated by only one tab:* When you're laying out text with tabs, it's easy to use two or three tabs between items, especially when you're working with default tab stops rather than custom tab stops placed where you need them. But if you convert material separated by multiple tabs, you'll get the wrong number of columns. (You can create the same problem with commas, but it's less likely that you'll add extra commas for layout purposes.)

- *Each cell's material consists of a single paragraph, not multiple paragraphs:* Make sure that no cell's material is broken onto multiple paragraphs—otherwise, you'll get the wrong number of rows.

Tap the Show/Hide button at the right end of the Home tab of the Ribbon if you need to see the tabs and paragraph marks in the document.

You can convert such text into a table by following these steps.

1. Look through the text you want to turn into a table and make sure the items that will become columns are separated consistently using tabs or commas. See the nearby sidebar for more detail.

2. Select the text.

3. Tap the Insert tab on the Ribbon to display its controls.

4. Tap the Table button.

> **Tip**   Word doesn't provide an easy way to convert a table into text. Your best option is to cut the table to the Clipboard and then paste it where you need the text. Word pastes in the table as a table. Tap the Paste Options button that appears at the lower-right corner of the pasted material, and then tap the Keep Text Only button to convert the material to paragraphs of text with the contents of the cells separated by tabs.

Using AutoFit

Word includes an AutoFit feature that you can use to adjust column width to fit the column width to the contents of the cells. Here's how to use AutoFit.

1. Tap anywhere in the table.

2. Tap the Table tab on the Ribbon to display its controls.

3. Tap the AutoFit button to display the AutoFit pop-up panel (see Figure 5-18).

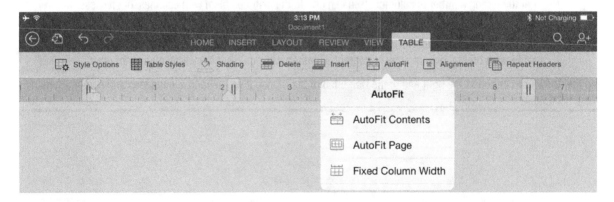

Figure 5-18. Use the buttons on the AutoFit pop-up panel to tell Word how to fit column width to contents

4. Tap the appropriate button:

   a. *AutoFit Contents*: Tap this button to adjust the width of each column to best fit its contents. Word may change the table's width.

   b. *AutoFit Page*: Tap this button to fit the table to the page on which it falls.

   c. *Fixed Column Width*: Tap this button to turn off AutoFit, fixing each column's width at its current width. You can adjust the column width manually as needed.

Repeating Table Headers on Each Page

If you create a table that runs from one page to the next (or to multiple pages), make Word continue the table's headers on each page. This is much better than creating a table header row manually on each page, because such rows can move from page to page as you create or edit your document.

Here's how to turn on repeat headers.

1. Tap in the header row. If you want to use multiple rows of headers, select the rows.

2. Tap the Table tab of the Ribbon to display its controls.

3. Tap the Repeat Headers button so that its background turns gray and it appears pushed in.

Using Sections to Create Complex Documents

When you need to create documents that use multiple layouts, you have to put each layout in a separate section. Here are examples of documents that use multiple layouts:

- A newsletter may need different numbers of columns on different pages (or on the same page).

- A report may require different headers and footers for different chapters.

- A business letter may need to contain an envelope page as well.

Word's sections are essential for creating complex documents, but they're tricky both to see and to grasp. Word makes matters worse by automatically creating sections when your documents need them—for example, when you apply columns to part of a document, as discussed later in this chapter—but not making clear what it's doing.

Here are the essentials:

- *Each new blank document has a single section at first*: When you create a new blank document, Word creates it as a single section until you add further sections. By contrast, documents you create based on a template contain however many sections the template has.

- *When you need to give part of the document a different layout, you create a new section*: For example, if you need to create a landscape page in a document that uses portrait orientation, you put the landscape page in a separate section so that you can change the layout.

- *A section can start on the same page or on a different page*. Word gives you four kinds of section breaks:

  - *Continuous*: The new section starts on the same page as the previous section. This type of break is useful for creating multi-column layouts on part of a page that also has one or more single-column layouts.

  - *Next page*: The new section starts on the next page after the previous section ends. This is the kind of break you use for putting a new chapter on a new page or for changing layout from portrait to landscape.

  - *Even page*: The new section starts on the next even page after the previous section ends. This may mean having a blank page in the printed document.

  - *Odd page*: The new section starts on the new odd page after the previous section ends. This too may mean a blank page appears in the printed document.

- *A section break divides one section from the next*: When you create a section (or Word creates one automatically for you), you add a section break to the document. A section break is normally hidden, but if you display paragraph marks and other invisible characters, it appears as a dotted double line with the words Section Break and the type in the middle—for example, Section Break (Continuous).

Once you know all this, inserting a section break is simplicity itself.

1. Place the insertion point where you want the new section to start. It's best to put the insertion point at the beginning of a paragraph.

2. Tap the Insert tab of the Ribbon to display its controls.

3. Tap the Breaks button to display the Breaks pop-up panel (see Figure 5-19).

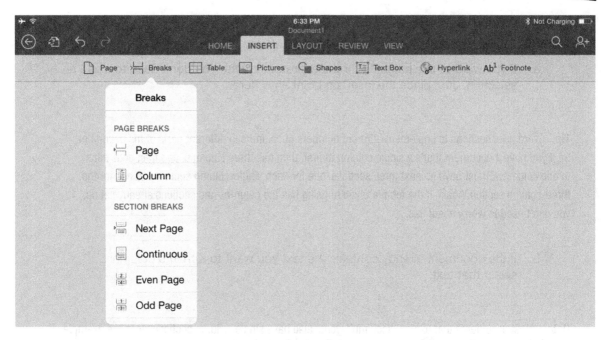

Figure 5-19. You can insert any of the four types of section breaks from the Section Breaks pop-up panel

4.   Tap the Next Page button, the Continuous button, the Even Page button, or the Odd Page button, as needed. Word inserts the break.

To see the break, tap the Show/Hide button at the right end of the Home tab of the Ribbon.

Creating Columns of Text

When you're creating a publication such as a newsletter, you may find it useful to create columns of text like those used in newspapers or magazines, where the text runs all the way down one column and then starts at the top of the next column.

> **Note**   Some templates have columns already set up, so you can simply add text to create the layout. For example, the Business Newsletter template includes a three-column layout.

Here's how to create columns of text.

1. Select the part of the document you want to affect.

    a. If you want to use columns for the entire document, you don't need to make a selection. Just place the insertion point anywhere.

Tip Word uses sections to implement different numbers of columns in different parts of the document. So if you have a document that's a single column at first, then has three columns, and then goes back to one column, it must have at least three sections: one for each single-column section and one for the three-column section. Again, if the template you're using has the columns and sections already set up, you don't need to worry about this.

---

    b. If the document already contains the text you want to turn into columns, select that text.

Note Most documents that use multicolumn layouts also have single-column sections, as in the example shown in this section. If you use a multicolumn layout all the way through a document, you can use the header (or the footer) to implement a single-column section if needed.

---

    c. If you want to create columns at the end of the document, select a paragraph at the end of the document. (If there is no blank paragraph at the end of the document, create a new paragraph and then select it.)

2. Tap the Layout tab of the Ribbon to display its controls.

3. Tap the Columns button to display the Columns pop-up panel (see Figure 5-20).

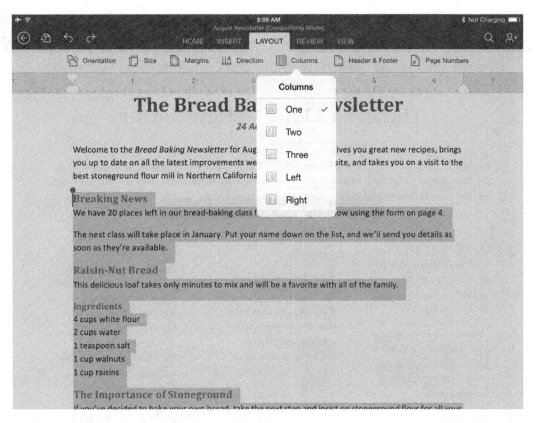

Figure 5-20. *Tap the Columns button on the Layout tab of the Ribbon to display the Columns pop-up panel, and then tap the number of columns to use*

4. Tap the appropriate button:

    a. *One*: Tap this button to change back from a multi-column layout to a single-column layout.

    b. *Two*: Tap this button to create two columns of the same width.

    c. *Three*: Tap this button to create three columns of the same width.

    d. *Left*: Tap this button to create a narrower column to the left of a wider column.

    e. *Right*: Tap this button to create a narrower column to the right of a wider column.

The columns appear in the document (see Figure 5-21), and you can judge how well they work.

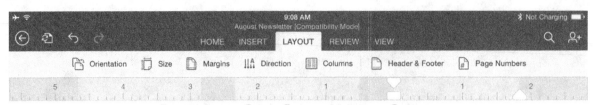

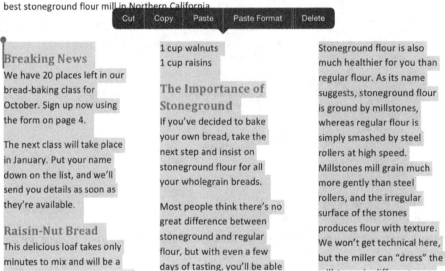

Figure 5-21. *Word converts the selected text to newspaper-style columns*

Note You can change the indents of the paragraphs in columns by tapping the paragraph you want to affect and then dragging the Left Indent marker, the First-Line Indent marker, or the Right Indent marker, as needed. If you don't have the ruler displayed, tap the View tab of the Ribbon and then set the Ruler switch to the On position to display it.

Wrapping Text Around Objects

You can insert objects, such as photos or shapes, in your documents by using the techniques explained in Chapter 2. After inserting an object, you can change the text wrapping if necessary by tapping the Wrap Text button on the Picture tab or Shape tab of the Ribbon and then tapping the wrap type you want on the Wrap Text pop-up panel (see Figure 5-22).

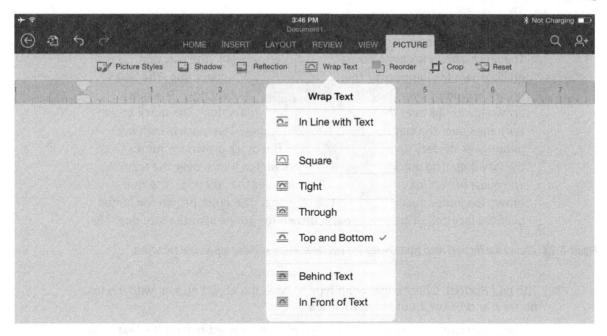

Figure 5-22. Use the Wrap Text pop-up panel on the Picture tab of the Ribbon to control text wrapping around a picture. For shapes and text boxes, the Wrap Text button appears on the Shape tab

These are the wrap types:

- *In Line with Text*: Choose this wrap type to place the object in the text layer, making Word treat the object as a character. Word moves the object with the text stream, so if you insert a character before the object, the object moves to the right. Inline placement is mostly useful for small objects.

- *Square*: Choose this wrap type to wrap the text around the border of the object. This is the wrap type you'd normally use for wrapping around an object.

- *Tight*: Choose this wrap type to wrap the text tightly around the border of the object. This wrap type is useful for irregularly shaped objects.

- *Through*: Choose this wrap type to wrap the text tightly around the border of the object and in any white space. Figure 5-23 shows a shape that uses the Through wrap type.

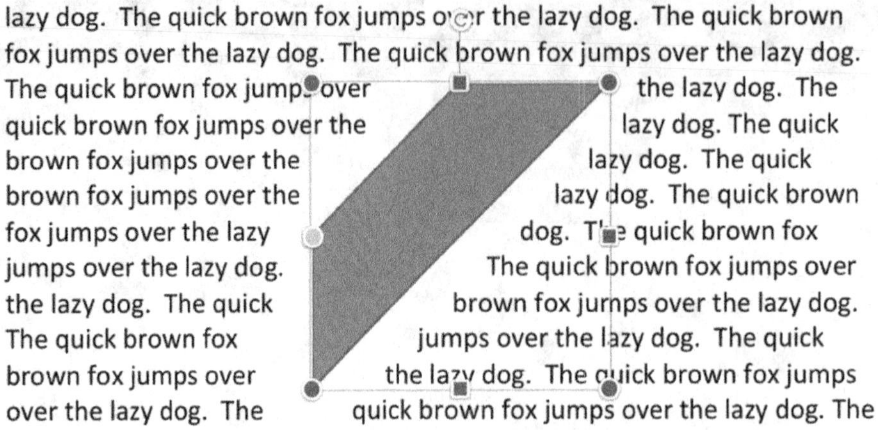

lazy dog. The quick brown fox jumps over the lazy dog. The quick brown fox jumps over the lazy dog. The quick brown fox jumps over the lazy dog. The quick brown fox jumps over the lazy dog. The quick brown fox jumps over the lazy dog. The quick brown fox jumps over the brown fox jumps over the lazy dog. The quick brown fox jumps over the lazy dog. The quick brown fox jumps over the lazy dog. The quick brown fox jumps over the lazy dog. The quick brown fox jumps over the lazy dog. The quick brown fox jumps over the lazy dog. The quick brown fox jumps over the lazy dog. The quick brown fox jumps over the lazy dog. The quick brown fox jumps over the lazy dog. The quick brown fox jumps over the lazy dog. The quick brown fox jumps over the lazy dog. The quick the lazy dog. The quick brown fox jumps over the lazy dog. The quick over the lazy dog. The quick brown fox jumps over the lazy dog. The

Figure 5-23. *Choose the Through wrap type to wrap the text through any white space around the object*

- *Top and Bottom*: Choose this wrap type to have the object appear with the text above it and below it but not at its sides.

- *Behind Text*: Choose this wrap type to position the object behind the text layer. You can then move the object freely so that it appears where you want it. If text appears in front of the object, it obscures it.

- *In Front of Text*: Choose this wrap type to position the object in front of the text layer. You can then move the object freely so that it obscures or enhances the text.

Summary

In this chapter, you learned how to lay out your documents and format them. You now know how to set page size, orientation, and margins and how to format using styles and direct formatting. You can also use Word's features for tables, create newspaper-style columns, divide your documents into sections, and make the most of Word's tricks with wrapping text around objects.

Chapter 6

Revising and Completing Your Documents

You may create some documents on your own, but most likely you'll work with other people on many documents. That may mean either sharing the documents via a OneDrive account or via a SharePoint server or using e-mail to send the documents back and forth.

This chapter will first show you how to add headers, footers, and page numbers to your documents and how to work with footnotes and endnotes. You will then learn how to work with comments; how to use the Track Changes feature to mark revisions in your documents and integrate input from multiple authors; and how to edit your documents simultaneously with your colleagues, resolving any editing conflicts that arise within a document.

Adding Headers, Footers, and Page Numbers

If you're planning to print out a multipage document, or to distribute it as a PDF file, it's often a good idea to add headers, footers, and page numbers to make the pages easy to identify.

Adding Headers and Footers to a Document

A header appears across the top of a page, and a footer appears across the bottom of a page. You can use headers and footers to add information such as the document name and file name, author name, date, and page numbers—or any other information that you need to make available to the reader.

Word gives you plenty of flexibility with headers and footers. If a document needs the same header (or footer) all the way through, you can quickly add one. But you can also use different headers or footers on the odd pages of the document to the even pages, and use different headers and footers from one section of a multisection document to the next. You can also prevent the header or footer from appearing on the first page of a document, which is useful for documents such as letters.

> **Note**   Word's templates come with built-in headers and footers that you can quickly add to give your documents a standard look. These headers and footers range from the straightforward Blank one to stylish designs that can look good in a variety of documents. Many of the headers and footers come with odd-page and even-page versions so that you can create effective page spreads.

Here's how to add a header or a footer.

1. Tap the Layout tab of the Ribbon to display its controls.

2. Tap the Header & Footer button to display the Header & Footer pop-up panel (see Figure 6-1).

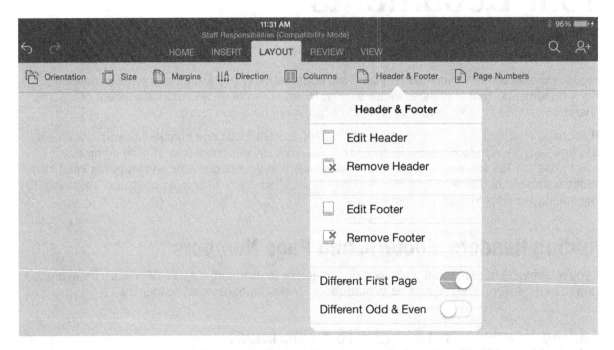

Figure 6-1. To start creating a header or footer, tap the Header & Footer button on the Layout tab of the Ribbon, and then tap the Edit Header button or the Edit Footer button on the Header & Footer pop-up panel

3. Set the Different First Page switch to the On position if you want the first page to have a different header or footer (or no header or footer).

4. Set the Different Odd & Even switch to the On position if you want to have different headers and footers on the odd pages than on the even pages.

5. Tap the Edit Header button or the Edit Footer button, depending on which element you want to edit. Word displays the header area (see Figure 6-2) or the footer area, as appropriate.

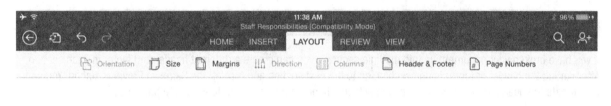

5 March 2015

Staff Responsibilities

Figure 6-2. Type or paste the text of the header or footer in the header or footer area, and then click the Close button

6. Type or paste in the text you want.

Tip Text is good for a plain header or footer, but you can also insert tables, pictures, shapes, text boxes, or hyperlinks in a header or footer by using the controls on the Insert tab of the Ribbon.

Note You can add page numbers to a header or footer by tapping the Page Numbers button on the Layout tab of the Ribbon and then working in the Page Numbers pop-up panel. The next main section shows you the detail of adding and formatting page numbers.

---

7. Format the text as necessary by using the controls on the Home tab of the Ribbon.

Tip Many templates include a Header style designed for the header area and a Footer style for the footer area.

---

8. Tap the Close button to close the header area or footer area and return to your document. The Close button appears beneath the header area or above the footer area.

USING DIFFERENT HEADERS AND FOOTERS IN DIFFERENT SECTIONS

If you have broken your document up into multiple sections, you can create a different header and footer in each section. After setting the header or footer in one section, go to the next section and turn off the Same as Previous setting. You can then create the header or footer for this section without changing the header or footer in the previous section.

At this writing, you need to use a desktop version of Word to turn off the Same as Previous setting. The Same as Previous button appears in Word for iPad, but as yet it is a status readout rather than a button for toggling the Same as Previous setting on or off.

Removing a Header or Footer

You can get rid of an unwanted header or footer by deleting it, but there's an easier way to remove it: tap the Layout tab of the Ribbon, tap the Header & Footer button, and then tap the Remove Header button or the Remove Footer button on the Header & Footer pop-up panel.

Adding Page Numbers to a Document

You can add page numbers to a document to help its readers keep its printed pages in the right order or simply see which point they've reached in it. Word's Page Numbers feature makes it easy to add page numbers by putting a page number field in the header or footer. Word then repeats the page number on each page, inserting the correct value.

Inserting Page Numbers

Here's how to insert page numbers.

1. Tap the Layout tab of the Ribbon to display its controls.

2. Tap the Page Numbers button to display the Page Numbers pop-up panel. When page numbering is off, the Page Numbers pop-up panel contains only the Numbering switch.

3. Set the Numbering switch to the On position. The remaining controls appear on the Page Numbers pop-up panel (see Figure 6-3).

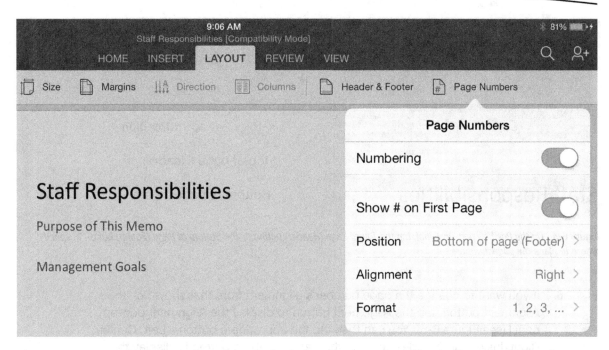

Figure 6-3. *In the Page Numbers pop-up panel, set the Numbering switch to the On position, and then choose the position, alignment, and format for the page numbers*

4. Set the Show # on First Page switch to the On position if you want to include the page number on the first page.

Tip   When the document's first page is obviously the first, such as when you use letterhead or other special paper for a printed document, you may want to omit the page number from the first page.

---

5. If you want to change the page number's position from that shown on the Position button, tap the Position button to display the Position pop-up panel (see Figure 6-4). You can then tap the Top of Page (Header) button or the Bottom of Page (Footer) button, as needed. Tap the Page Numbers button to return to the Page Numbers pop-up panel.

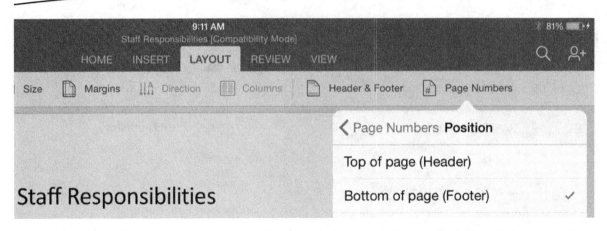

Figure 6-4. *On the Position pop-up panel, tap the Top of Page (Header) button or the Bottom of Page (Footer) button to specify where to place the page numbers*

6. If you want to change the page number's alignment from that shown on the Alignment button, tap the Alignment button to display the Alignment pop-up panel (see Figure 6-5). You can then tap the appropriate button—Left, Center, Right, Inside, or Outside—and tap the Page Numbers button to display the Page Numbers pop-up panel again.

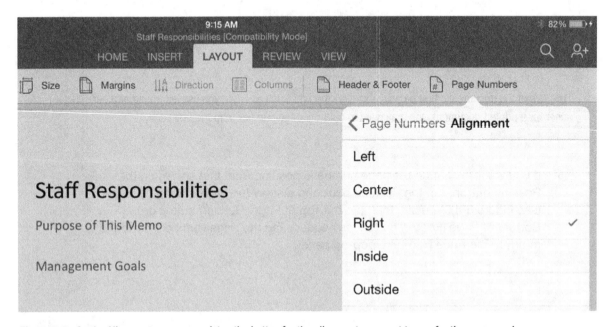

Figure 6-5. *On the Alignment pop-up panel, tap the button for the alignment you want to use for the page number*

Note   The Inside and Outside options on the Alignment pop-up panel are for facing-page spreads such as those in books or magazines. Using the Inside option puts the page numbers on the right side of the left-hand page and the left side of the right-hand page; using the Outside option puts the page numbers on the left side of the left-hand page and the right side of the right-hand page.

7.   If you want to change the page number's format from that shown on the Format button, tap the Format button to display the Format pop-up panel (see Figure 6-6). You can then tap the appropriate button—1, 2, 3, . . .; a, b, c, . . .; A, B, C, . . .; i, ii, iii, . . .; or I, II, III, . . . —and tap the Page Numbers button to return to the Page Numbers pop-up panel.

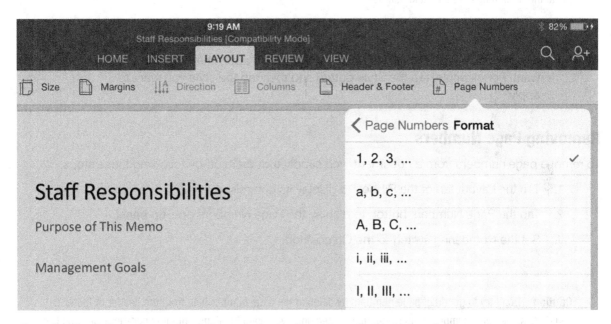

Figure 6-6. On the Format pop-up panel, choose the number format to use for the page numbers

8.   When you finish specifying the page numbers you want, tap in the document to close the Page Numbers pop-up panel.

Formatting Page Numbers

After inserting page numbers in a document, you can format them by applying a style or applying direct formatting. Follow these steps.

1. Scroll the document up or down as needed until you can see one of the page numbers.

2. Double-tap near the page number to open the header or footer for editing.

3. Double-tap the page number to select it. The Edit menu appears.

> **Tip**   If you've copied formatting from elsewhere, you can tap the Paste Format button on the Edit menu to paste the formatting onto the page number.

4. Use the controls on the Home tab of the Ribbon to apply the formatting you want. For example, tap the Style button and then tap the style you want to apply.

Removing Page Numbers

To remove page numbers from a document, you simply turn them off by following these steps.

1. Tap the Layout tab of the Ribbon to display its controls.

2. Tap the Page Numbers button to display the Page Numbers pop-up panel.

3. Set the Numbering switch to the Off position.

> **Caution**   Don't try to get rid of page numbers by deleting the page number field from the header or footer. If you do this, the Page Numbers feature remains turned on. If you open the Page Numbers pop-up panel, you'll see the message "Your page numbering format isn't editable." This is because the page number field is no longer there.

Working with Footnotes and Endnotes

If you create professional or academic documents, you may need to add footnotes or endnotes to provide extra information or show your sources.

Deciding Between Footnotes and Endnotes

A *footnote* is a note that appears at the foot of the page that refers to it, while an *endnote* is a note that appears at the end of a section or document. Normally, you use footnotes when it's likely the reader will want to read the information, and the chunks of information are short enough to fit at the bottom of pages. You use endnotes for information that you think only a few readers will need to consult or for longer pieces of information.

At this writing, Word for iPad complicates the decision between footnotes and endnotes because it enables you to create footnotes but not endnotes. But Word for iPad does display endnotes correctly, so it's possible that an update will add the ability to create endnotes. So when you're working on your iPad, you can create only footnotes—unless you use a desktop version of Word to place endnote markers where you need endnotes. You can then fill in the text for the endnotes using your iPad.

> **Tip**   You can convert footnotes to endnotes, or endnotes to footnotes, by using a desktop version of Word.

Inserting a Footnote

Here's how to insert a footnote in a document.

1. Tap the appropriate point in the document. Normally, you place the insertion point immediately after the last word of the text to which you want the footnote to refer.

2. Tap the Insert tab of the Ribbon to display its controls.

3. Tap the Footnote button. Word inserts the footnote mark and displays the footnote area of the document. This area is separated from the document text by a short horizontal line.

4. Type or paste the text for the footnote (see Figure 6-7).

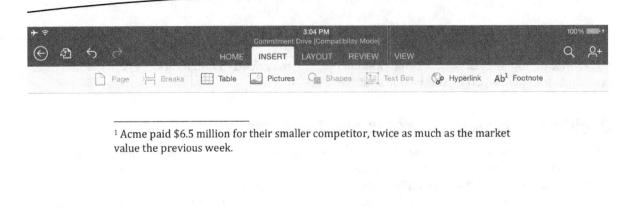

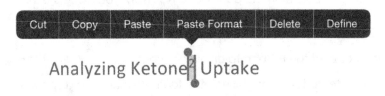

¹ Acme paid $6.5 million for their smaller competitor, twice as much as the market value the previous week.

Figure 6-7. Type the content for the footnote in the footnote area at the bottom of the page

5.   Tap in the document text to return to editing the document.

Editing and Deleting Footnotes and Endnotes

You can edit a footnote by going to the footnote area, positioning the insertion point at the point where you want to edit, and then making the changes needed. Similarly, you can edit an endnote in the endnotes area.

To delete a footnote or an endnote, double-tap the note's reference number in the text, and then tap the Delete button on the Edit menu that appears (see Figure 6-8). Word deletes the note text from the footnote area or endnote area along with the reference number.

Figure 6-8. Double-tap a footnote reference number and then tap the Delete button on the Edit menu to delete the footnote

Working with Comments

You and your colleagues can attach comments to items in the document to offer opinions or suggest changes, without actually changing the text itself. You can then view the comments and remove them once you've dealt with them.

Adding a Comment

You can quickly add a comment to a part of a document by following these steps.

1. Select the part of the document to which the comment will refer. You can simply tap to place the insertion point in the text, but if your comment refers to a specific section, it's usually clearer to select that section.

2. Tap the Review tab of the Ribbon to display its controls.

3. Tap the New Comment button. A new comment balloon appears in the revisions pane on the right.

4. Type the text of the comment (see Figure 6-9).

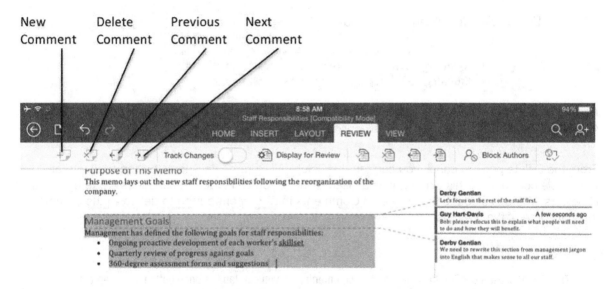

Figure 6-9. Type the text of your comment in the comment balloon

5. Touch elsewhere in the document to deselect the comment.

Viewing and Deleting Comments

When you receive a document that contains comments, use the buttons at the left end of the Review tab of the Ribbon to work through them. Tap the Previous Comment button or the Next Comment button to select the comment you want to affect, or simply tap the comment in the revisions pane.

After selecting a comment and dealing with it (for example, by editing the text), you can delete the comment. Tap the Delete Comment button to display the Delete pop-up panel (see Figure 6-10), and then tap the Delete Comment button.

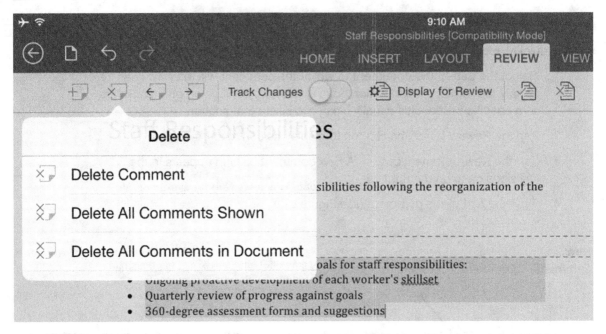

Figure 6-10. From the Delete panel, you can delete the selected comment, delete all the comments shown, or delete all the comments in the document

From the Delete pop-up panel, you can tap the Delete All Comments Shown button to delete all the visible comments. This command is available only if you've hidden the changes made by some reviewers. You can also tap the Delete All Comments in Document button to delete all the comments (even if some of them are hidden).

Tip   Word doesn't confirm the deletion of all comments, but you can tap the Undo button if you tap the Delete All Comments in Document button by mistake.

Tracking Changes in Your Documents

When you need to work with other people on creating or revising a document, use Word's Track Changes feature. Track Changes can automatically track almost all the changes in the document so that you can review them, see who made which changes when, accept the changes you want to keep, and reject the rest.

You can choose which types of changes to track and which to ignore. For example, you may want to track only the edits to the text of a document and let your colleagues handle the formatting.

Turning on Track Changes and Working with It

To turn on Track Changes, tap the Review tab of the Ribbon, and then set the Track Changes switch to the On position. With Track Changes turned on, you can write and edit as normal. As you work, Word marks changes as follows:

- *Insertions:* Inserted text appears in color with an underline.

> **Note**   For revisions, Word uses a different color for each of the first eight authors to help you distinguish each author's work. If there are more than eight authors, Word starts reusing the colors for the ninth and subsequent authors.

- *Deletions:* Deleted text appears in color with a single strikethrough.

> **Tip**   You can choose which tracked changes to display in a document. See the section "Choosing What to Display for Review," later in this chapter, for details.

- *Moved Text:* Text you have moved (by using Cut and then immediately using Paste) appears in green with a double underline.
- *Moved From:* Text that you have moved elsewhere appears in green with a double strikethrough.

> **Caution**   When you move text, you must perform the Paste operation next after the Cut operation for Word to register the move and use the correct revision marks. If you cut text, do something else (such as type some characters), and then paste in the cut material, Word marks the cut text as a deletion and the pasted text as an insertion.

- *Changed lines:* Word places a vertical line to the left of each line that contains revision marks. These changed lines give you a quick indication where to look for changes on the page.
- *Formatting changes:* Word displays the resulting formatting. The details of the formatting change appear in the revisions pane.

Integrating Tracked Changes into a Document

When everyone has made their edits to the document with Track Changes on, you can go through the changes and accept those you want to keep and reject the others. To review the changes, you use the controls on the right side of the Review tab on the Ribbon. But before you get started, you may want to specify which items Word should display for review.

Choosing What to Display for Review

To speed up your review of a document that uses Track Changes, you can change how Word displays the markup for review. For example, you can show the document as it will appear with all the markup accepted, or show the document's original version to see how it was.

To control which markup appears, tap the Review tab of the Ribbon to display its controls, and then tap the Display for Review button. In the Display for Review pop-up panel that appears (see Figure 6-11), you can choose which view of the document to use:

- *All Markup:* Choose this item to see the document's final text with all the markup displayed. This is the default setting, and the one you'll probably want to use most of the time while marking up the document.

- *No Markup.* Choose this item to see the document's final text with no markup appearing. Use this view when you want to read the document without the visual distraction of markup. This is the best view for catching errors, omissions, and grammar and logic problems.

- *Original with Markup:* Choose this item to see the document's original text with the markup displayed. Use this view when you want to focus on the changes made to the original text.

- *Original:* Choose this item to see the document's original text before any of the changes were made. By switching among this view and the No Markup view, you can judge the extent and success of the edits to the document.

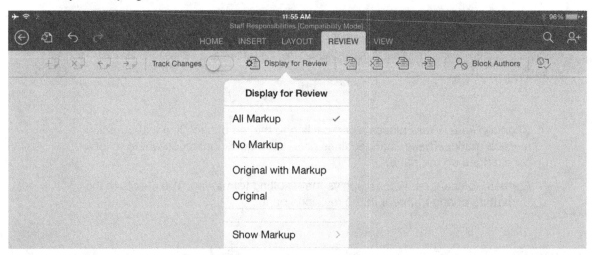

Figure 6-11. The Display for Review pop-up panel enables you to view the original document or the final document in a clean state, or view either the final document or the original document with markup showing the changes

You can also tap the Show Markup button at the bottom of the Display for Review pop-up panel to display the Show Markup pop-up panel (see Figure 6-12). Here, you can tap the buttons to place or remove the check marks to specify exactly which markup items you want to see:

- *Comments:* Choose whether comments appear. Turning off the display of comments in a busy document can help you to see the contents more clearly.

- *Insertions and Deletions:* Choose whether markup appears indicating text and other items inserted in the document, deleted from it, or moved from one place in the document to another.

- *Formatting:* Choose whether Word displays changes to formatting, such as the application or a style or the addition of direct formatting.

- *Show Revisions in Balloons:* Place a check mark on this item to use balloons to display the details of revisions as well as comments and formatting changes. The upper screen in Figure 6-11 shows revisions in balloons.

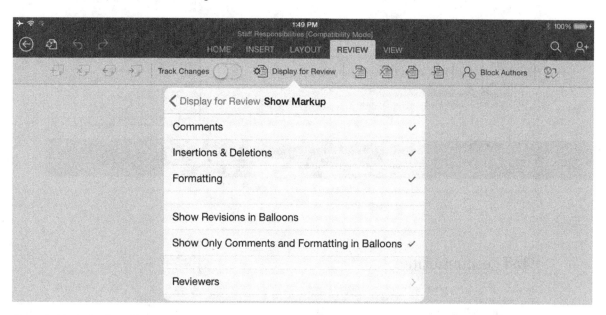

Figure 6-12. In the Show Markup pop-up panel, you can choose whether to display comments, insertions and deletions, and formatting changes. You can also choose what appears in revision balloons

Note   The Show Revisions in Balloons button and the Show Only Comments and Formatting in Balloons button are a pair of option buttons. Only one can be selected at once, so placing the check mark on one of these buttons removes the check mark from the other.

- *Show Only Comments and Formatting in Balloons:* Place a check mark on this item to use balloons to display only comments and formatting changes. When you use this option, the revisions in the document text itself. The lower screen in Figure 6-13 shows revisions inline and comments and formatting in balloons.

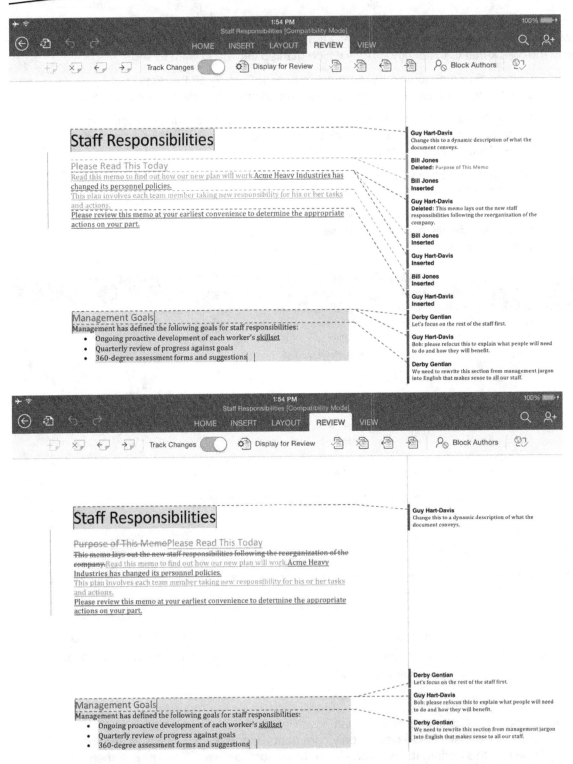

Figure 6-13. *Choosing Show Revisions in Balloons (above) makes your document look substantially different than choosing Show Only Comments and Formatting in Balloons (below)*

From the Show Markup pop-up panel, you can also choose which reviewers' comments and changes appear. Tap the Reviewers button to display the Reviewers pop-up panel (see Figure 6-14), and then tap to place or remove check marks on the reviewers' buttons to control which appear and which don't. This setting is useful when multiple colleagues have reviewed a document and you need to tune out some of them.

Figure 6-14. On the Reviewers pop-up panel, tap to place or remove check marks to control whose edits Word displays. Tap the All Reviewers button to place or remove the check marks for all reviewers at once

Accepting and Rejecting Tracked Changes

To work through the tracked changes in a document, first select a change by tapping the Next button or the Previous button. If you're using the Show Revisions in Balloons setting, you can also tap the revision balloon for the change.

You can then accept changes by tapping the Accept button and then tapping the appropriate button on the Accept pop-up panel (see Figure 6-15): the Accept & Move to Next button, the Accept Change button, the Accept All Changes Shown button, the Accept All Changes in Document button, or the Accept All Changes & Stop Tracking button.

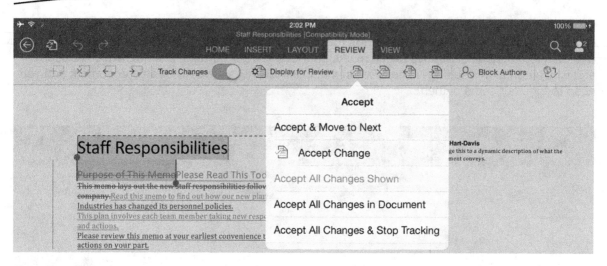

Figure 6-15. *On the Accept pop-up panel, tap the Accept & Move to Next button or the Accept Change button to accept the currently selected change. You can also accept all the changes shown or all the changes in the document*

Note   Tap the Accept & Move to Next button or the Reject & Move to Next to move quickly from one change to the next.

The Accept All Changes Shown command and the Reject All Changes Shown command are available only when you have hidden changes from some reviewers.

Similarly, you can reject changes by tapping the Reject button and then tapping the appropriate button on the Reject pop-up panel (see Figure 6-16), which offers corresponding buttons to those on the Accept pop-up panel: the Reject & Move to Next button, the Reject Change button, the Reject All Changes Shown button, the Reject All Changes in Document button, or the Reject All Changes & Stop Tracking button.

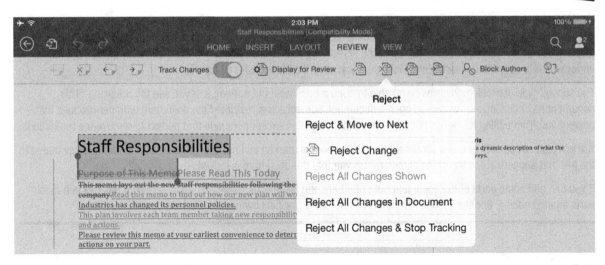

Figure 6-16. *On the Reject pop-up panel, you can reject a single change or all changes at once*

> **Caution**   Word doesn't confirm any of the "All" commands, such as the Accept All Changes in Document command or the Reject All Changes & Stop Tracking command. If you touch any of these four buttons by accident, touch the Undo button immediately.

When you've finished accepting or rejecting changes, save the document. You may want to use the Duplicate command to save it under a different name if the document is now ready for another stage in its evolution.

Editing Your Documents Simultaneously with Colleagues

Word for iPad makes it easy to edit your documents simultaneously with your colleagues. To enable simultaneous editing, you put the document in a shared location, such as a shared folder on your OneDrive account or on a SharePoint server. Your colleagues can then access it with most versions of Word—with the desktop versions, with the online version, and with Word on the iPad.

RESOLVING PROBLEMS THAT PREVENT SIMULTANEOUS EDITING

Simultaneous editing normally works pretty well on Word for iPad. But sometimes you may find you can't work together on a document with others. Here are the two things that typically go wrong, and what to do when you run into them.

The first thing that goes wrong is that you find you can't open the document for editing. When this happens, check the type of document. It must be a .docx file for simultaneous editing to be available on Word for iPad. Normally, this problem occurs if you've opened a macro-enabled document in Word for iPad. This file has the .docm file extension, but you won't see this on the file management screen. (If you need to see the file extension for the current document, tap the File button and then tap Properties on the File menu to open the Properties pop-up panel.)

If the document has the .doc file type, you'll need to update it to the .docx file format to make it available for simultaneous editing. You'll know that the document has a different file type because when you open the document, Word displays the Convert and Edit bar at the top of the screen. Tap the Convert and Edit button, and then choose the name under which to save the converted file. Make sure you save the file in a shared location.

The second type of problem involves being able to open a document but not edit it. If you see the message "This document has been locked" when you open a document, someone has restricted the document with permissions that prevent you from editing it. There's nothing you can do about this except persuade that person to remove the restrictions.

You will also not be able to edit a document that someone has marked as final. In this case, tap the Edit Anyway button in the bar that appears at the top of the screen telling you that the document is locked.

If you can edit some parts of the document but not others, the issue is normally that another author has blocked those parts against editing. See the section "Working with Blocking" for full coverage of blocking.

Editing a Document Simultaneously

To edit a document simultaneously with others, you open the document as normal from the shared location in which it is stored. Word displays the Other Authors Are Editing This Document bar (see Figure 6-17) at the top of the screen to alert you to other authors editing the document.

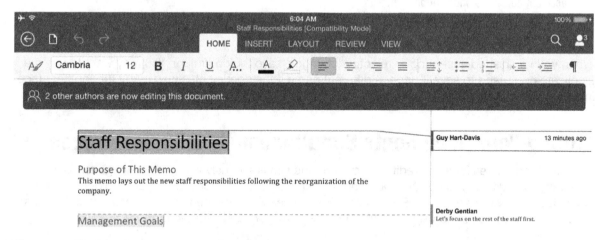

Figure 6-17. *The Other Authors Are Editing This Document bar alerts you to the virtual presence of other authors or editors*

To see who else is editing the document, tap the Share button to display the Share pop-up panel, and then tap the Authors Editing button to display the list of authors (see Figure 6-18).

Figure 6-18. Tap the Share button and then tap the Authors Editing button to display the list of authors working on the document

You can edit the document as normal unless other authors have blocked off parts for their own use. The section "Working with Blocking" covers this topic.

Saving Your Changes

Word turns off the AutoSave feature (if it was on) when you are editing a document simultaneously with others. You can tap the File button and then tap the Save and Refresh button on the File menu to force Word to save your changes and refresh the document with others' changes at any point.

Updating the Document with Other Authors' Changes

When another author has updated the document, Word displays the Updates Available bar (see Figure 6-19) to let you know. Tap the Save and Refresh button to save your changes and refresh your copy of the document with the changes the other authors have made.

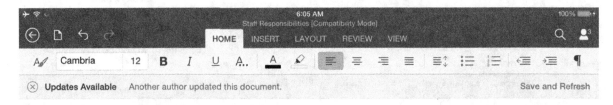

Figure 6-19. When the Updates Available bar appears, tap the Save and Refresh button to save your changes and get the latest changes from other authors

After saving and refreshing the document, Word displays the message "This document was refreshed with updates made by other authors" (see Figure 6-20) to make sure you're up to date on what's happened.

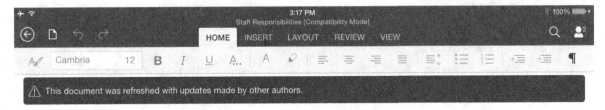

Figure 6-20. Word confirms that the refresh operation is complete

Working with Blocking

You can block other authors from working on particular parts of a document. This is useful when you're focusing on a section of a document and need to be able to write or edit without interference.

Similarly, others can block you from parts of the document.

Blocking Others from Part of a Document

To block others, follow these steps.

1. Select the part of the document that you want to protect.

2. Tap the Review tab on the Ribbon to display its contents.

3. Tap the Block Authors button to display the Block Authors pop-up panel (see Figure 6-21).

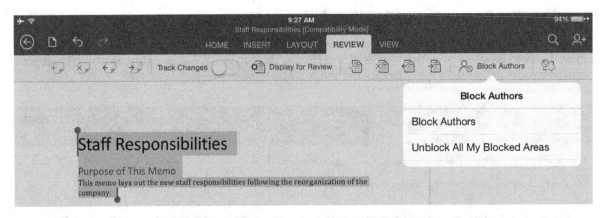

Figure 6-21. Tap the Block Authors button on the Block Authors pop-up panel to block other people from working on the section you've selected

4. Tap the Block Authors button.

After you finish working in the blocked section, remove the block by tapping the Block Authors button again and then tapping the Unblock All My Blocked Areas button in the Block Authors pop-up panel.

Being Blocked

When someone else has blocked others from editing part of the document, that part appears with a bracket beside it, with the blocking author's name in a bubble and a blocking symbol (a person with a struck-through circle). Figure 6-22 shows an example.

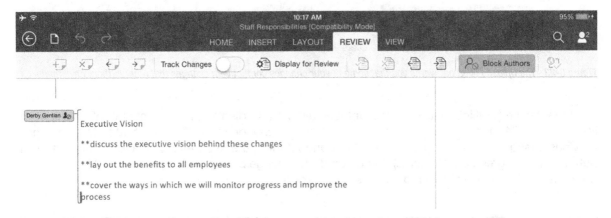

Figure 6-22. Word displays the name of the blocking author next to each section she has blocked

When you're blocked from a section, you can't edit it until the blocking author releases the block.

Resolving Conflicts

When you and others work on a document simultaneously, conflicts can occur if two or more people change the same part of the document within the same update cycle. When conflicts occur, you'll see a notification such as the Upload Failed bar shown in Figure 6-23.

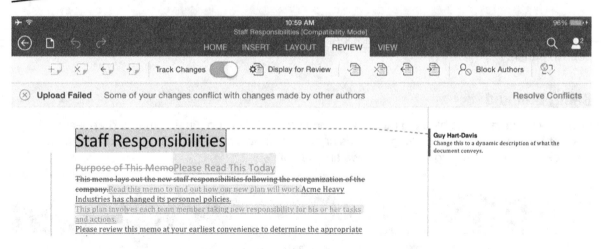

Figure 6-23.   The Upload Failed bar warns you that some of your changes conflict with changes that other authors have made

Tap the Resolve Conflicts button on the Upload Failed bar to display the Conflicts tab of the Ribbon (see Figure 6-24). Tap the Next button to select the next change or the Previous button to select the previous change, and then tap the Keep My Change button, the Keep All My Changes button (the All button with two green check marks), the Discard My Change button, or the Discard All My Changes button (the All button with two red crosses), as needed.

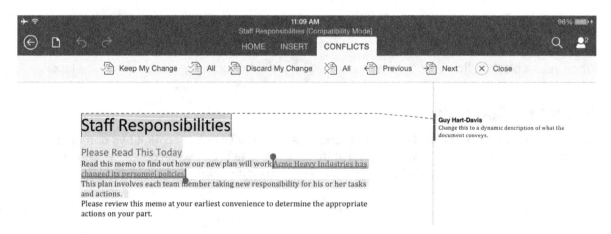

Figure 6-24.   Use the buttons on the Conflicts tab of the Ribbon to resolve the editing conflicts in the document

Note   When Word displays the Conflicts tab of the Ribbon, it hides the Layout tab, the Review tab, and the View tab, leaving only the Home tab and the Insert tab along with the conflicts tab. This slimming down of the Ribbon is to help you avoid causing any more conflicts before you resolve the existing ones.

When the Conflicts Resolved bar appears (see Figure 6-25), tap the Save And Close View button. Word saves your changes; removes the Conflicts tab from the Ribbon; and restores the Layout tab, the Review tab, and the View tab.

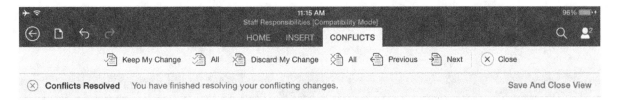

Figure 6-25. Tap the Save And Close View button on the Conflicts Resolved bar to close the Conflicts view and return to editing your document

Summary

In this chapter, you learned how to work with footnotes and endnotes and how to add headers, footers, and page numbers to your documents. This chapter also showed you how to use the Track Changes feature to mark revisions in your documents, how to view only those revisions you need to see at any given point, and how to accept and reject revisions as needed. You also learned how to add, review, and delete comments and how to use Word's powerful features for editing documents simultaneously with your colleagues.

Chapter 7

Getting Started with Excel for iPad

In this chapter, you will get up and running with Excel for iPad. First, the chapter will briefly cover the app's features and its limitations so that you know what's there and what's missing. After that, the chapter will show you how to create a new workbook and navigate the Excel interface. You will also learn how to enter data in a worksheet—by typing, by pasting, or by using the Fill feature—and how to customize Excel's view to suit your preferences.

Understanding Excel for iPad's Features and Limitations

As you'd probably expect, Excel for iPad is a more compact app than Excel for Windows and Excel for the Mac, the two desktop versions of Excel. Excel for iPad provides all the features you need to create and edit the most widely used types of workbooks, including about 9 in 10 of the massive range of functions that Excel supports.

Note Microsoft has added various features to Excel for iPad since launching the app, and is continuing to add features, so the details in this section may no longer be accurate by the time you read it. For example, soon after the first release, Microsoft added printing, improved support for external keyboards, and support for PivotTables whose source data is in the same workbook. So it is a good idea to update Excel on your iPad to the latest version, either by running the App Store app on your iPad and looking on the Updates tab or by using iTunes on your computer.

This section first discusses the features that Excel has and the features it lacks, then explains briefly what happens to workbook content that Excel for iPad doesn't support.

Which Features Does Excel for iPad Have and Lack?

Excel for iPad enables you to perform all the essential actions with workbooks. You can create a new workbook, save it either online (on OneDrive or SharePoint) or on your iPad; you can open and close existing workbooks, edit them, print them, and save changes; and you can duplicate a workbook or restore a workbook to an earlier version to recover from mishaps or unfortunate edits.

At this writing, Excel for iPad is missing or has only partial support for various major features that the desktop versions of Excel offer. Here is a list of the main features:

- *Templates*: Excel for iPad enables you to create workbooks based on the range of templates that come with the app, but you can't create a workbook based on a template of your own. Excel for iPad also cannot create templates yet.

- *Views*: The desktop versions of Excel enable you to switch between Normal view and Page Layout view as needed. By contrast, Excel for iPad has only a single view, a layout view that shows objects on screen as closely as possible to how they will appear in either a printout or a PDF file.

- *Outlines*: The desktop versions of Excel enable you to group rows or columns to create collapsible outlines. This feature is especially useful with large worksheets in which it is hard to see the wood for the trees. Excel for iPad doesn't have this feature.

- *Advanced charts and sparklines*: Excel for iPad has good support for charts, but it doesn't offer all the chart types that the desktop versions of Excel have. Excel for iPad also doesn't have sparklines, mini-charts that you can insert in a single cell.

- *Track Changes and protection*: The desktop versions of Excel enable you to track changes made in a workbook and to protect worksheets or entire workbooks against unauthorized changes. Excel for iPad doesn't have these capabilities; at this writing, its only review tool is comments.

- *What-if analysis and validation*: Excel for iPad doesn't have advanced data tools such as what-if analysis and data validation.

- *External data*: Excel for iPad cannot connect to external data sources as the desktop versions can.

- *SmartArt*: Excel for iPad doesn't have SmartArt diagrams, which you can use in the desktop versions to create process diagrams, list diagrams, and relationship diagrams.

- *Conditional formatting*: Excel for iPad doesn't offer conditional formatting. This is formatting that changes depending on the conditions that you specify. For example, you can use conditional formatting to apply striking formatting to suspiciously high values so that they jump out at you.

- *Macros and VBA*: Excel for iPad doesn't have the Visual Basic for Applications (VBA) programming language, which enables you to automate tasks using macros and user forms (custom dialog boxes).

What Happens to Content That Excel for iPad Does Not Support?

When you open a workbook that contains items that Excel for iPad doesn't support, the app deals with them as smartly as possible. Excel for iPad correctly displays many items that it doesn't enable you to create, and it even lets you edit them. For example, if you open a workbook that contains sparklines, Excel for iPad not only displays them correctly but also updates the sparklines if you change the values on which they are based; however, you cannot change the sparkline type or the range of cells it uses.

If a workbook contains data that Excel for iPad can't display, it leaves that content unchanged in the file so that it is still there when you open the workbook in a desktop version of Excel. For example, Excel for iPad leaves VBA code untouched when you edit a workbook and save it.

Creating a New Workbook on Your iPad

To create a new workbook on your iPad, tap the New button on the file management screen, and then tap the button for the appropriate template on the New screen (see Figure 7-1).

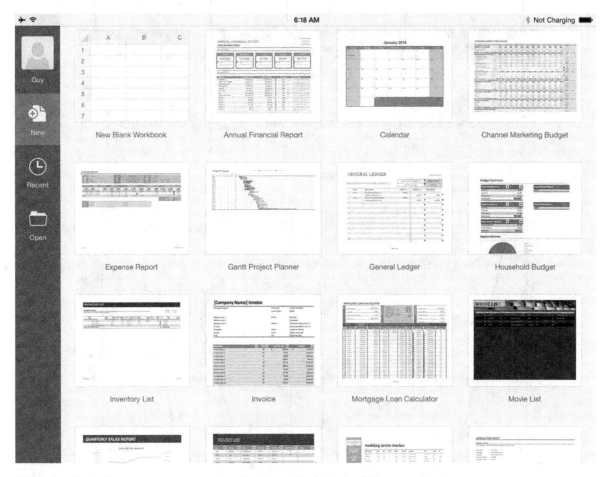

Figure 7-1. On the New screen, tap the template for the type of workbook you want to create

Tap the New Blank Workbook button if you want to create a workbook with no contents. This is good when you want to create a workbook from scratch or when you're coming to grips with Excel.

Otherwise, tap the template that looks most suitable for the type of workbook you want to create. Excel for iPad provides a good range of templates, ranging from business-oriented templates such as the Annual Financial Report template and the Channel Marketing Report template to personal templates such as the Movie List template and the Wedding Invite Tracker template. But you can adapt any template as needed, so don't feel constrained by the names.

Navigating the Excel Interface

Once you've created a workbook, you'll see the Excel interface (see Figure 7-2). The following list explains the main elements in the Excel interface.

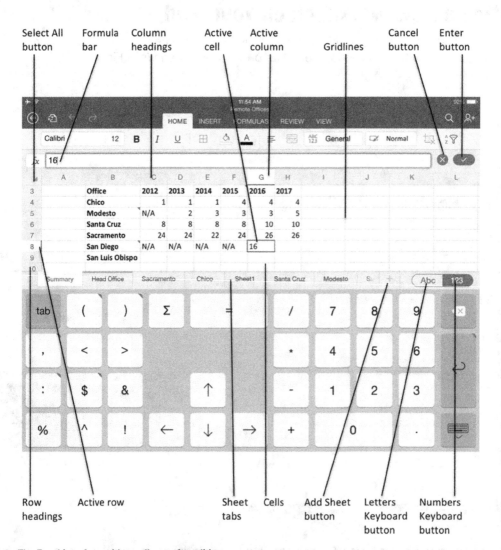

Figure 7-2. The Excel interface with a cell open for editing

Apart from the Ribbon, which you know all about already, these are the main elements of the Excel screen:

- *Formula bar*: This is the bar directly below the Ribbon. This bar shows the data or formula in the active cell. It is where you enter and edit data.

- *Enter button*: This is the green button with the white check mark that appears at the right end of the Formula bar when you are entering or editing the data in a cell. Tap this button to enter what you have typed, or the edits you have made, and to close the cell for editing.

- *Cancel button*: This is the red circle with the white cross that appears to the left of the Enter button at the right end of the Formula bar. You tap this button to cancel entering your text or edits and to close the cell for editing. Canceling out of a cell returns its contents (if any) to how they were before.

- *Row headings*: These are the numbers at the left side of the screen that identify each row. The first row is 1, the second row 2, and so on.

- *Column headings*: These are the letters at the top of the worksheet grid that identify the columns. The first column is A, the second column is B, and so on.

- *Cells*: These are the boxes formed by the intersections of the rows and columns. Each cell is identified by its column letter and row number. For example, the first cell in column A is cell A1, and the second cell in column B is cell B2.

- *Gridlines*: These are the light-gray lines that separate the cells. Excel displays the gridlines by default so that you can see where each cell falls. You can turn off the gridlines by displaying the View tab of the Ribbon and setting the Gridlines switch to the Off position.

- *Active cell*: This is the cell you're working in. Excel displays a heavy green rectangle around the active cell.

- *Active row*: This is the row that contains the active cell. Excel displays the row heading for the active row with a lighter gray background, the number in green rather than gray, and a green line on the right side of the heading to help you pick out the active row easily.

- *Active column*: This is the column that contains the active cell. As with the active row, Excel displays the column heading for the active row with a lighter gray background, the number in green rather than gray, and a green line at the bottom for easy identification.

- *Select All button*: Tap this button at the intersection of the row headings and column headings to select all the cells in the worksheet.

- *Sheet tabs*: To display a worksheet or a chart sheet, you tap its sheet tab on the Sheet tab bar.

- *Add Sheet button*: Tap this button to add a new worksheet after the current sheet.

- *Letters Keyboard button*: Tap this button to display the letters keyboard. You will learn about the Excel keyboard later in this chapter.

- *Numbers Keyboard button*: Tap this button to display the numbers keyboard.

Navigating Workbooks and Worksheets

Each workbook consists of one or more worksheets or other sheets, such as chart sheets, macro sheets, or dialog sheets. To display the sheet you want to view, tap its tab in the Sheet Tabs bar at the bottom of the Excel screen. If the sheet's tab isn't visible, scroll the Sheet Tabs bar left or right until you can see the right tab.

> **Note** A *chart sheet* is a separate sheet that contains a chart. A *macro sheet* is a sheet that contains macros, sequences of commands. A *dialog sheet* is a sheet that contains custom dialog boxes for purposes such as controlling the running of macros. Macro sheets and dialog sheets are for the desktop versions of Excel.

Each worksheet contains 16,384 columns and 1,048,576 rows, giving a grand total of 17,179,869,184 cells. Normally, you'll use only a small number of these cells—perhaps a few hundred or a few thousand—but there's plenty of space should you need it for large worksheets.

Each column is identified by one, two, or three letters:

- The first 26 columns use the letters A to Z.
- The next 26 columns use AA to AZ, the following 26 BA to BZ, and so on.
- When the two-letter combinations are exhausted, Excel uses three letters: AAA, AAB, and so on.

Each row is identified by a number, from 1 up to 1048576.

Each cell is identified by its column lettering and its row number. For example, the cell at the intersection of column A and row 1 is cell A1, and the cell at the intersection of column ZA and row 2256 is ZA2256.

Moving the Active Cell

In Excel, you usually work in a single cell at a time. That cell is called the *active cell* and receives the input from the keyboard. You move the active cell by tapping the cell that you want to make active. To make a cell active and open it for editing, you double-tap it. If the cell you want to open for editing is already the active cell, tap the Formula bar to open it for editing. (You can also double-tap the active cell if you prefer.)

When you have opened the active cell for editing, you can tap the arrow buttons on the numbers keyboard to move from cell to cell. Tap the Up arrow button to move the active cell up to the cell in the next row, tap the Right arrow button to move the active cell to the next column, and so on.

If you connect a hardware keyboard to your iPad, you can move the active cell by using the keys and keyboard shortcuts explained in Table 7-1.

Table 7-1. Keyboard Shortcuts for Moving the Active Cell

To Move the Active Cell Like This	Press This Key or Keyboard Shortcut
Up one row	Up arrow
Down one row	Down arrow
Left one column	Left arrow
Right one column	Right arrow
To the last row in the worksheet	Command+Down arrow
To the last column in the worksheet	Command+Right arrow
To the first row in the worksheet	Command+Up arrow
To the first column in the worksheet	Command+Left arrow

Tip   Tap the Excel title bar to scroll up quickly to the top rows of the active worksheet.

Selecting Cells and Ranges

To work with a single cell, you simply tap it. When you need to affect multiple cells at once, you select the cells. For example, you can select multiple cells so that you can apply formatting to them.

Excel calls the selection of cells a *range*. In Excel, a range can consist of either a rectangle of contiguous cells or various cells that aren't next to each other. At this writing, Excel for iPad enables you to select only ranges of contiguous cells, and only one range at a time, unlike the desktop versions of Excel, which let you select ranges of noncontiguous cells and multiple ranges at once.

To select a range, tap the cell at one corner of the range to make it the active cell. Then tap the corner handle on the active cell and drag it until the selection encompasses all the cells you want in the range (see Figure 7-3).

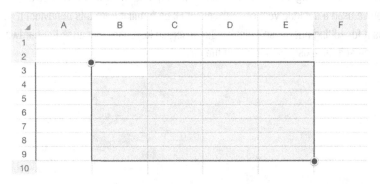

Figure 7-3. To select a range, tap any corner handle on the active cell and drag until the selection encompasses the cells you want

> **Tip**   If you connect a hardware keyboard to your iPad, you can select text by holding down the Shift key and pressing the keys or shortcuts shown in Table 7-1. For example, hold down the Shift key and press the Right arrow key to extend the selection to the right by one column, or press the Down arrow key to extend the selection to the next row. The Command+Up arrow keyboard shortcut (select to the first row) and the Command+Left arrow shortcut (select to the first column) tend to be more useful than the Command+Down arrow shortcut (select to the last row) and the Command+Right arrow shortcut, which usually select galaxies of emptiness.

To select an entire row, tap its row heading. Similarly, to select an entire column, tap its column heading.

To deselect the range you've selected, tap any cell either inside or outside the range.

Entering Data in a Worksheet

You can enter data in your worksheets by typing it, by pasting it, or by using drag and drop to move or copy it. Excel also includes a feature called Fill that automatically fills in series data for you based on the input you've provided.

Opening a Cell for Editing

Before you can enter data in a cell using the onscreen keyboard, you need to open the cell for editing. To do so, you double-tap the cell. Excel automatically displays the onscreen keyboard so that you can enter the data with it.

> **Note**   When you have a hardware keyboard connected to your iPad, you can simply select the cell and start typing to open the cell for editing and enter data in it. Entering data this way overwrites any existing contents in the cell. (If you've used a desktop version of Excel, you'll be familiar with this behavior.) If you double-tap a cell, Excel opens it for editing but doesn't display the onscreen keyboard (because the hardware keyboard is there). You can then edit the existing contents of the cell.

Meeting Excel's Numbers Keyboard

As well as the default iOS keyboards, Excel for iPad has a custom onscreen numbers keyboard to help you enter data more quickly. Tap the 123 button at the right end of the Sheet Tabs bar to display the numbers keyboard (see Figure 7-4), which is largely self-explanatory except for these features:

- *SUM key*: Tap this key to enter the SUM() function in the active cell. SUM() is the most widely used function, so it's great to have it at your fingertip.

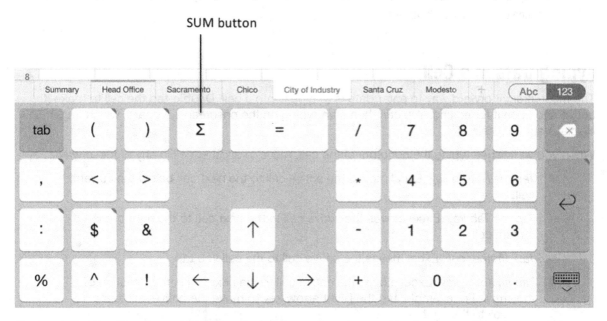

Figure 7-4. Excel provides a customized numbers keyboard to enable to you enter data, functions, and formulas more easily

- *Green-triangle keys*: The green triangles in the upper-right corner of a key indicate that the key has a pop-up panel with alternate characters. Table 7-2 shows you the alternate characters available. Tap and hold the key to display the pop-up panel, slide your finger to the character you want, and then lift your finger.

Table 7-2. Alternate Keys on the Number Keyboard

Key	Alternate Keys
(	[{
)	] }
,	;
:	@ #
$	¢ ¥ € £ ₩
Return	Carriage return within a cell

■ *Tab key*: Tap this key to move the active cell one column to the right.

■ *Arrow keys*: Tap an arrow key to move the active cell one column or row in the direction shown on the key.

> **Note**   You can use the standard iOS numbers and symbols keyboards if you prefer. To display the numbers keyboard, tap the .?123 button on the letters keyboard as usual; and to display the symbols keyboard, tap the #+= button on the numbers keyboard.

Typing Data in a Cell

The most straightforward way to enter data is to type it into a cell. Double-tap the cell to make it active and open it for editing. You can then start typing on the onscreen keyboard, which Excel displays automatically.

When you've finished typing the contents of the cell, move to another cell in any of these ways:

■ *Tap the Return key*: Excel moves the active cell to the next cell below the current cell.

■ *Tap the Tab key*: Excel moves the active cell to the next cell to the right of the current cell.

■ *Tap another cell*: Excel moves the active cell to the cell you tap.

■ *Tap an arrow key*: Excel moves the active cell to the next cell in the direction of the arrow. For example, tap the Right arrow key to move the active cell to the next cell to the right.

Excel automatically opens the cell you move to, so you don't need to double-tap it.

When you finish your editing session, tap the Enter button at the right end of the Formula bar to accept the current entry and close the cell for editing. Excel hides the onscreen keyboard.

Editing a Cell's Contents

When you need to edit the existing contents of a cell, double-tap the cell to open it for editing. Excel displays the cell's contents in the Formula bar (see Figure 7-5), and you can edit them there using the onscreen keyboard, which appears automatically.

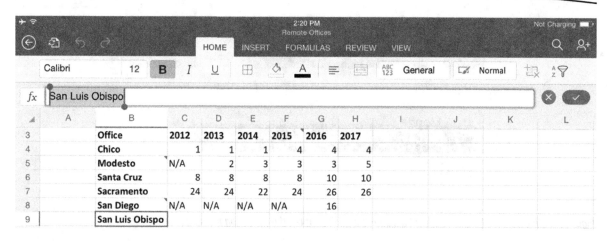

Figure 7-5. Double-tap a cell to open it for editing. You can then edit the cell's contents in the Formula bar

When you finish editing the cell, either move to another cell you want to edit as described in the previous section, or tap the Enter button to close the cell for editing.

Entering Data Quickly Using the Fill Feature

When you need to fill in a series of data, see if Excel's Fill feature can enter it for you. To use Fill, you enter the base data for the series in one or more cells. You then select the cells, activate Fill, and then drag the Fill handle in the direction you want to fill. Fill checks your base data, works out what the other cells should contain, and fills it in for you.

To get the hang of Fill, try the following example on a blank worksheet in a practice workbook. If you're currently working on a valuable workbook, tap the Back button to return to the file management screen, tap the New button, and then tap the New Blank Workbook button to create a new blank workbook.

The first example uses the days of the week. Follow these steps.

1. Double-tap cell A1 to open the cell for editing.

2. Type **Monday** in the cell.

3. Tap the Enter button to close the cell for editing. The cell remains active.

4. Tap the cell again to display the Edit menu (see Figure 7-6).

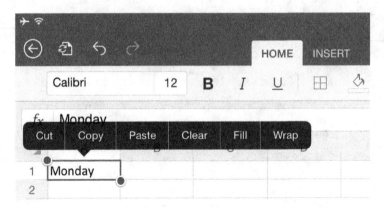

Figure 7-6. Tap the active cell to display the Edit menu, and then tap the Fill button to turn on Fill

5. Tap the Fill button on the Edit menu to activate the Fill feature. Fill arrows (green circles containing white arrows) appear showing the directions in which you can drag (see Figure 7-7).

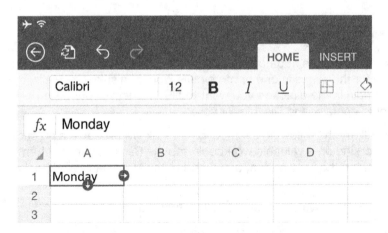

Figure 7-7. The Fill arrows indicate that Fill is active

6. Tap a Fill arrow and drag it to select the range of cells you want to fill with data (see Figure 7-8).

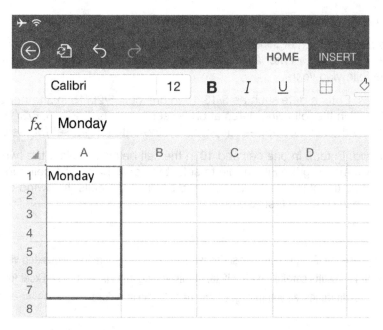

Figure 7-8. Drag a Fill arrow to select the cells you want to fill

7. Lift your finger from the screen. Excel fills the cells with data—in this case, the days Tuesday through Sunday (see Figure 7-9).

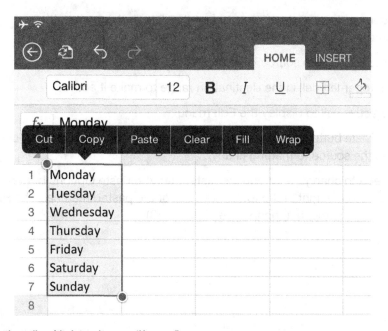

Figure 7-9. Excel fills the cells with data when you lift your finger

Here are three examples of data you can complete using the Fill feature:

- *Months and years*: Enter **January** in a cell and use the Fill feature to enter the remaining months. Or enter **2015** in one cell, **2016** in the next cell, and use Fill to fill in the following years.

- *Date series*: Enter a date such as 5/13/15 in one cell, 5/20/15 in another cell, and use Fill to fill in the following dates at one-week intervals: 5/27/15, 6/3/15, and so on. (How these dates appear depends on the date format set for the cells.)

- *Linear trend*: Enter **5** in one cell and **10** in the cell below it. Select the two cells, turn on Fill, and drag the Fill handle to select the cells below the cell containing 10. Fill enters the numbers 15, 20, 25, and so on in the cells, following the linear trend suggested by the first two cells.

Caution   If you're used to filling in complex series with the AutoFill feature in the desktop versions of Excel, check through your Fill results carefully on the iPad. At this writing, the Fill feature on Excel for iPad cannot fill in series such as growth trends, so you may get some unwelcome surprises.

Pasting Data into a Worksheet

If the data you need to add to a worksheet is already in another document, you can copy it and paste it into the worksheet. Follow these steps.

1. In the source document and app, select the data and copy it to the Clipboard.

2. Switch to Excel if the source is another app.

3. Tap the upper-left cell in the destination range to make it active.

4. Tap the active cell to display the Edit menu.

5. Tap the Paste button. Excel pastes the data using default settings, which includes the source formatting (if any).

6. If you need to change what you've pasted, tap the Paste Options button below and to the right of the lower-right cell of the pasted material. The Paste Options pop-up menu appears (see Figure 7-10).

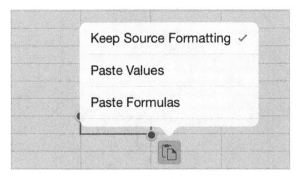

Figure 7-10. *To change what you've pasted, tap the Paste Options button, and then tap the button for the appropriate paste option*

7. Tap the button for the paste option you want to use. Your options vary depending on what you've pasted, but you'll frequently see some of the following options:

    ■   *Keep Source Formatting*: Tap this button to preserve the source formatting of what you pasted, keeping the item looking as it did when you copied it.

    ■   *Use Destination Theme*: After pasting an object, such as a chart or a shape, tap this button to apply the formatting theme of the destination range to the object.

    ■   *Paste Values*: Tap this button to paste the values with no formatting.

    ■   *Paste Formulas*: Tap this button to paste the formulas and constants without formatting.

    ■   *Paste as Picture*: Tap this button to paste in the copied object as a picture rather than as editable text.

Moving Data with Cut and Paste and Drag and Drop

When you need to move data to a different location, you can use either cut and paste or drag and drop.

To use cut and paste, select the data in its source and copy it to the Clipboard. Then tap the upper-left cell in the destination range, tap again to display the Edit menu, and tap the Paste button.

To move data with drag and drop, follow these steps.

1. Select the cell or range you want to move.

2. Tap and hold the selection until it becomes mobile.

3. Drag the selection to the destination (see Figure 7-11) and then lift your finger.

4				
5		Smith	887	
6		Jones	913	
7		Ramirez	1018	
8				
9			Smith	887
10			Jones	913
11			Ramirez	1018
12				
13				

Figure 7-11. You can use drag and drop to move a selection to a different location in the same worksheet

Creating Tables

When you create a worksheet that contains many related items in a single range, you may benefit from creating a table. For example, if you need to record data such as purchase orders or customer details, you can put each item in a separate row and then create a table that contains all the rows. The table enables you to treat each row as a record and to sort and filter the rows to show the information you need.

> **Note**   Some of the templates in Excel for iPad contain tables already set up for you to use.

To create a table, follow these steps.

1. Open the workbook you want to use. Create a new workbook if necessary.

2. If you need to add a worksheet, click the New Sheet button. Name the worksheet so that you can easily identify it.

3. Type the headings for the table. For example, if the table will contain customer names and addresses, you'd type fields such as Last Name, First Name, Middle Initial, Title, Address 1, and so on.

4. Tap the row heading for the headings row and then apply formatting to the row to distinguish it from the following rows. For example, tap the Bold button on the Home tab of the Ribbon to apply boldface.

5. Enter the first record in the first row below the headings. (If you don't have records yet, enter sample data—but remember to remove it after creating the table.) You can enter multiple records if you want, but you don't need to. Add to this row any number formatting or other formatting the table's cells will need. The rows you add subsequently will pick up the formatting from this row.

6. Select the headings and the row of data below them. If you've entered multiple records, select them all.

7. Tap the Insert tab of the Ribbon to display its controls (see Figure 7-12).

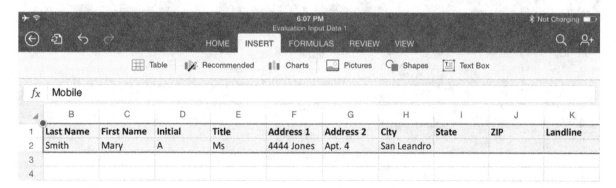

Figure 7-12. *Tap the Table button on the Insert tab of the Ribbon to convert the selected headings and data into a table*

8. Tap the Table button. Excel converts the headings and data into a table and adds the Table tab to the Ribbon (see Figure 7-13).

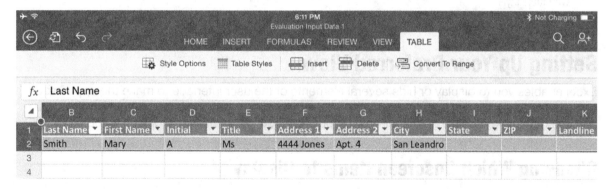

Figure 7-13. *Each heading cell in the table becomes a pop-up menu that you can use to sort and filter the table*

Note   See Chapter 9 for sorting and filtering in Excel worksheets and tables.

You can now add further records to the table. As long as you put the next record in the row immediately under the last existing row, Excel automatically adds it to the table. You can also add rows within the table if you prefer by tapping the Insert button on the Table tab of the Ribbon and then tapping the appropriate item on the Insert pop-up panel (see Figure 7-14).

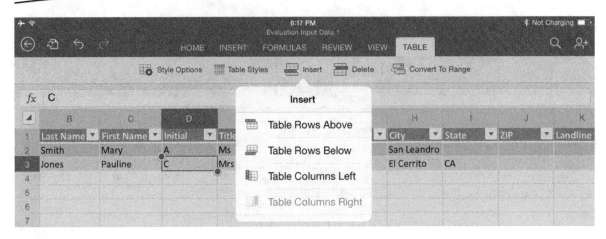

Figure 7-14. You can insert rows inside the table by tapping the appropriate button on the Insert pop-up panel

> **Note**   See the section "Applying Table Formatting" in Chapter 8 for details on how to format tables with table styles.

Setting Up Your Preferred View

Excel enables you to display or hide several elements of the user interface to make the app look and behave the way you want it to. You can also freeze the panes in a worksheet so that specific rows and columns remain visible no matter how far down or how far across the worksheet you scroll.

Choosing Which Onscreen Items to Display

To choose which onscreen items to display, tap the View tab of the Ribbon to display its controls (see Figure 7-15). You can then set the following four switches to the On position or to the Off position, as needed:

- *Formula Bar*: You can hide the Formula bar when you have finished entering data and you need more space on screen. Excel automatically displays the Formula bar if you open a cell for editing.

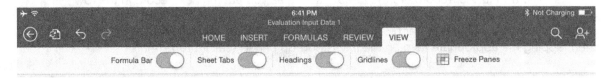

Figure 7-15. On the View tab of the Ribbon, you can toggle the display of the Formula bar, Sheet tabs, row and column headings, and gridlines

- *Sheet Tabs*: You can hide the sheet tabs to get more space on screen or to hide the other worksheets while displaying the worksheet to others on your iPad.

- *Headings*: You can hide the row and column headings when you don't want others to see them. The usual reason for hiding the headings is to prevent others from seeing that you have hidden some rows, columns, or both.

- *Gridlines*: You can hide the gridlines if your worksheet looks better without them. If you want gridlines on some cells but not on the rest of the worksheet, use the Borders button on the Home tab of the Ribbon to apply borders to those cells.

Freezing Panes

To keep your data headings on screen when you scroll down or to the right on a large worksheet, you can freeze the heading rows and columns in place. For example, if you have headings in column A and row 1, you can freeze column A and row 1 so that they remain on screen.

You can quickly freeze the first column, the top row, or your choice of rows and columns:

- *Freeze the first column*: Tap the Freeze Panes button, and then tap the Freeze First Column button on the Freeze Panes pop-up panel (see Figure 7-16).

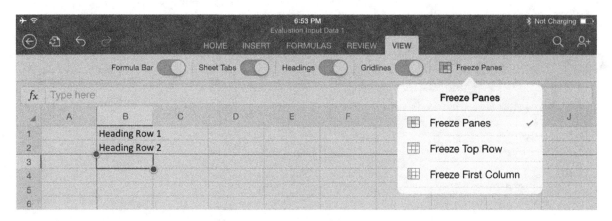

Figure 7-16. From the Freeze Panes pop-up panel, you can freeze the top row, the first column, or your choice of rows and columns

- *Freeze the first row*: Tap the Freeze Panes button, and then tap the Freeze Top Row button on the Freeze Panes pop-up panel.

- *Freeze your choice of rows and columns*: Tap the cell below the row and to the right of the column you want to freeze. For example, to freeze the top two rows and column A, tap cell B3. Then tap the Freeze Panes button and tap the Freeze Panes button on the Freeze Panes pop-up panel.

Summary

In this chapter, you got off to a running start with Excel for iPad. You now know what features and limitations the app has compared to the desktop versions. You can create workbooks, navigate the Excel interface, and enter data in a worksheet using several essential techniques. You also learned how to use the View controls to make Excel look the way you prefer.

In the next chapter, you will learn how to build worksheets and format them to look the way you want.

Chapter 8

Building and Formatting Worksheets

In this chapter, you will examine how to build and format worksheets quickly and efficiently in Excel for iPad. You will start by creating the structure of your workbook, inserting and deleting worksheets as needed, and renaming and rearranging them. You will move on to inserting and deleting rows, columns, and cells; setting column height and row width; and hiding any rows or columns you don't want people to see. After that, you will dig into formatting cells and ranges, using the Find and Replace features, and sorting and filtering your data to show the records you need. You will finish by looking at how to work with comments and how to print all or part of a workbook.

Creating the Structure of Your Workbook

Excel for iPad gives each new blank workbook you create a single worksheet, but you can easily insert other worksheets as needed. If you find you have surplus worksheets, you can delete them. You can rename the worksheets with descriptive names, and you can reshuffle them into the order that makes most sense.

Inserting, Deleting, and Duplicating Worksheets

When you need a new worksheet, you can either insert a new worksheet after an existing worksheet or duplicate an existing worksheet so that you can reuse its content or formatting. You can delete any worksheet that you no longer need.

Inserting a Blank Worksheet

Here's how to insert a new worksheet.

1. Tap the tab of the existing worksheet after which you want to position the new worksheet. (If the workbook contains only a single worksheet, you don't need to do this.)

2. Tap the + button after the last worksheet in the Worksheets bar. Excel inserts the worksheet after the current worksheet, giving it a default name such as Sheet2.

3. Double-tap the default name to select it.

4. Type the name you want to give the worksheet (see Figure 8-1).

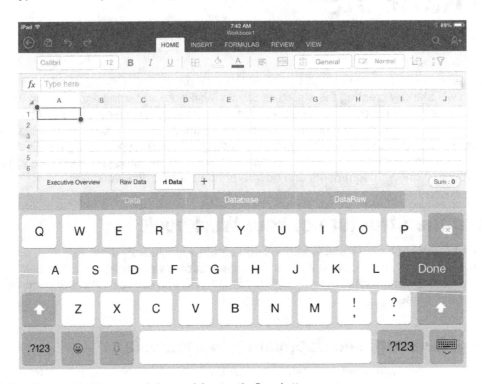

Figure 8-1. Type the name for the new worksheet and then tap the Done button

> **Note**   You can use the same technique to rename the first sheet (or any sheet) in a workbook: double-tap its current name to select it, type the new name, and then tap the Done button on the keyboard or simply tap in the worksheet.
>
> Worksheet names can be up to 31 characters long, so you have enough space for several words. Excel for iPad displays only about the first 20 characters of longer names, truncating them with an ellipsis (…). So put the key words at the beginning of the name rather than the end to enable yourself to identify your worksheets easily. For example, the name "2015 Sales by Territory" works better than the name "Sales by Territory 2015" because you can see the year even when Excel truncates the name.

5.   Tap the Done button on the keyboard.

Deleting a Worksheet

Here's how to delete a worksheet.

1.   Tap the worksheet's tab to select it.

2.   Tap the tab again to display the Edit menu (see Figure 8-2).

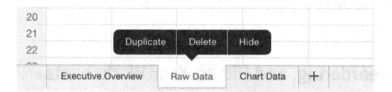

Figure 8-2.   To delete a worksheet, tap the active worksheet's tab, and then tap the Delete button on the Edit menu

3.   Tap the Delete button. Excel displays the Delete the Selected Sheet? dialog box (see Figure 8-3).

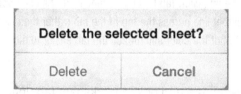

Figure 8-3.   Tap the Delete button in the Delete the Selected Sheet? dialog box to delete the selected worksheet and all its data

4.   Tap the Delete button.

> **Tip**   If you delete the wrong worksheet, you can't use Undo to recover it. Instead, tap the File button on the Ribbon, tap Restore, and then tap the latest version of the workbook to go back to that version. You'll lose any other changes you've made since that version was saved, so be sure that recovering the deleted worksheet is worth this cost.

Duplicating a Worksheet

Often, you can save time by duplicating an existing worksheet and then making any necessary changes to the duplicate rather than creating a new worksheet and entering data on it.

Here's how to duplicate a worksheet.

1. Tap the worksheet's tab to select it.

2. Tap the tab again to display the Edit menu.

3. Tap the Duplicate button. Excel creates a duplicate of the worksheet, placing it before the original worksheet and adding " (2)" to its name—for example, the duplicate of a worksheet named Summary receives the name Summary (2).

4. Double-tap the duplicate sheet's tab to select its name.

5. Type the new name.

6. Tap the Done button.

Renaming, Reordering, and Hiding Your Worksheets

To rename a worksheet, double-tap its tab button, type the new name of up to 31 characters, and then tap the Done button.

> **Tip**   If you need to make a particular worksheet tab stand out, use a desktop version of Excel to change its color. Right-click or Ctrl+click the tab, click Tab Color, and then click the color you want to apply. Excel for iPad displays the color as a discreet line across the top of the tab rather than as the background for the whole tab (as the desktop versions do), but the color still makes the tab easier to pick out in a busy workbook.

To change the order of worksheets, tap and hold a worksheet tab until it becomes mobile, drag it to its new position, and then drop it there.

Note   At this writing, Excel provides no easy way to copy or move a worksheet into another workbook. To work around this, select all the data on the appropriate worksheet, copy it, and then move to the destination workbook and paste in the data. If necessary, tap the Paste Options button and tap Keep Source Formatting or Match Destination Formatting to fix any formatting problems. If you're moving the worksheet rather than copying it, you can now go back to the source workbook and delete the worksheet from it.

When you don't want a worksheet to be visible, but you want to keep it in the workbook rather than remove it, you can hide the worksheet. Follow these steps.

1. Tap the worksheet's tab to make the worksheet active.

2. Tap the tab again to display the Edit menu.

3. Tap the Hide button. Excel hides the worksheet.

Excel doesn't display any indicator to show that a workbook contains hidden worksheets. To find out if it does, tap the current worksheet tab to display the Edit menu and see if it contains the Unhide button (see Figure 8-4).

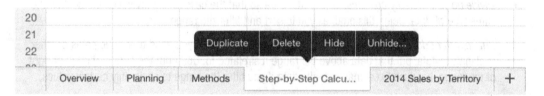

Figure 8-4. The Unhide button on the Edit menu for a worksheet tab indicates that the workbook contains one or more hidden worksheets

Tap the Unhide button to display a menu of the hidden worksheets (see Figure 8-5). You can then tap the worksheet you want to unhide.

Figure 8-5. Tap the Unhide button on the Edit menu to display the menu of hidden worksheets, and then tap the worksheet you want to unhide

---

> **LAYING OUT YOUR WORKSHEETS THE SMART WAY**

Excel gives you a great deal of flexibility in how you lay out your worksheets. Each worksheet contains more than 16 billion cells, and you can put pretty much as many worksheets in a workbook as you want—although if you want to keep Excel on your iPad running snappily, you'll do well to keep the number of worksheets and the number of occupied cells down to a small fraction of the limits.

To make your worksheets easy to use, follow these suggestions for laying them out:

- *Put different topics on different worksheets*: Split your data up by topic (or by date, if that makes more sense) and put different topics on different worksheets. Usually, it's best to keep the most important data in the upper-left corner of any worksheet, where you can most easily access it, rather than having to trek off into the wilds of high-numbered rows or exotically lettered columns.

- *Name the worksheets clearly*: Give the worksheet tabs descriptive labels so you can easily pick the worksheet you want.

- *Provide navigation tools*: If a workbook has so many worksheets that navigating with worksheet tabs is awkward, create a summary worksheet at the front containing a list of the other worksheets and their contents—and hyperlinks you can tap to jump directly to each sheet. To add a hyperlink to a cell, you insert the HYPERLINK() function in the cell. Chapter 9 explains how to use functions.

- *Divide up your data by columns*: Lay out the data so that the cells in any given column contain the same type of data. Doing this enables you to sort and filter the range by rows.

- *Put important data above the range rather than beside it*: When you need to include notes or other explanatory data, put that data above the range it's related to. Don't put the data to the left or right of the range, because Excel may hide the data if you filter the range to show only certain values.

- *Separate your data ranges from each other*: If you include several different types of data in the same worksheet, put each type in a separate range, with one or more blank columns and one or more blank rows between the ranges. Having this extra space makes it easier for both Excel and you to identify and select the ranges individually.

Inserting and Deleting Rows, Columns, and Cells

As you lay out the data in your worksheets, you may need to insert and delete rows, columns, or blocks of cells. Often, inserting or deleting rows or columns is easier than moving your existing data, especially when there's a large amount of data involved.

Sometimes you may also need to insert or delete a block of cells without inserting or deleting entire columns or rows.

Inserting Rows or Columns

The easiest way to insert a row or column is to tap the heading of the existing row or column before which you want to insert the new one and then tap the Insert button on the Edit menu, which appears automatically. For rows, this button is called Insert Above (see Figure 8-6); for columns, it's called Insert Left.

Figure 8-6. Tap a row heading and then tap the Insert Above button on the Edit menu to insert a new row above the existing row

To insert more than one column or row, select the same number of columns or rows first. For example, here's how to insert three columns before column F.

1. Tap the heading for column F to select it. The Edit menu appears automatically.

2. Drag the right-hand selection handle to the right to expand the selection to columns G and H as well.

3. Tap the Insert Left button on the Edit menu (see Figure 8-7). Excel inserts the new columns to the left of the existing ones.

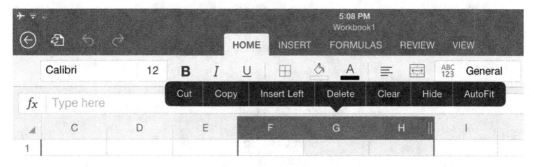

Figure 8-7. You can insert multiple columns or rows at once by selecting the same number of existing rows or columns before giving the Insert command

Note Excel selects the new columns or rows after it inserts them. If the columns or rows you had previously selected are blank, it may appear that Excel hasn't inserted the new items. If cells onscreen have contents, you'll be able to see the change more clearly.

You can also insert a column or row by using the Insert & Delete Cells pop-up panel by following these steps.

1. Tap a cell in the column or row before which you want to insert the column. You can also tap the column heading or row heading.

2. If the Home tab of the Ribbon isn't currently displayed, tap the Home tab to display its controls.

3. Tap the Insert & Delete Cells button to display the Insert & Delete Cells pop-up panel (see Figure 8-8).

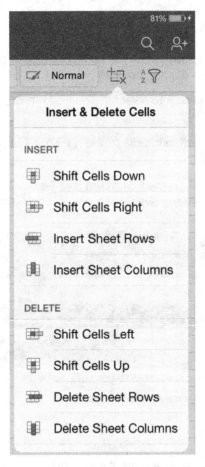

Figure 8-8. *You can insert cells, rows, or columns by using the Insert & Delete Cells pop-up panel on the Home tab of the Ribbon*

4. Tap the Insert Sheet Columns button or the Insert Sheet Rows button.

> **Note** When the selection is one or more columns, tapping the Shift Cells Right command has the same effect as the Insert Sheet Columns command. Similarly, when the selection is one or more rows, tapping the Shift Cells Down command has the same effect as the Insert Sheet Rows command.

Deleting Rows and Columns

To delete a row or column, tap the heading for the row or column, and then tap the Delete button on the Edit menu. Excel deletes the row or column without further confirmation.

To delete multiple rows or columns, tap the heading of the first row or column, drag the selection handle through the other rows or columns, and then tap the Delete button on the Edit menu. You can also select the row, rows, column, or columns; tap the Insert & Delete Cells button on the Home tab of the Ribbon; and then tap the Delete Sheet Rows button or the Delete Sheet Columns button, as appropriate.

Inserting Individual Cells and Blocks of Cells

When you don't need insert entire rows or columns, you can insert an individual cell or a block of cells. Follow these steps.

1. Select the existing cell or cells before which you want to insert the new cell or cells.

2. If the Home tab of the Ribbon isn't currently displayed, tap the Home tab to display its controls.

3. Tap the Insert & Delete Cells button to display the Insert & Delete Cells pop-up panel.

4. Tap the Shift Cells Down button or the Shift Cells Right button, as needed.

Similarly, you can delete an individual cell or a block of cells without deleting the entire row or column.

1. Select the cell or cells you want to delete.

2. Tap the Home tab of the Ribbon to display its controls.

3. Tap the Insert & Delete Cells button to display the Insert & Delete Cells pop-up panel.

4. Tap the Shift Cells Left button or the Shift Cells Up button, as needed.

Setting Column Width and Row Height

To set the width of a column, tap the column heading, and then drag the sizing handle to the right or left as needed.

To have Excel resize a column to fit its contents, tap the column heading, and then tap the AutoFit button on the Edit menu that appears (see Figure 8-9).

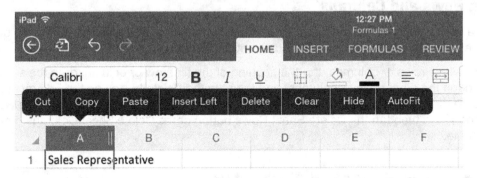

Figure 8-9. Tap the AutoFit button on the Edit menu to resize a column to fit its contents

> **Note**   AutoFit works only for the current contents of the column or row—it's not a persistent setting, so if you add an entry that's wider or taller than the contents to which you applied AutoFit, Excel doesn't adjust the width or height to accommodate the new entry. Instead, you need to apply AutoFit again—preferably after entering all the items in the column or row, or at least entering the widest and tallest items.

Similarly, you can change a row's height by tapping the row heading and then dragging the sizing handle up or down as needed. To have Excel adjust the row's height to fit its contents, tap the row heading, and then tap the AutoFit button on the Edit menu.

Hiding Rows and Columns

Sometimes it's helpful to hide particular columns and rows so that they're not visible in the worksheet. You may want to do this to keep sensitive data from showing or simply to make the part of the worksheet you're actually using fit on the iPad's screen all at once.

To hide a column or row, tap its column heading or row heading, and then tap the Hide button on the Edit menu. Excel hides the row or column, but you can easily tell it's gone; first, the column letter or row number is missing in the sequence; and second, Excel makes the border between the columns or rows before and after the hidden one heavy and bold. Figure 8-10 shows a worksheet with column B and row 2 hidden.

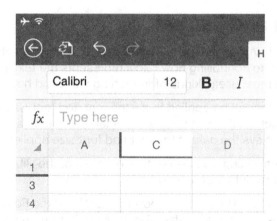

Figure 8-10. Excel displays a heavier border between row or column headings to indicate a hidden row or column, as with row 2 and column B here

Tip   If you don't want other people to be able to see that you've hidden rows or columns, turn off the display of row headings and column headings. Tap the View tab of the Ribbon and then set the Headings switch to the Off position. Turning off the display of headings makes it harder to determine cell references, so don't hide the headings if anyone will be editing the structure of the workbook.

To display a hidden row or column again, you unhide it. Tap the heavy row border or column border to display the Edit menu, and then tap the Unhide button (see Figure 8-11). If you find it hard to tap the border of the hidden column or row, select the columns or rows before or after the hidden one, and then tap Unhide on the Edit menu.

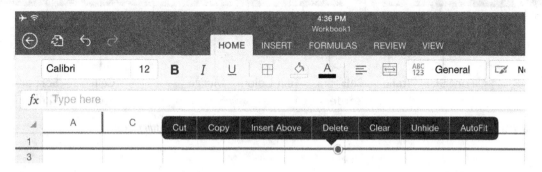

Figure 8-11. To unhide a row or column, tap the heavy row border or column border, and then tap the Unhide button on the Edit menu

Formatting Cells and Ranges

In Excel, you can format cells in a wide variety of ways—everything from choosing how to display the borders and background to controlling how Excel represents the text you enter in the cell. This section shows you how the most useful kinds of formatting work and how to apply them.

Each cell comes with basic formatting applied to it—the font and font size to use and usually the General number format, which you'll meet shortly. So when you create a new workbook and start entering data in it, Excel displays the data in the font and font size applied to the cells you use.

Excel for iPad puts all the formatting options on the Home tab of the Ribbon, as you can see in Figure 8-12. These break down into four categories:

- *Character Formatting*: Use the Fonts pop-up panel and the Font Size pop-up panel to select the font and font size. Tap the Bold button, the Italic button, or the Underline button to apply those attributes where needed.

- *Cell Formatting*: Use the Cell Borders pop-up panel, the Fill Color pop-up panel, and the Text Color pop-up panel to control the appearance of cells. Tap the Alignment button and select the appropriate horizontal and vertical alignment on the Alignment panel. If you need to merge cells together, select them, and then tap the Merge button.

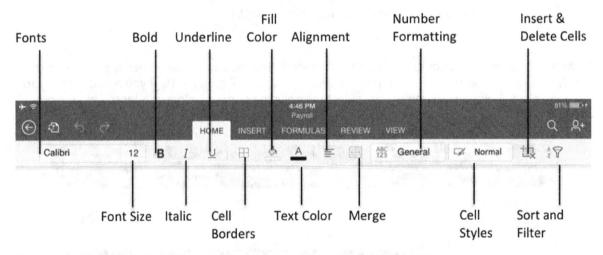

Figure 8-12. The Home tab of the Ribbon gives you quick access to Excel for iPad's formatting tools

Caution   When you merge together cells that contain data values, Excel keeps only the data value in the upper-left cell in the range. Excel displays the Merging Multiple Data Values dialog box to warn you of this change. Tap the Continue button to continue with the merge or tap the Cancel button if you want to move the data from the other cells before merging the cells.

- *Number Formatting*: Tap the Number Formatting button and then select the number format on the Number Formatting pop-up panel and its subpanels. You'll learn about the number formatting options a little later in this chapter.

- *Cell Styles*: Tap the Cell Styles button and then tap the appropriate style on the Cell Styles pop-up panel. The cell styles are preformatted appearance settings that you can apply quickly to cells.

Understanding How Formatting Works in Excel

In Excel, you can apply direct formatting just as you can in most other apps. For example, you can select a cell and then tap the Bold button on the Home tab of the Ribbon to make the cell's contents bold, or tap the Fill Colors button and use the Fill Colors pop-up panel to choose a fill color for the cell.

Direct formatting is easy, but you can usually save time and effort—and make your formatting more consistent—by using the cell styles that Excel provides. A cell style is a complete set of formatting for a cell, including any font formatting, number formatting, borders, alignment, fills, and protection needed.

UNDERSTANDING HOW EXCEL STORES DATES AND TIMES

Excel stores dates as serial numbers starting from 1 (Sunday, January 1, 1900) and running way into the future. To give you a couple of points of reference, 42005 represents Thursday, January 1, 2015, while 42370 represents Friday, January 1, 2016.

You can enter a date by typing the serial number (if you know it or care to work it out), but it's much easier to type a date in a conventional format, because Excel recognizes most of them. For example, if you type **1/1/2016**, Excel converts it to 42370 and displays the date in whichever format you've chosen.

Excel stores times as decimal parts of a day. For example, 42370.25 is 6 a.m. (one quarter of the way through the day) on January 1, 2016.

Controlling How Data Appears by Applying Number Formatting

When you enter a number in a cell, Excel displays it according to the number formatting applied to that cell. For example, if you enter **42300** in a cell formatted with General formatting, Excel displays it as 42300. If the cell has Currency formatting, Excel displays a value such as $42,300.00 (depending on the details of the format). And if the cell has Date formatting, Excel displays a date such as 23 October 2015 (again, depending on the details of the format). In each case, the number stored in the cell remains the same—so if you change the cell's formatting to a different type, the way that Excel displays the data changes to match.

Table 8-1 explains Excel's number formats, with brief examples.

Table 8-1. Excel's Number Formats

Number Format	Explanation	Examples
General	Excel's default format for all cells in new worksheets. No specific format, but displays up to 11 digits per cell and uses no thousands separator. For any entry longer than 11 digits, General format uses scientific notation (see the "Scientific" entry later in this table).	1234567 Industry
Number	Displays the number of decimal places you choose. You can choose whether to use the thousands separator and how to display negative numbers.	1000 1,000 1,000.00
Currency	Displays the number of decimal places you choose, using the thousands separator. You can choose which currency symbol to display (for example, $) and how to display negative numbers. The currency symbol appears before the first digit in the cell.	$2,345.67 −$2,345.67
Accounting	Displays the number of decimal places you choose, using the thousands separator. You can choose which currency symbol to use. The symbol appears aligned at the left edge of the cell. Decimal numbers are aligned on the decimal point. Negative numbers appear with parentheses around them.	$ 1,000,000 $ (99.999.00)
Date	Displays any of a variety of date formats.	7/30/2015 Thursday, June 30, 2015
Time	Displays any of a variety of date formats.	11:59:59 PM 23:59:59
Percentage	Displays a percent sign and the number of decimal places you choose.	78.79% 200%
Fraction	Displays the number as a fraction. Fractions tend to be visually confusing, so use them only if you must—for example, for betting charts.	1/2 1 ¼
Scientific	Displays the number in exponential form, with E and the power to which to raise the number. You can choose how many decimal places to use.	1.2346E+08 −9.8765E+07
Text	Displays and treats the data as text, even when it appears to be another type of data (for example, a number or date).	Product List 18
Special	Displays the data in the format you choose: ZIP Code, ZIP Code + 4, Phone Number, or Social Security Number.	10013 10013-8295 (212) 555-9753 722-86-8261
Custom	Displays the data in the custom format you choose. Excel provides dozens of custom formats, but you can also create your own formats. Custom formats are available only in the desktop versions of Excel.	[Various]

> **Tip**   Excel for iPad displays custom formats correctly, and the word Custom appears in the Number Formatting box and on the Number Formatting pop-up panel when a cell with a custom format is selected, but you cannot edit the custom format. You can apply a custom format to another cell by copying and pasting the format from the cell that contains it.

Here's how to apply a number format.

1. Select the cell or cells that need the format.

2. Tap the Home tab of the Ribbon to display its controls, if it is not already displayed.

3. Tap the Number Formatting button to display the Number Formatting pop-up panel (see Figure 8-13).

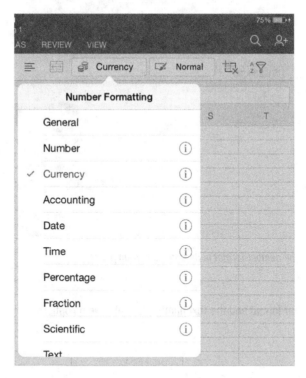

Figure 8-13. *To apply a number format to selected cells, tap the Number Formatting button, and then tap the appropriate number format on the Number Formatting pop-up panel*

4. Tap the number format you want. This example uses the Currency number format. Excel applies the number format to the cell or cells.

5. If the cells now look the way you want them to, tap in the worksheet to close the Number Formatting pop-up panel. Otherwise, tap the Options button (the button with the *i* icon) on the right of the button for the number format you selected in Step 4. Excel displays the Options pop-up panel for the number format—for example, the Currency Options pop-up panel (see Figure 8-14).

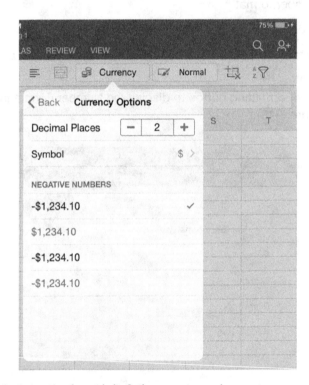

Figure 8-14. *Choose options for the number format in its Options pop-up panel*

Note   The General number format and the Text number format have no options.

6. Use the controls in the Options pop-up panel to specify how you want the number format to appear. For example, in the Currency Options pop-up panel, you can choose these options:

    a. *Decimal Places*: Tap the + button or the – button to adjust the number of decimal places.

    b. *Symbol*: Tap this button to display the Symbols pop-up panel (see Figure 8-15), tap the symbol you need, and then tap the Back button.

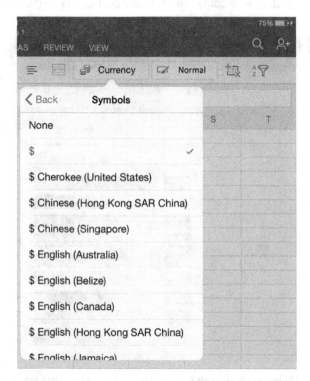

Figure 8-15. For number formats such as Currency and Accounting, use the Symbols pop-up panel to specify the currency symbol to display

    c. *Negative Numbers*: In this list, tap the format to use for negative numbers. Your options include showing negative numbers in red instead of the default color, either with or without a leading minus sign.

7. Tap outside the Options pop-up panel to close the pop-up panel and return to your worksheet.

Applying Direct Formatting

You can quickly format a cell, or its contents, by tapping the cell and then tapping the appropriate button on the Home tab of the Ribbon. For example, you can apply a fill color by following these steps.

1. Tap the cell to select it. Alternatively, select a range of cells.

2. Tap the Home tab of the Ribbon to display its controls, if it is not already displayed.

3. Tap the Fill Color button to display the Fill Color pop-up panel (see Figure 8-16).

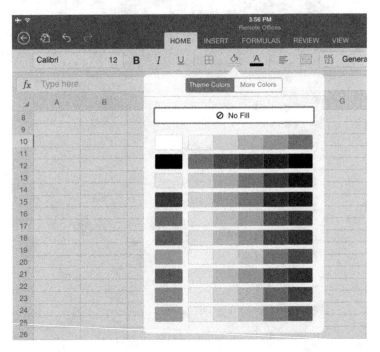

Figure 8-16. You can apply direct formatting in seconds by using the controls on the Home tab of the Ribbon

4. Tap the Theme Colors tab or the More Colors tab, as needed.

5. Tap the color you want to apply.

> **Note**   In Excel for iPad, you can't format part of the text in a cell—you must format the entire contents, even if you select part of it before giving the formatting command. If you open a workbook with cells that include text with different formatting in the same cell, Excel for iPad displays the cells correctly, but any formatting changes you make to such a cell apply to all its text.

Formatting with Cell Styles

As you've seen earlier in this chapter, you can give any cell exactly the formatting you want by using the controls on the Home tab of the Ribbon. But applying formatting one aspect at a time—font, font size, alignment, and so on—is slow work, and it's easy to apply formatting inconsistently.

To save time and ensure your formatting is consistent, you can use Excel's cell styles. Each cell style is a collection of formatting that you can apply to one or more cells and contains six types of formatting:

- *Number:* For example, General, Currency, or Percentage.

> **Note**   At this writing, Excel for iPad enables you to apply existing cell styles but not to edit them or create new cell styles. To create or edit cell styles, you must use a desktop version of Excel.

- *Alignment*: Horizontal alignment (for example, General, Center, or Justify), vertical alignment (for example, Top, Center, or Bottom), and other alignment formatting (such as wrapping the text to the window).
- *Font*: The font, font size, font color, and so on.
- *Border*: Any borders included in the cell style, or No Borders if it has no borders.
- *Fill*: Any fill included in the cell style, or No Shading if it's plain.
- *Protection*: Locked, Hidden, both, or No Protection.

Here's how to apply a cell style.

1.   Select the cell or the range to which you want to apply the cell style.

2.   Tap the Home tab of the Ribbon to display its controls.

3.   Tap the Cell Styles button to display the Cell Styles pop-up panel (see Figure 8-17).

Figure 8-17. The quick way to format cells or ranges is to apply a cell style from the Cell Styles pop-up panel

4. Tap the cell style you want to apply. These are the four main categories of
    cell styles:

    ▪ *Good, Bad, and Neutral*: This category has Good, Bad, and Neutral cell styles that
    you can use to apply color coding to cells. Here is also where you will find the
    Normal cell style that Excel applies to any cell that doesn't have another
    cell style.

    ▪ *Data and Model*: This category contains the Calculation, Check Cell, Explanatory,
    Followed Hyperlink, Hyperlink, Input, Linked Cell, Note, Output, and Warning Text
    cell styles. Most of these cell styles are used for data modeling. Excel automatically
    applies the Hyperlink cell style to cells containing hyperlinks you have not clicked
    yet, changing their cell style to Followed Hyperlink once you have clicked them.

    Note   The Hyperlink cell style appears in the Data and Model category in the Cell Styles panel only if the
    workbook contains hyperlinks. Similarly, the Followed Hyperlink cell style appears only if the workbook
    contains hyperlinks you've followed.

- *Titles and Headings*: This category contains four cell styles for descending levels of headings (Heading 1, Heading 2, Heading 3, and Heading 4), the Title cell style for giving a worksheet a title, and the Total cell style for easily formatting cells that contain totals.

- *Themed Cell Styles*: This category contains four shaded cell styles featuring six of the theme colors, with four degrees of shading for each. Each color's cell styles are named 20%, 40%, 60%, and 100%, so there's a 20% blue cell style, a 20% red cell style, a 20% green cell style, and so on, depending on the theme colors.

Applying Table Formatting

To save you time with formatting, Excel provides preset table styles that you can apply to a table to give it an overall look. After applying a table style, you can choose style options to customize the look.

Note   Chapter 7 explains how to insert a table.

Here's how to apply a table style.

1. Tap anywhere in the table you want to format. Excel adds the Table tab to the Ribbon and displays its controls.

2. Tap the Table Styles button to display the Table Styles pop-up panel (see Figure 8-18). This panel breaks up the styles into three categories: Light, Medium, and Dark. Scroll up or down if necessary to display styles that don't fit in the panel.

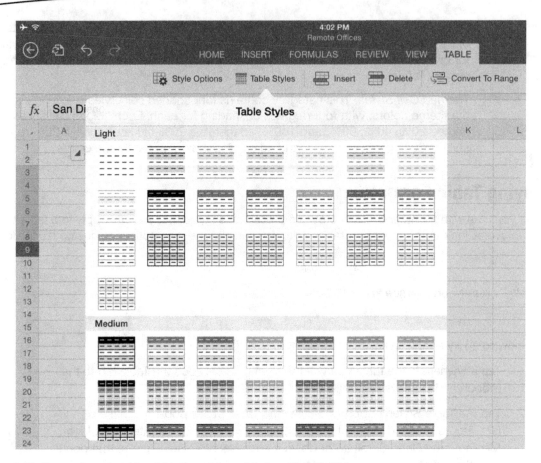

Figure 8-18. You can format a table quickly by applying a style from the Table Styles pop-up panel

3. Tap the table style you want to apply. The table takes on the style's formatting.

4. Tap the Style Options button to display the Style Options pop-up panel (see Figure 8-19).

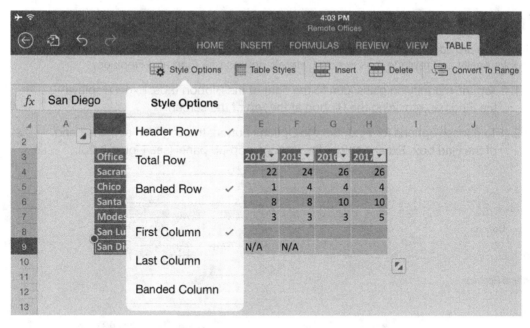

Figure 8-19. In the Style Options pop-up panel, tap to turn an option on or turn it off

5. Tap to place a check mark next to the options you want to use or to remove a check mark from an option that you want to stop using. These are the options:

    a. *Header Row*: Select this option to apply different formatting to the header row.

    b. *Total Row*: Select this option to apply different formatting to the total row.

    c. *Banded Row*: Select this option to apply different formatting to alternate rows, making the rows easier to distinguish from each other. Banded rows tend to be helpful on large worksheets, especially if you've suppressed the display of gridlines.

    d. *First Column*: Select this option to apply different formatting to the first column. You'd normally do this if the first column contains headings.

    e. *Last Column*: Select this option to apply different formatting to the last column. You might do this if the last column contains totals or some form of evaluation or summary.

    f. *Banded Column*: Select this option to apply different formatting to alternate columns, making it easier to distinguish one column from another.

Tip   Usually, it's best to use either the Banded Row option or the Banded Column option rather than both, but you can use both if you find the resulting look helpful.

Using Find and Replace

Excel for iPad provides Find and Replace features that enable you to locate specific text in your workbooks easily and replace it as needed. Here's how to use Find and Replace.

1. Tap the magnifying glass icon to the right of the Ribbon tabs. Excel displays the Find bar, replacing the Ribbon at the top of the screen.

2. To choose options for Find, tap the Options button, the cog icon at the left end of the Find box. Excel displays the Options pop-up panel (see Figure 8-20).

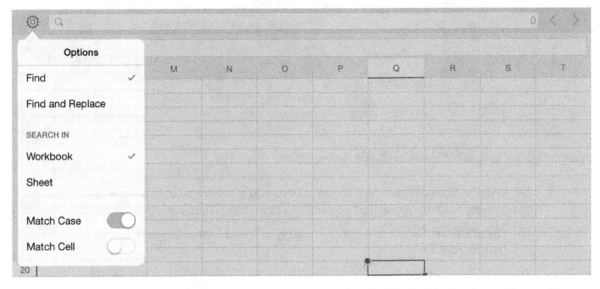

Figure 8-20. On the Options pop-up panel, choose between the Find feature and the Find and Replace feature, choose where to search, and select matching options

3. At the top of the Options pop-up panel, tap the Find button or the Find and Replace button to specify which feature you want to use.

4. In the Search In area, tap the Workbook button or the Sheet button to specify the area you want to search.

5. At the bottom of the Options pop-up panel, set the Match Case switch to the On position if you want Find to be case sensitive (for example, "Sales" matches "Sales" but not "sales," "SALES," or any other different capitalization).

6. Also at the bottom of the Options pop-up panel, set the Match Cell switch to the On position if you want to match only the entire contents of cells instead of finding matches within cell contents as well.

7. Tap in the Find box and type your search term. Excel searches automatically as you enter the term, displays the number of instances found at the right side of the Find box, and selects the cell containing the first instance (if there are any).

8. If you're using Find and Replace rather than Find, tap in the Replace box and type the replacement text.

9. Use the buttons on the Find bar or Find and Replace bar (see Figure 8-21) to work with what Excel has found:

    a. **>**: Tap this button to select the cell containing the next instance.

    b. **<**: Tap this button to select the cell containing the previous instance.

    c. *Replace*: Tap this button to replace the current instance of the Find text with the Replace text and select the cell containing the next instance.

    d. *All*: Tap this button to replace all instances of the Find text with the Replace text.

Figure 8-21. Use the > button, < button, Replace button, and All button to work through the instances of the search term

Tap in the worksheet when you're ready to close the Find bar or the Find and Replace bar.

Sorting and Filtering Your Data

After entering data on a worksheet or creating a table, you may need to sort the data so that you can see how the values relate to each other. You may also need to filter a table's data to make the table display only the records that you want to see.

Sorting Data

Excel for iPad enables your to sort your data by rows quickly by following these steps:

1. Tap a cell in the column you want to sort.

2. Tap the Home tab of the Ribbon to display its controls, if it's not already displayed.

3. Tap the Sort and Filter button to display the Sort And Filter pop-up panel (see Figure 8-22).

Figure 8-22. You can sort data in the selected column by opening the Sort and Filter pop-up panel and tapping the Ascending button or the Descending button

4. Tap the Ascending button (to sort A to Z, low values to high values, early dates to later dates, and so on) or the Descending button (high values to low, and so on).

Filtering Data

When you need to find records in a worksheet that match the terms you specify, you can *filter* it. Filtering makes Excel display only the records that match your search terms, hiding all the other records.

> **Tip**   Filtering tends to be most useful in tables, but you can use it in other data areas as well.

Here's how to filter data.

1. Tap a cell in the column by which you want to filter.

2. Tap the Home tab of the Ribbon to display its controls, if it's not already displayed.

3. Tap the Sort and Filter button to display the Sort And Filter pop-up panel.

4. Set the Filter switch to the On position. Excel displays a down-arrow button on the right of the heading of the data range in the column. If there's no heading, Excel displays a down-arrow button on the empty cell directly above the data range

5. Tap the down-arrow button. Excel displays another Sort And Filter pop-up panel, this time from the down-arrow button (see Figure 8-23).

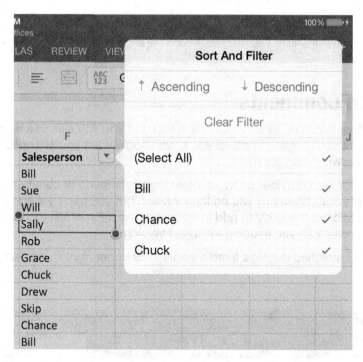

Figure 8-23. *Tap the down-arrow button to display the Sort And Filter pop-up panel, then place a check mark on each item you want to include in the filtered view*

6. Place a check mark on each item you want to include in the filtered view. If you want only a few items, tap the "(Select All)" button at the top of the list to deselect all the items and then tap to select each you want. Excel displays the filtered rows (see Figure 8-24).

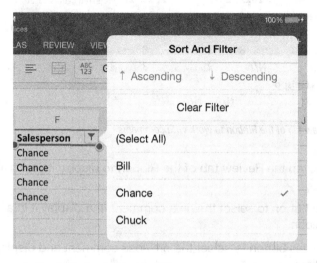

Figure 8-24. *Tap the down-arrow button to display the Sort And Filter pop-up panel, then place a check mark on each item you want to include in the filtered view*

> **Note**   Tap the Clear Filter button on the Sort And Filter pop-up panel when you want to remove the filtering.

Working with Comments

Excel provides comments mostly as a collaboration tool, but you can also use them to make notes for yourself about what you're trying to achieve in a workbook, what you still need to add, and other details that might otherwise slip your mind.

At this writing, Excel for iPad provides an incomplete implementation of comments: you can review the existing comments and delete any you no longer need, but you can't yet add new comments. This is a feature that Microsoft is likely to add in an update, so if Excel still can't add comments when you read this, make sure you're using the latest version.

A cell with a comment attached displays a red triangle in its upper-right corner, as you can see in Figure 8-25.

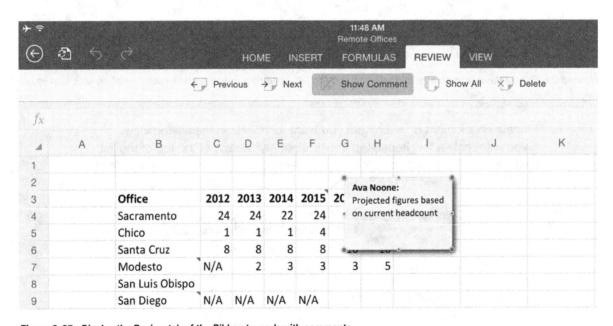

Figure 8-25. Display the Review tab of the Ribbon to work with comments

To work with comments, tap the Review tab of the Ribbon to display its controls. You can then use the buttons as follows:

- *Next*: Tap this button to select the next comment and display it in a comment balloon.

- *Previous*: Tap this button to select the previous comment and display it in a comment balloon.

> **Tip**   You can also display a comment by tapping its square and then tapping the comment symbol that appears above and to the right of the selected cell. After displaying a comment balloon, you can toggle its format between square-ish and a longer, flatter rectangle by tapping the balloon.

- *Show Comment*: Tap this button to toggle the display of the current comment balloon.

- *Show All*: Tap this button to toggle the display of all comments. Showing all comments can help you get an overview of what you have to deal with, but if the balloons are packed closely together, you may find it easier to work with one at a time.

- *Delete*: Tap this button to delete the selected comment.

Tap the Show Comment button again when you want to stop displaying comments.

Printing a Workbook

Excel enables you to print the parts you need of a workbook. You can choose what to print, choose between portrait orientation and landscape orientation, and print either at full size or scaled to fit the paper size you choose. You need to have either an AirPrint-compatible printer or another AirPrint technology; see Chapter 2 for more information.

Here's how to print part of the active worksheet or workbook.

1. If you want to print a worksheet, make it active. If you want to print only a selection, select the range that encompasses it.

2. Tap the File button to display the File menu.

3. Tap the Print button to display the Layout Options pop-up panel (see Figure 8-26).

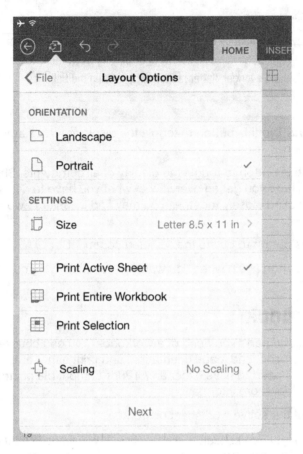

Figure 8-26. In the Layout Options pop-up panel, choose what to print, select the orientation and paper size, and apply any scaling needed

4. In the Orientation section, tap the Landscape button or the Portrait button as needed, placing a check mark on it.

5. If the Size button shows a different paper size than you want to use, tap the Size button, tap the appropriate size on the Size pop-up panel, and then tap the Layout Options button to return to the Layout Options pop-up panel.

6. Further down the Layout Options pop-up panel, specify what to print by tapping the Print Active Sheet button, the Print Entire Workbook button, or the Print Selection button.

7. If you need to apply scaling, tap the Scaling button to display the Scaling Options pop-up panel (see Figure 8-27); tap the Fit Sheet on One Page button, the Fit All Rows on One Page button, or Fit All Columns in One Page button; and then tap the Layout Options button to return to the Layout Options pop-up panel.

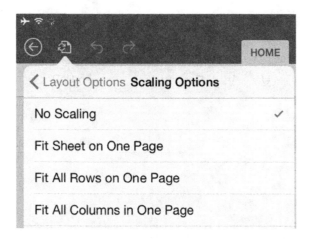

Figure 8-27. In the Scaling Options pop-up panel, choose any scaling needed for the printout

8. Tap the Next button to display the Printer Options pop-up panel.

9. If the Printer button doesn't show the right printer, tap the Printer button, tap the printer in the Printer pop-up panel, and then tap the Printer Options button.

10. If you need to adjust the range of pages, tap the Range button, use the controls in the Page Range pop-up panel to specify what to print, and then tap the Printer Options button.

11. Tap the + button or – button to adjust the number of copies as needed.

12. Tap the Print button.

Summary

In this chapter, you learned how to set up your workbooks with the worksheets they need; how to rearrange the rows, columns, and cells in those worksheets as needed; and how to hide rows and columns. You also learned how to format cells and ranges, use the Find and Replace features, and sort and filter data—not to mention how to work with comments and how to print your worksheets and workbooks.

Chapter 9

Using Formulas and Functions in Your Worksheets

Many of your worksheets will likely need to perform calculations with your data. To perform calculations in Excel, you enter formulas and functions in the appropriate cells in the worksheets. This chapter will explain what formulas and functions are, and what the difference between them is, and then shows you how to use each. Along the way, you will learn how to refer to cells and ranges, meet the calculation operators that Excel supports, and discover how to use them. You will also learn about common problems that occur with formulas and ways to troubleshoot them.

Understanding the Difference Between Formulas and Functions

In Excel, you can perform calculations in two main ways, each of which starts with an equal sign:

- **By using a function:** A *function* is a preset formula that performs a standard calculation. For example, when you need to add several values together, you use the SUM() function; for instance, **=SUM(1,2,3,4,5,6)** is simpler than **=1+2+3+4+5+6** but has the same effect.

- **By using a formula:** A *formula* is a custom calculation that you create when none of Excel's functions does what you need. At its simplest, a formula can be a straightforward calculation; for example, to subtract 50 from 100, you can type **=100-50** in a cell (the equal sign tells Excel you're starting a formula). Formulas can also be more complex, as you'll see in due course.

You can use functions as needed in your formulas. For example, say you need to add the contents of the cells in the range A1:A6 and then divide them by the contents of cell B1. Excel doesn't have a built-in function for doing this because it's not a standard calculation. So instead, you create a formula such as this: **=SUM(A1:A6)/B1**. (In this example, the / is the keyboard equivalent of the ÷ symbol.)

You will learn how to use both functions and formulas. I'll start with formulas, but first, let's go over the ways of referring to cells and ranges in formulas and functions.

Referring to Cells and Ranges in Formulas and Functions

To make your formulas and functions work correctly, you need to refer to the cells and ranges you want. This section makes sure you know how to refer to cells and ranges, both when they're on the same worksheet as the formula and when they're on a different worksheet.

Referring to a Cell

To refer to a cell on the same worksheet, simply use its column lettering and its row number. For example, use **=A10** to refer to cell A10.

To refer to a cell on a different worksheet, enter the worksheet's name followed by an exclamation point and the cell reference. For example, use **=Supplies!A10** to refer to cell A10 on the worksheet named Supplies. The easiest way to set up such a reference is via these steps.

1. Double-tap the cell in which you want to enter the formula. Excel displays the Formula bar and the keyboard.

2. If the letters keyboard is displayed, tap the 123 button in the upper-right corner of the keyboard to display the numbers keyboard. (Tapping the .?123 button gives you the regular numbers keyboard, which is less useful in Excel because it is not optimized for entering data and formulas).

3. Tap the = key. Excel automatically displays the Functions pop-up panel (see Figure 9-1).

Figure 9-1. Excel automatically displays the Functions pop-up panel when you double-tap a cell and type an equal sign

4. Tap anywhere in the spreadsheet to close the Functions pop-up panel.

5. Tap the worksheet tab for the worksheet that contains the cell you want to refer to.

6. Tap the cell.

7. Tap the Enter button, the green button with the white check mark at the right end of the Formula bar, to enter the reference. Excel returns you to the worksheet on which you're creating the formula.

8. Double-tap the cell to resume editing its contents.

9. Finish creating the formula, and then tap the Enter button. You can also tap the Return key on the keyboard.

Note Tapping the Return key on the keyboard enters the formula in the cell and moves the active cell down by one cell. If necessary, you can double-tap the previous cell to edit its contents.

Instead of using the method just described to enter a reference to another worksheet, you can type in the worksheet's name and the reference. There's one complication: if the worksheet's name contains any spaces, you must put the name inside single quotes, for example, **='Sales Results'!A10** rather than **=Sales Results!A10**. You can also use the single quotes on worksheet names that don't have spaces if you find it easier to be consistent. If you omit the single quotes when they're needed, Excel displays an error message.

Note If you refer to a named cell in a formula, the formula displays that name, not the reference.

CREATING A FORMULA USING A HARDWARE KEYBOARD

If you're using a hardware keyboard with your iPad, you can enter a formula using different techniques from using the touchscreen:

- Tap the target cell instead of double-tapping it. When using a hardware keyboard, you don't need to open the cell for editing; simply select the cell and then type **=**.

- Alternatively, use the arrow keys to move the active cell to the target cell. You can also press the Tab key to move the active cell to the right by one cell or press the Enter key to move the active cell down by one cell.

- Press the Enter key to enter the formula in the cell instead of tapping the Enter button on the Formula bar.

DEALING WITH EXTERNAL REFERENCES IN WORKBOOKS

The desktop versions of Excel enable you to create external references, references to cells and ranges in other workbooks. This type of reference also has a strict format: first the workbook's path, then the file name in brackets, then the worksheet's name, and then the cell reference. For example, the reference **='Common:Spreadsheets:[Results.xlsx]Sales!'AB12** refers to cell AB12 on the worksheet named Sales in the workbook Results.xlsx in the Common:Spreadsheets folder on a Mac.

Excel for iPad cannot handle external references at this writing. When you open a workbook that contains an external reference, Excel displays the Cannot Update Workbook dialog box to warn you of the problem. When you dismiss this dialog box, Excel lets you work in the workbook, but it's best not to continue, for two reasons. First, the data may not be current, so your calculations may contain unknown horrors; and second, changes you make to the workbook may break references, which can cause you trouble when you next open the workbook on your PC or Mac.

Excel for iPad allows you to create external links in your workbooks, but because the data is not available, Excel displays the value 0 (zero) for those links. It is best not to create external links on Excel for iPad because you can't see the results until you open the workbook in a desktop version of Excel.

Referring to a Range

To refer to a range that consists of a block of cells, enter the addresses of the first cell and the last cell, separating them with a colon. For example, to refer to the range from cell P10 to cell Q12, use **=P10:Q12**. You can enter the range address in several ways:

- ▨ Type in the range address, including the colon.
- ▨ Tap the first cell in the range, type the colon, and then tap the last cell.
- ▨ Tap the first cell in the range and drag through to the last cell.

To refer to a range that consists of individual cells, give the address of each cell, separating the addresses with commas. For example, to add the values in cell J14, cell K18, and cell Z20, use **=SUM(J14,K18,Z20)**.

To refer to a range on a different worksheet, use the technique explained in the previous section. For example, if you need to work out the average value of the values in the range P10 to P22 on the worksheet named Stock Listing, use **=AVERAGE('Stock Listing'!P10:P22)**.

Making One Row or Column Refer to Another Row or Column

Sometimes you may need to make the contents of one row or column refer to another row or column. For example, say you need to make each cell in column J refer to the corresponding cell in column C, so that cell J1 refers to cell C1, cell J2 to cell C2, and so on.

To do this, follow these steps.

1. Tap the first cell in the column in which you want to enter the data—in this case, cell J1.

2. Tap in the Formula bar to display the keyboard.

3. Tap the = button to start creating the formula. The Functions pop-up panel appears.

4. If the Functions pop-up panel is in the way, tap anywhere in the worksheet to close it.

5. Tap the column heading for column C to make Excel enter the formula =C:C.

6. Tap the Enter button at the right end of the Formula bar to enter the formula.

7. Use AutoFill to copy the formula to the other cells in column J.

Similarly, you can refer to a whole row by entering its letter designation, a colon, and the letter designation again; for example, **2:2**.

Understanding Absolute References, Relative References, and Mixed References

Using cell addresses or range addresses is straightforward enough, but when you start using formulas, there's a complication. When you copy a formula and paste it in a different location, you need to tell Excel whether the pasted formula should refer to the cells it originally referred to, or the cells in the same relative positions to the cell where the formula now is, or a mixture of the two. (If you move a formula to another cell by using drag and drop or cut and paste, Excel keeps the formula as it is.)

To make clear exactly what each reference refers to, Excel uses three types of references:

- **Absolute reference:** A reference that always refers to the same cell, no matter where you copy it. Excel uses a dollar sign ($) to indicate that each part of the reference is absolute. For example, B3 is an absolute reference to cell B3.

- **Relative reference:** A reference that refers to the cell by its position relative to the cell that holds the reference. For example, if you select cell A3 and enter **=B5** in it, the reference means "the cell one column to the right and two rows down." So if you copy the formula to cell C4, Excel changes the cell reference to cell D6, which is one column to the right and two rows down from cell C4. To indicate a relative reference, Excel uses a plain reference without any dollar signs, such as B5.

- **Mixed reference:** A reference that is absolute for either the column or the row and relative for the other. For example, $B4 is absolute for the column (B) and relative for the row (4), while B$4 is relative for the column and absolute for the row. When you copy and paste a mixed reference, the absolute part stays the same, but the relative part changes to reflect the new location.

If you're typing a reference, you can type the $ sign into the reference to make it absolute or mixed. If you're entering references by selecting cells, follow these steps to change the reference type.

1. Tap the cell to which you want to refer, or tap and drag to select a range. The reference appears in the Formula bar.

2. Tap the reference in the Formula bar to select it. The reference changes color.

3. Tap the selected reference to display the Edit menu.

4. Tap the Reference types button to display the Cell Reference Types pop-up panel.

5. Tap the reference you want: Relative Column, Relative Row; Absolute Column, Absolute Row; Relative Column, Absolute Row; or Absolute Column, Relative Row.

> **Note**   If a formula refers to multiple cells, you need to alter the reference for each cell separately. There's no mechanism for altering each reference to the same type in a single move.

Referring to Named Cells and Ranges

If your workbook contains named cells or ranges, you can refer to them easily in formulas by entering their names. For example, if you have named one cell Income and another cell Expenditure, you can use a formula such as =Income – Expenditure to calculate the net remaining.

> **Tip**   Names for cells and ranges must be unique within a workbook, so you don't need to specify the worksheet when referring to a named cell or range.

At this writing, Excel for iPad cannot create named cells or ranges, so you need to create them in a desktop version of Excel instead.

Creating Formulas to Perform Custom Calculations

When you need to perform a custom calculation in a cell, you create a formula that tells Excel what you want to do. The formula uses the appropriate calculation operators, such as + signs for addition and – signs for subtraction. In this section, you will meet the calculation operators, try using them in a worksheet, and learn the order in which Excel applies them and how to change that order.

Understanding Excel's Calculation Operators

To perform calculations in Excel, you need to know the operators for the different operations— addition, division, comparison, reference, and text. Table 9-1 explains the full set of calculation operators you can use in your formulas in Excel.

Table 9-1. Excel's Calculation Operators

Calculation Operator	Operation	Explanation or Example
Arithmetic Operators		
+	Addition	=1+2 adds 2 to 1.
−	Subtraction	=1−2 subtracts 2 from 1.
*	Multiplication	=2*2 multiplies 2 by 2.
/	Division	=A1/4 divides the value in cell A1 by 4.
%	Percentage	=B1% returns the value in cell B2 expressed as a percentage. Excel displays the value as a decimal unless you format the cell with the Percentage style.
^	Exponentiation	=B1^2 raises the value in cell B1 to the power 2.
Comparison Operators		
=	Equal to	=B2=15000 returns TRUE if cell B2 contains the value 15000. Otherwise, it returns FALSE.
<>	Not equal to	=B2<>15000 returns TRUE if cell B2 does not contain the value 15000. Otherwise, it returns FALSE.
>	Greater than	=B2>15000 returns TRUE if cell B2 contains a value greater than 15000. Otherwise, it returns FALSE.
>=	Greater than or equal to	=B2>=15000 returns TRUE if cell B2 contains a value greater than or equal to 15000. Otherwise, it returns FALSE.
<	Less than	=B2<15000 returns TRUE if cell B2 contains a value less than 15000. Otherwise, it returns FALSE.
<=	Less than or equal to	=B2<=15000 returns TRUE if cell B2 contains a value less than or equal to 15000. Otherwise, it returns FALSE.
Reference Operators		
[cell reference]:[cell reference]	The range of cells between the two cell references	A1:G5 returns the range of cells whose upper-left cell is cell A1 and whose lower-right cell is cell G5.
[cell reference],[cell reference]	The range of cells listed	A1,C3,E5 returns three cells: A1, C3, and E5.
[cell or range reference] [space][cell or range reference]	The range (or cell) that appears in both cells or ranges given	=A7:G10 B10:B12 returns the cell B10, because this is the only cell that appears in both the ranges given. If more than one cell appears in the range, this returns a #VALUE! error.
Text Operator		
&	Concatenation (joining values as text)	=A1&B1 returns the values from cells A1 and B1 joined together as a text string. For example, if A1 contains "South America " (including a trailing space) and B1 contains "Sales", this formula returns "South America Sales." If A1 contains 100 and B1 contains 50, this formula returns 10050.

Using the Calculation Operators

Now that you know what the calculation operators are, try the following example of creating a worksheet (see Figure 9-2) with formulas that use the four most straightforward operators—addition, subtraction, multiplication, and division.

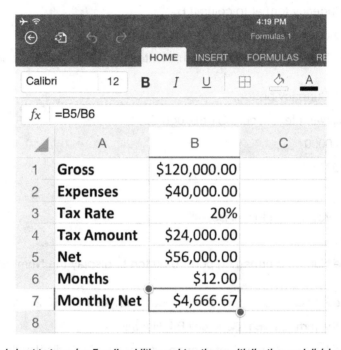

Figure 9-2. *Create this worksheet to try using Excel's addition, subtraction, multiplication, and division operators*

To create the worksheet, follow these steps.

1. Create a new workbook.

   a. If you're currently in a workbook, tap the Back button.

   b. Tap the New tab in the tab bar to display the New screen.

   c. Tap the New Blank Workbook icon.

2. Type the following text in cells A1 through A7:

   ▦   *A1*: Gross

   ▦   *A2*: Expenses

   ▦   *A3*: Tax Rate

   ▦   *A4*: Tax Amount

   ▦   *A5*: Net

   ▦   *A6*: Months

   ▦   *A7*: Monthly Net

3. Apply boldface to column A.

    a. Tap the column heading to select the column.

    b. Tap the Home tab of the Ribbon to display its controls.

    c. Tap the Bold button.

4. Apply the Currency format to column B.

    a. Tap the column heading to select the column.

    b. Tap the Number Formatting pop-up button to display the Number Formatting pop-up panel.

    c. Tap the Currency button.

5. Type the following text in cells B1 through B3:

    ▨ *B1*: 120000

    ▨ *B2*: 40000

    ▨ *B3*: 0.2

6. Apply the Percent style to cell B3.

    a. Tap cell B3.

    b. Tap the Number Formatting pop-up button to display the Number Formatting pop-up panel.

    c. Tap the Percentage button. The readout changes from $0.20 to 20%.

7. Now enter the formula **=B1*B3** in cell B4, like this:

    a. Double-tap cell B4 to select it, open it for editing, and display the keyboard.

    b. Type = to start creating a formula in the cell. The Functions pop-up panel appears.

    c. Tap anywhere in the worksheet to close the Functions pop-up panel.

    d. Tap cell B1 to enter it in the formula. Excel displays a shimmering dotted blue outline around the cell and adds it to the formula in the cell and to the Formula bar (see Figure 9-3).

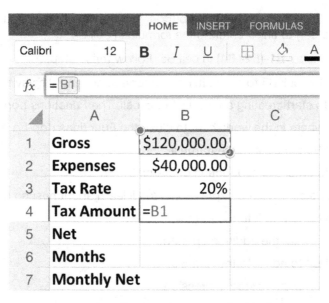

Figure 9-3. *When you tap cell B1, Excel adds it to the formula in both the cell and the Formula bar and displays a dotted blue outline around it*

    e.   Type * to tell Excel you want to multiply the value in cell B1. Excel enters the asterisk in the formula and changes the outline around cell B1 to solid blue.

    f.   Tap cell B3 to enter it in the formula. Excel displays a shimmering dotted outline (red this time) around the cell and adds it to the formula in the cell and in the formula bar (see Figure 9-4).

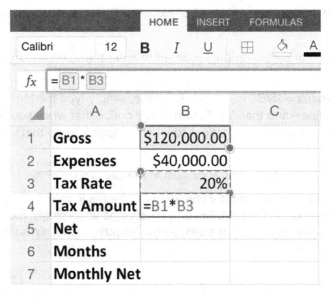

Figure 9-4. *Tap cell B3 to add it to the formula*

    g. Tap the Enter button (the green button with the check mark at the right end of the Formula bar) to finish entering the formula in cell B4.

8. Enter the formula **=B1-(B2+B4)** in cell B5. Follow these steps.

    a. Double-tap cell B5 to select it, open it for editing, and display the keyboard.

    b. Type = to start creating a formula in the cell. The Functions pop-up panel appears.

    c. Tap anywhere in the worksheet to close the Functions pop-up panel.

    d. Tap cell B1 to add it to the formula.

    e. Type – to enter the subtraction operator.

    f. Type (to start a nested expression. (You'll learn about nesting shortly.)

    g. Tap cell B2 to add it to the formula.

    h. Type + to enter the addition operator.

    i. Tap cell B4 to add it to the formula.

    j. Type) to end the nested expression.

    k. Tap the Enter button to finish entering the formula.

9. Enter **12** in cell B6 and apply General formatting to it. Follow these steps.

    a. Tap cell B6 to select it.

    b. Tap the Number Formatting pop-up button to display the Number Formatting pop-up panel.

    c. Tap the General button.

    d. Double-tap cell B6 to select it, open it for editing, and display the keyboard. The Functions pop-up panel opens.

    e. Tap anywhere in the worksheet to close the Functions pop-up panel.

    f. Type **12**.

    g. Tap the Enter button on the keyboard to enter the value and move the active cell to cell B7.

10. Enter the formula **=B5/B6** in cell B7. This time, simply type the formula in—lowercase is fine—and then tap Return. You'll notice that when you type each cell reference, Excel selects that cell to let you check visually that you have the right cell.

11. Tap the Enter button to enter the formula in the cell. You're done.

Now that you've created the worksheet, try changing the figures in cells B1, B2, and B3. You'll see the results of the formulas in cells B4, B5, and B7 change accordingly. Excel recalculates the formulas each time you change a value in a cell, so the formula results remain up to date.

Note The desktop versions of Excel enable you to turn off automatic recalculation and force recalculation manually. Turning off automatic recalculation is useful for large workbooks containing many calculated values, especially when one recalculated value causes many other values to need recalculation. Excel for iPad does not let you turn automatic recalculation on or off at this writing. But if you open a workbook that has automatic recalculation turned off, you can recalculate it manually: tap the Formulas tab to display its controls, and then tap the Recalculate button, the button on the far right that shows a calculator icon.

Overriding the Order in Which Excel Evaluates Operators

When you need to use multiple operators in a formula, you must understand the order in which Excel evaluates the operators so that you can get the calculation correct. You can also override the default evaluation order to make your formulas work the way you intend.

In the previous example, you entered the formula **=B1-(B2+B4)** in cell B5. The parentheses are necessary because the calculation has two separate stages—one stage of subtraction and one stage of addition—and you need to control the order in which they occur.

Try changing the formula in cell B5 to **=B1-B2+B4** and see what happens. Follow these steps.

1. Double-tap cell B5 to open it for editing.

2. Tap in the Formula bar to start editing the formula there.

3. Delete the opening and closing parentheses.

4. Tap the Enter button at the right end of the Formula bar.

You'll notice that the Net amount (cell B5) jumps substantially. This is because you've changed the meaning of the formula.

- *=B1-(B2+B4).* This formula means "add the value in cell B2 to the value in cell B4, and then subtract the result from the value in cell B1."

- *=B1-B2+B4.* This formula means "subtract the value in cell B2 from the value in cell B1, and then add the value in cell B4 to the result."

Double-tap cell B5 to open the cell for editing. Position the insertion point before **B2** and type **(;** then position the insertion point after **B4** and type **)**. Then tap the Enter button to enter the formula in the cell.

The order in which Excel evaluates the operators is called *operator precedence*, and it can make a huge difference in your formulas, so it's vital to know both how it works and how to override it. Table 9-2 shows you the order in which Excel evaluates the operators in formulas.

Table 9-2. Excel's Operator Precedence in Descending Order

Precedence	Operators	Explanation
1	–	Negation
2	%	Percentage
3	^	Exponentiation
4	* and /	Multiplication and division
5	+ and –	Addition and subtraction
6	&	Concatenation
7	=, <>, <, <=, >, and >=	Comparison operators

When two operators are at the same level, Excel performs the operator that appears earlier in the formula first.

Nesting Parts of a Formula to Control Operator Precedence

You can control operator precedence in any formula by nesting one or more parts of the formula in parentheses. For example, as you just saw, using **=B1-(B2+B4)** makes Excel evaluate **B2+B4** before the subtraction.

You can nest parts of the formula several levels deep if necessary. For example, the following formula uses three levels of nesting and returns 180:

```
=10*(5*(4/(1+1))+8)
```

> **Note** If you've ever worked out math equations by hand, you know how you start by calculating the innermost (most deeply nested) set of parentheses and then work outward, applying the order of operator precedence within each level of nesting. Excel works in just the same way, following common mathematical rules.

Breaking Up a Complex Formula into Separate Steps

Excel enables you to create a highly complex formula in a single cell. If you like math, science, or logic, you may enjoy creating such formulas. It's certainly satisfying when they work, but they can be hard to troubleshoot when they don't.

To make troubleshooting (or simply changing) your formulas easier, consider breaking up any complex formula into separate steps, putting each step in its own cell or row. For example, you could break up that =10*(5*(4/(1+1))+8) formula like this:

- Cell B1. =1+1

- Cell B2. =4/B1

- Cell B3. =5*B2

- Cell B4. =B3+8

- Cell B5. =10*B4

Broken up like this, each formula is easy to read, and you can easily see if any of the steps gives the wrong result. You can type a text description of each step in the next cell for reference, or (more discreetly) insert a comment describing the step.

When you've checked that the formula works, you have the option of creating a new version of the formula that goes into a single cell. But if you want to keep the worksheet easy to read and easy to audit, leave the formula in its step-by-step form.

Entering Formulas Quickly Using Copying and AutoFill

In many worksheets, you'll need to enter related formulas in several cells. For example, say you have the worksheet shown in Figure 9-5, which lists a range of products with their prices and sales. Column D needs to show the total revenue derived by multiplying the Units figure by the Price value.

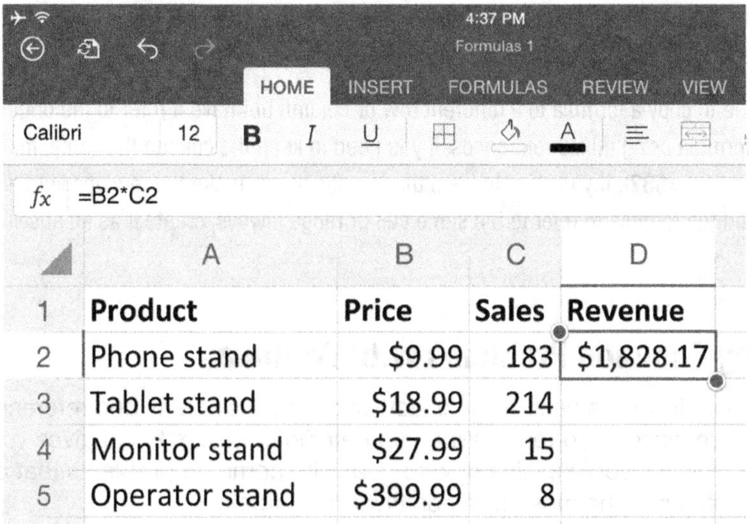

Figure 9-5. When a worksheet needs similar formulas in a column or row, you can enter one formula manually and then use the AutoFill or Copy and Paste features to enter it quickly in the other cells

Each cell in column D needs a different formula: Cell D2 needs =B2*C2, Cell D3 needs =B3*C3, and so on. Because the formula is the same except for the row number, you can use either AutoFill or Copy and Paste to enter the formula from cell D2 into the other cells as well.

To enter the formula using AutoFill, follow these steps.

1. Tap the cell that contains the formula—in this case, cell D2.

2. Tap the cell again to display the Edit menu.

3. Tap the Fill button to display the AutoFill handles.

4. Drag the appropriate handle (in this case, the downward handle) down through cell D5. Excel automatically fills in the formulas, adjusting each for the change in row.

To enter the formula using Copy and Paste, use the Copy and Paste commands.

1. Tap the cell that contains the formula.

2. Tap the cell again to display the Edit menu.

3. Tap the Copy command.

4. Tap to select the first cell in the destination range.

5. Drag a selection handle to select the rest of the destination range. The Edit menu appears automatically.

6. Tap the Paste button. Excel pastes in the formulas.

Note   If you need to copy a formula to a different row or column but have it refer to the original column or row, create the formula using mixed references. If you need to keep the column the same, make the column absolute (for example, =$B2); if you need to keep the row the same, make the row absolute (for example, =B$2). If you need the formula to refer to the same cell or range always, create it as an absolute reference.

Troubleshooting Common Problems with Formulas

Like most calculations, formulas need to be exactly correct. A single wrong reference or a typo can prevent a formula from working correctly. When something is wrong, Excel gives you as much help as possible to fix it. This section explains how to deal with common problems that occur in formulas. Table 9-3 shows solutions to the most common error messages.

Table 9-3. How to Solve Excel's Eight Most Common Errors

Error	The Problem	The Solution
#####	The formula result is too wide to fit in the cell.	Make the column wider—for example, double-click the column head's right border to AutoFit the column width.
#NAME?	A function name is misspelled, or the formula refers to a range that doesn't exist.	Check the spelling of all functions; correct any mistakes. If the formula uses a named range, check that the name is right and that you haven't deleted the range.
#NUM!	The function tries to use a value that is not valid for it—for example, returning the square root of a negative number.	Give the function a suitable value.
#VALUE!	The function uses an invalid argument—for example, using =FACT() to return the factorial of text rather than a number.	Give the function the right type of data.
#N/A	The function does not have a valid value available.	Make sure the function's arguments provide values of the right type.
#DIV/0	The function is trying to divide by zero (which is mathematically impossible).	Change the divisor value from zero. Often, you'll find that the function is using a blank cell (which has a zero value) as the argument for the divisor; in this case, enter a value in the cell.
#REF!	The formula uses a cell reference or a range reference that's not valid—for example, because you've deleted a worksheet.	Edit the formula and provide a valid reference.
#NULL!	There is no intersection between the two ranges specified.	Change the ranges to produce an intersection.

Caution   This section shows you how to troubleshoot problems that Excel can identify because they prevent your calculations from working. But what can be much more dangerous are mistakes in formulas that *don't* cause errors but instead give the wrong results; because the formulas work correctly, Excel can't detect the errors and so raises no objections, but the values you get aren't what you intend. If having your calculations give the correct results is important to you (as is usually the case), have a competent colleague check your worksheets for mistakes. You may also want to get a book such as *Spreadsheet Check and Control* (O'Beirne, Systems Publishing), which teaches you how to audit Excel worksheets.

> **Note**   The =SUM() function ignores any text values in the ranges you set it to add. This is because many spreadsheets contain labels in areas that you may want to add.

If you create an error when entering a formula, Excel may display the Formula Error dialog box when you tap the Enter button. Read the details to see what the problem is, and then resolve it; if you can tap the Enter button without the Formula Error dialog box appearing again, chances are you've solved the problem.

> **Tip**   At this writing, Excel for iPad doesn't provide features for auditing formulas or tracing errors except for circular references (discussed next). If you run into errors that you cannot resolve on Excel for iPad, troubleshoot the workbook using a desktop version of Excel (assuming that you have access to one).

Removing Circular References

Even if you're careful, it's easy enough to create a *circular reference*—a reference that refers to itself.

Circular references most often occur when you enter a formula that refers to a cell that itself refers to the cell in which you're entering the formula. For example, say cell A1 contains the formula **=B1**. If you enter the formula **=A1** in cell B1, you've created a circular reference: cell B1 gets its value from cell A1, which gets its value from cell B1, and so on.

You can also enter a circular reference by making a cell refer to itself. For example, if you enter **=A1/B1** in cell A1, you've created a circular reference in that cell, because cell A1 refers to itself. This type of circular reference is usually easier to avoid than the previous type.

Circular references can be useful in some specialized circumstances, such as when you need to perform iterations of a calculation, but normally you don't want them in your worksheets, so Excel warns you about them. For circular references involving multiple cells, Excel displays blue arrows indicating the cells involved (see Figure 9-6).

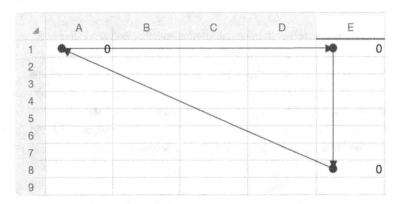

Figure 9-6. Excel displays arrows to indicate a circular reference among multiple cells

If you create a circular reference within a cell (making the cell refer to itself), Excel displays the Excel Cannot Calculate Formula dialog box (see Figure 9-7). Tap the OK button, and then remove the circular reference.

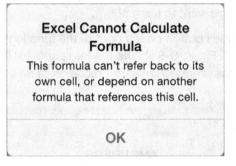

Figure 9-7. The Excel Cannot Calculate Formula dialog box warns you about a circular reference within a cell

Inserting Functions to Perform Standard Calculations

A function is a predefined formula for performing a standard calculation. Excel includes several hundred built-in functions that you can simply insert in a cell and provide with the data they need to deliver the result. Functions save you time and effort and help you avoid the mistakes that can occur when you create formulas. Excel also makes functions easy to use, so when you need to perform a standard calculation, check whether Excel has a function for it—most likely, it does.

In this section, you will learn how to insert functions into your worksheets, how to find the functions you want, and how to use arguments to give the functions the data they require for the calculations.

Once you're comfortable with how functions work, I'll review the different categories of functions that Excel provides, such as database functions, logical functions, and math and trigonometric functions. I'll explain the functions you're most likely to find useful, giving examples where they'll be helpful.

Understanding Function Syntax

In Excel, a function has a name written in capitals followed by a pair of parentheses, which enclose any pieces of data the function needs. Here are three examples:

- SUM( ): This widely used function adds together two or more values that you specify.

- COUNT( ): This function counts the number of cells that contain numbers (as opposed to text, blanks, or other data types) in the range you specify.

- TODAY( ): This function enters the current date in the cell.

Most functions take *arguments*, pieces of information that tell the function what you want it to work on. Excel's two main tools for inserting functions, the Functions pop-up panel and the AutoSum Functions pop-up panel, both give you easy access to help information that lists the arguments required for each function.

To see the help about a function and a list of its arguments, follow these steps.

1. Double-tap the cell to open it for editing.

2. Tap the = key to display the Functions pop-up panel.

3. Locate the function you want to learn about.

4. Tap the Info button (the i button on the right of the function's button) to display the Info panel. Figure 9-8 shows the Info panel for the AMORDEGRC function, which returns prorated linear depreciation of an asset.

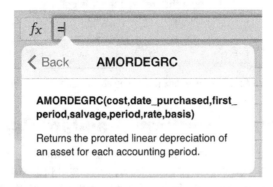

Figure 9-8. Open the Info panel for a function to see its argument list and a brief description of what it does

5. Tap the Back button to return to the Functions pop-up panel.

When you've identified the function you want to use, tap its button on the Functions pop-up panel to insert the function into the Formula bar. Excel displays the function's arguments in gray boxes. For example, in Figure 9-9 the Formula bar shows the SUM() function. This function has one required argument and one optional argument, and you can add further arguments as needed:

- **Required argument:** Each required argument appears with its name in standard-weight type, like the argument *number1* in the figure. You separate the arguments with commas, as in the example in the next paragraph. For example, you can use SUM() to add the values of cells in a range: SUM(C1:C10). Here, C1:C10 is a single argument, the required argument.

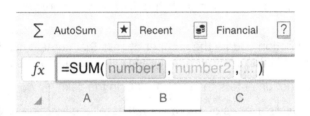

Figure 9-9. When you insert a function in the Formula bar, Excel displays a list of its arguments, showing which are required, which are optional, and whether you can use extra arguments

- **Optional argument:** Each optional argument appears in fainter type, like the argument *[number2]* in the figure. For example, you can use SUM() to add the values of two cells: SUM(C1,C3). Here, C1 is the required argument, and C3 is the first optional argument.

- **Extra arguments:** The ellipsis (…) shows that you can enter extra arguments of the same type. For example, you can use SUM() to add the values of many cells: SUM(C1,C3,D4,D8,E1,XF202). Here, C1 is the required argument, and all the other cell references are optional arguments.

Note   Several functions take no arguments. For example, the TODAY() function simply returns the current date and requires no more information. Similarly, the NOW() function needs no arguments to return the current date and time, and the NA() function simply enters #(N/A) in a cell to indicate that the information is not available. But even when a function takes no arguments, you must include the parentheses to make Excel recognize the function.

Inserting a Function

You can insert a function in a worksheet either by using one of the Functions panels or by typing it the function into the cell. As you've seen, Excel automatically displays the main Functions panel when you type = to start creating a formula in a cell. But normally you'll want to use the individual Functions panels, such as the AutoSum Functions panel or the Financial Functions panel, which you access from the Formulas tab of the Ribbon.

Inserting a Function Using the Functions Panels

To insert a function using one of the Functions panels, tap the Formulas tab of the Ribbon to display its controls (see Figure 9-10). You can then tap the button for the Functions panel you need.

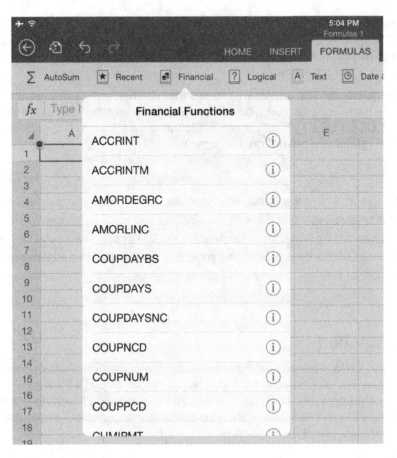

Figure 9-10. On the Formulas tab of the Ribbon, tap the button for the Functions panel you want to display. For example, tap the Financial button to display the Financial Functions panel

- **AutoSum:** This Functions panel enables you to enter the widely-used functions SUM(), AVERAGE(), COUNT(), MAX(), or MIN() in your worksheets.

> **Note**   In landscape orientation, the Formulas tab of the Ribbon displays the names of all the buttons except the More Functions button and the Recalculate button (the button at the right end). In portrait orientation, the Formulas tab displays the names of only the AutoSum button and the Recent button.

- **Recent:** This Functions panel provides quick access to the functions you've used most recently, enabling you to quickly insert a function again.

- **Financial:** This Functions panel contains functions for financial calculations—for example, calculating the payments on your mortgage or the depreciation on an asset.

- **Logical:** This Functions panel contains functions for performing logical tests—for example, testing whether a particular cell contains an error.

- **Text:** This Functions panel contains functions for manipulating text, such as the TRIM() function (for trimming off leading and trailing spaces) and the LEFT() function, which returns the leftmost part of the value.

- **Date & Time:** This Functions panel contains functions ranging from returning the current date with the TODAY() function to using the WEEKDAY() function to return the day of the week for a particular date.

- **Lookup & Reference:** This Functions panel contains functions for looking up data from other parts of a worksheet or referring to other cells in it.

- **Math & Trigonometry:** This Functions panel contains mathematical functions, such as the SQRT() function for returning a square root, and trigonometric functions, such as the ACOS() function for calculating the arccosine of a number.

- **More Functions:** (This is the … button to the right of the Math & Trigonometry button.) Tap this button to display the More Functions panel (see Figure 9-11), which gives you access to the following Functions panels:

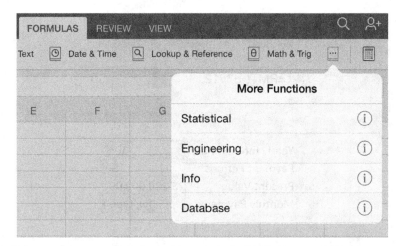

Figure 9-11. Open the More Functions panel to access the Statistical Functions panel, the Engineering Functions panel, the Info Functions panel, and the Database Functions panel

- **Statistical:** This category contains functions for performing statistical calculations, such as working out standard deviations based on a population or a sample.

- **Engineering:** This category contains functions including the DEC2HEX() function (for converting a decimal number to hexadecimal, base 16) and the HEX2OCT() function (for converting a hexadecimal number to octal, base 8).

■ **Information:** This category contains functions for returning information about data, such as whether it is text or a number.

■ **Database:** This category contains functions for working with databases—for example, returning the average of values in a column or list or the count of cells containing numbers in a field.

Tip If you want to browse the full list of functions in alphabetical order, double-tap the cell to open it for editing and then tap the = key on the onscreen keyboard to display the Functions panel. Scroll down past the Recently Used Functions list at the top to reach the All Functions list, where you can browse the functions.

When you find the function you need, tap it to insert it in the cell and in the Formula bar. Excel highlights the first required argument, and you can tap the cell that contains the value you want to use. Tap the next argument and then tap the appropriate cell (see the example in Figure 9-12). When you finish specifying the data to use for the function, tap the Enter button at the right end of the Formula bar to enter the function in the cell. The result then appears, and you can verify whether the formula is working.

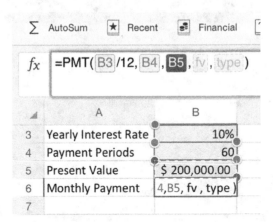

Figure 9-12. Tap an argument in the Formula bar and then tap the cell to use for the argument. Tap the Enter button to enter the function in the cell

Typing a Function Directly into a Cell

Typing a function into a cell works well when you know which function you want and you remember which arguments it requires. Usually, you'll want to type in only simple functions, such as TODAY() or ROUND(), and take advantage of Excel's help in entering other functions.

When you type the = sign to start the function, Excel displays the Functions pop-up panel. As you continue typing, the Functions pop-up panel narrows down the list to show only functions matching what you have typed. You can tap a function to insert it in the cell and the Formula bar with its arguments list or simply finish typing the function's name; if you continue typing, Excel hides the Functions pop-up panel when you type the opening parenthesis for the function.

Nesting One Function Inside Another Function

Many calculations require only a single function, but for others, you will need to use multiple functions. You can combine functions as needed, using them in much the same way that you use values. For example, the AVERAGE( ) function calculates the average (the arithmetic mean) of the values of the arguments, so AVERAGE(1,2,3) returns 2; and the ROUND( ) function returns the value of the first argument rounded to the number of digits specified by the second argument, so ROUND(2.418, 0) returns 2. To add the results of the two functions together, you create a formula like this, giving the result 4:

```
=AVERAGE(1,2,3) + ROUND(2.418,0)
```

When you need one function to work on the value that a second function returns, you can nest that second function inside the first function. For example, if you need to return the current hour, you can nest the NOW( ) function in the HOUR( ) function. The NOW( ) function returns the current date and time, and the HOUR( ) function returns the hour from a given time (in 24-hour format; if you need the hour in AM/PM format, change the number format by tapping the cell, tapping the Number Formatting button, tapping the Info icon on the Time button, and then tapping the time format).

Here's the NOW( ) function nested in the HOUR( ) function:

```
=HOUR(NOW( ))
```

As with formulas, you can nest functions many layers deep if you need to. Here's an example with three layers of nesting:

```
=INT(AVERAGE(ROUND(SUM(C1:C6),2),ROUND(SUM(D1:D6),2)))
```

As explained earlier in this chapter, Excel starts by evaluating the most deeply nested expressions. Here's what happens:

- **SUM(C1:C6):** This SUM function adds the values in the range C1:C6. Similarly, SUM(D1:D6) adds the values in the range D1:D6.

- **ROUND(SUM(C1:C6),2):** This ROUND function rounds the result of the SUM(C1:C6) formula to two decimal places. Similarly, ROUND(SUM(D1:D6),2) rounds the result of the SUM(D1:D6) formula to two decimal places.

- **AVERAGE:** This function returns the average of the results returned by the two ROUND functions.

- **INT:** This function returns the integer portion of the result from the AVERAGE function.

Meeting Excel's Most Useful Functions

In this section, you meet 21 of Excel's most widely useful functions. Excel has hundreds of functions, but many of them are highly specialized; for example, the AMORLINC function calculates an asset's prorated linear depreciation for each accounting period in the French accounting system, and the BESSELJ function calculates the Bessel function Jn(x), also called cylindrical harmonics. Unless you work in French accounting or cylindrical harmonics or specialize in confusing your colleagues, chances are that you'll use these functions seldom if ever.

By contrast, the 21 functions in this section turn up in a wide variety of workbooks, so you'll likely use at least some of them.

SUM

The SUM function is so widely used that you'll find it hard to avoid—and in fact you've already met it in this chapter. SUM calculates the sum of the specified numbers. For example, =SUM(1,2,3) returns 6.

AVERAGE, MEDIAN, and MODE

The AVERAGE function calculates the average of the specified values, cells, ranges, or arrays. For example, =AVERAGE(1,2,3) returns 2, and =AVERAGE(B1:B6) returns the average of the range B1:B6.

The MEDIAN function returns the median (the number in the middle of the given set) of the numbers or the values in the specified cells. For example, =MEDIAN(1,2,2,3,4,4,6) returns 3.

The MODE function returns the mode, the value that occurs most frequently in the specified values or range of cells. For example, =MODE(1,1,2,2,2,3,3,4,18) returns 2, because 2 is the number that occurs most frequently among the given numbers.

MAX and MIN

The MAX function returns the largest value in the specified range. For example, =MAX(C1:C6) returns the largest value in the range C1:C6.

The MIN function returns the smallest value in the specified range.

DAY, MONTH, and YEAR

The DAY function returns a serial number between 1 and 31, representing the day of the month for the specified serial date. For example, =DAY(42363) returns 25, indicating that the date falls on the 25th day in the month.

Similarly, the MONTH function returns a serial number between 1 and 12, representing the month in which the specified serial date falls. For example, =MONTH(42363) returns 12, indicating that the date is in December.

As you'd guess from the previous two functions, the YEAR function returns the four-digit number for the specified serial date. For example, =YEAR(42363) returns 2015, indicating that the date is in 2015.

IF

The IF function returns the first of the specified values if the condition is TRUE and the second of the specified values if the condition is FALSE. For example,
=IF(HOUR(NOW( ))<12,"AM","PM") displays "AM" if the current hour is less than 12 and "PM" otherwise.

ISBLANK, NA, and ISNA

The ISBLANK function returns TRUE if the cell is blank and FALSE if it has contents. For example, =ISBLANK(A24) returns TRUE if cell A24 is blank.

The NA function causes a cell to display #(N/A). You use it to indicate that a value is not available.

The ISNA function returns TRUE if the specified cell contains #N/A, entered either via the NA function or as text, and FALSE if it doesn't.

LEFT, RIGHT, and MID

The LEFT function returns the specified number of characters from the beginning of the text string. For example, =LEFT("Product Ratings",7) returns "Product."

Similarly, the RIGHT function returns the specified number of characters from the end of specified text string. For example, =RIGHT("Product Ratings",7) returns "Ratings."

In between LEFT and RIGHT, the MID function returns the specified number of characters after the starting point given in the specified text string. For example, =MID("Human Heart-Rate Monitor",7,10) returns "Heart-Rate."

TRIM

The TRIM function gives you an easy way to remove unwanted spaces from text strings. TRIM returns the specified text string with spaces removed from the beginning and ends, and extra spaces between words removed to leave one space between words. For example, =TRIM(4512 Christy Blvd.   ) strips out the superfluous spaces and returns "4512 Christy Blvd."

PI

The PI function returns the value of Pi to 15 digits (3.14159265358979).

ROUND, ROUNDDOWN, and ROUNDUP

The ROUND function returns the specified number rounded to the specified number of digits. For example, =ROUND(3.33333,2) returns 3.33.

The ROUNDDOWN function returns the specified number rounded down to the specified number of digits. For example, =ROUNDDOWN(18.57321,2) returns 18.57.

The ROUNDUP function returns the specified number rounded up to the specified number of digits. For example, =ROUNDUP(18.57321,2) returns 18.58.

Summary

In this chapter, you learned how to use formulas and functions to perform calculations in your workbooks. You know that a formula is the recipe for a calculation, and that a function is a preset formula built into Excel. You know how to put together a formula using an equal sign, cell or range references, operators, and other components. And you know how to insert functions in your worksheets and how to provide the arguments they require to work. You also met Excel's most widely useful functions—at least, according to me.

Chapter 10

Creating Effective Charts

Excel for iPad gives you all the features you need to create attractive and compelling charts directly on your iPad. You can choose from a wide variety of chart types and subtypes to find the chart that presents your data clearly and persuasively. After creating a chart, you can change its type and subtype as needed, switch its source data or transpose its rows and columns, and give it the layout and style that will work most effectively.

After creating a chart, you can paste it into a Word document or a PowerPoint presentation in moments—and even change the chart type, layout, and appearance in that app.

Learning the Essentials of Charts in Excel

This section goes quickly through the essentials that you need to know to use charts effectively in Excel. It starts with the difference between embedded charts and charts on chart sheets and then cover the various components of charts—the chart area, plot area, axes, categories, data series, and so on.

Understanding Embedded Charts and Chart Sheets

In the desktop versions of Excel, you can create a chart either embedded on a worksheet or on a separate chart sheet. Placing a chart on a worksheet enables you to look at the chart alongside the data that produces it, which is often helpful when you're creating the chart and deciding which data to include. Placing the chart on a separate chart worksheet lets you view or present the chart separately from its data.

At this writing, Excel for iPad can create only embedded charts, but it can display and edit charts on chart sheets as well. So if you need to create a chart on a chart sheet, you need to use a desktop version of Excel. You can then work with it on your iPad as needed.

> **Tip**   You can use a desktop version of Excel to switch an embedded chart you've created in Excel for iPad to a chart sheet. In Excel on Windows or the Mac, right-click or Ctrl+click the chart, and then click Move Chart on the contextual menu to open the Move Chart dialog box. Click the New Sheet option button, type the name for the chart sheet, and click the OK button.
>
> Similarly, you can move a chart from a chart sheet to a worksheet so that you can manipulate it more easily in Excel for iPad. In the Move Chart dialog box, click the Object In option button, select the worksheet in the drop-down list, and then click the OK button.

Understanding the Components of a Chart

Excel's charts vary widely in looks and uses, but most of them use the same set of components. Figure 10-1 shows a column chart of rainfall data for six months for seven weather stations, with the main parts of the chart labeled.

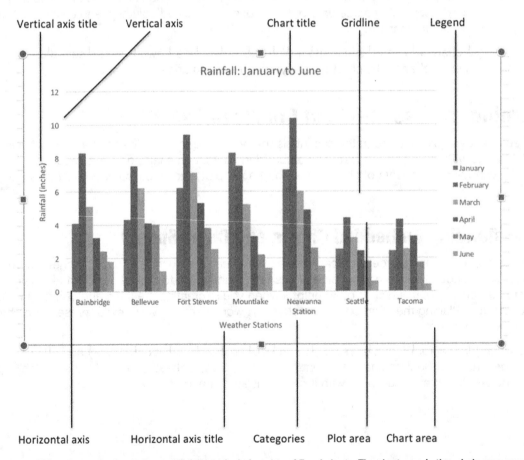

Figure 10-1. This column chart contains most of the typical elements of Excel charts. The chart area is the whole area occupied by the chart, and the plot area is where the data series are plotted

Chart Area and Plot Area

The *chart area* is the whole area occupied by the chart. If the chart has a white background, the easiest way to see the extent of the chart area is to tap the chart so that Excel displays a border around it.

The *plot area* is the area of the chart that contains the plotted data—in other words, the main part of the chart area, excluding the areas occupied by the chart title, the axis titles, and the legend (if it appears outside the plot area).

Chart Axes

Most charts have one, two, or three axes:

- *Horizontal axis*: This is the axis along which the data categories are laid out—for example, the weather stations in the sample chart. This axis is also called the *category axis* or the x-*axis*.

- *Vertical axis*: This is the axis along which the data series are laid out. This axis is also called the y-*axis*.

- *Depth axis*: In 3-D charts, this is the axis that provides the third dimension. This axis is also called the z-*axis*. Figure 10-2 shows a 3-D version of the rainfall chart.

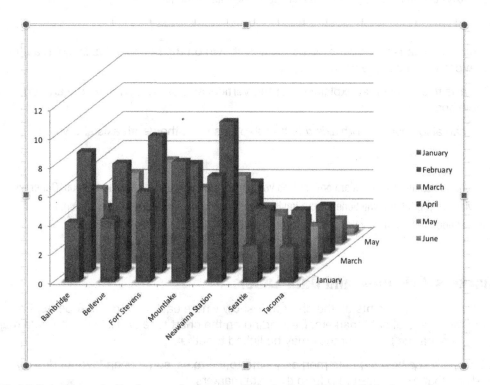

Figure 10-2. A 3-D chart has a depth axis, or z-axis, as well as the horizontal axis and vertical axis

Each axis has tick marks that show where the values appear on it.

Categories and Data Series

The *categories* are the subdivisions of data that appear on the horizontal axis. For example, in the sample chart, each weather station is a category.

The *data series* are the sets of data used to create the chart. For example, in the sample chart, the data series contain the rainfall measurements.

Chart Title and Axis Titles

The *chart title* is text that identifies the chart as a whole. The most straightforward position for the chart title is at the top of the chart, where the reader will see it immediately, but sometimes you may want to place it elsewhere. For example, you may place the chart title in open space in the chart area so that you can make the chart itself larger without the title making it taller.

> **Note**   In charts you create in Excel for iPad, the chart layout that you apply controls whether the chart title and axis titles appear and (if so) where they appear. In the desktop versions of Excel, you can toggle the chart title and axis titles off manually, reposition them as needed, and reformat them.

The *horizontal axis title* is text that explains what is shown on the horizontal axis, such as the weather stations in the sample chart.

The *vertical axis title* is text that explains what the vertical axis shows, such as the amount of rainfall in the sample chart.

A 3-D chart can also have a *depth axis title* that explains what the depth axis shows.

> **Note**   Chart titles and axis titles are optional, so you can include only those your chart needs. Generally, people viewing your charts will benefit from having clear chart titles and axis titles. But if a chart's content is obvious without them, you may prefer to let it speak by itself.

Data Markers, Gridlines, and Data Labels

The *data markers* are the points on the chart that show where each data point appears. Each series typically contains several data markers. Depending on the chart type and layout, the data markers may appear as separate points, or they may be linked together.

To make it easy to see how the data markers relate to the axes, some chart layouts display *gridlines*—lines that run across or up from the data markers.

Data labels are text items that display the exact value of data points. Data labels appear in some chart layouts and help viewers to see the exact figure for each data point rather than judging the value from the chart.

> **Note** In Excel for iPad, you control whether data markers, gridlines, and data labels appear by choosing a layout that includes the items you want to show. In the desktop versions of Excel, you can toggle these items on and off individually.

Choosing the Best Chart Type for Your Data

Excel enables you to create an impressive variety of different types of charts. Some of the charts are useful for many purposes, whereas others are highly specialized. Table 10-1 describes the types of charts that Excel provides and suggests typical uses for them.

Table 10-1. Excel's Chart Types and Suggested Uses

Chart Category	Description	Suggested Uses
Column	Displays data in vertical bars.	Comparing equivalent items (such as sales results) or sets of data that change over time (such as rainfall).
Line	Displays each series in a line.	Showing evenly spaced values that change over time, such as temperatures.
Pie	Displays a single data series as a pie divided up by the contribution of each data point.	Showing how much each item contributes to the whole; for example, breaking down expenses by department.
Bar	Displays data in horizontal bars.	Comparing similar items or indicating progress.
Area	Displays data as lines but with the areas between the lines shaded.	Showing how values have changed over time, especially the contribution of different data points in the series.
Scatter	Displays each data point as a point (or cross, or similar marker) on the plot area. Also known as an XY chart.	Showing values sampled at different times or that are not directly related to each other.
Stock	Displays each data series as a vertical line or bar indicating three or more prices or measurements (such as high, low, and closing prices).	Showing the daily prices of stocks. Also suitable for some scientific data.
Surface	Displays the data points as a three-dimensional surface.	Comparing two sets of data to find a suitable combination of them.

(continued)

Table 10-1. (*continued*)

Chart Category	Description	Suggested Uses
Doughnut	Displays the data series as a sequence of concentric rings.	Showing how much each item contributes to the whole—like a pie chart, but it works with two or more data series.
Bubble	Displays the data points as bubbles of different sizes depending on their values.	Showing the relative importance of each data point.
Radar	Displays the combined values of different data series.	Showing how the combined values of separate data series compare to each other (for example, the sales contributions of several different products over several periods of time).

Note   The table lists the charts in the same order as Excel for iPad's Charts pop-up panel except for the following chart types: the Donut chart type appears in the Pie category, the Bubble chart type appears in the Scatter category, and the Stock, Surface, and Radar chart types appear in the Others category.

Creating, Laying Out, and Formatting a Chart

In this section, you'll look at how to create a chart from your data, lay it out with the components and arrangement you want, and format it using a style and a set of colors.

Creating a Chart

Here's how to create a chart.

1. Select the cells that contain the data for the chart. Normally, it's easiest to tap the first cell, and then drag the selection handle to select the rest of the range.

2. Tap the Insert tab of the Ribbon to display its contents.

3. Tap the Recommended button to display the Recommended panel, which shows the chart types that Excel recommends based on a quick analysis of the selected data. Figure 10-3 shows an example. If one of the recommended charts is suitable, tap it and skip the rest of the steps in this list.

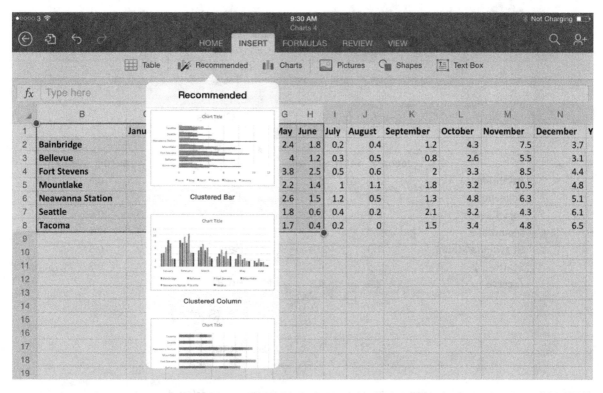

Figure 10-3. *Look at the charts on the Recommended pop-up panel to see if any suit your needs*

Note The Recommended chart types tend to be a bit hit and miss, because Excel doesn't actually understand what your data represents. But it's well worth looking at the recommendations, because doing so takes only a second and the previews give you a good idea of what the chart will look like.

4. Tap the Charts button to display the Charts pop-up panel (see Figure 10-4), which gives you access to the full range of charts that Excel for iPad offers.

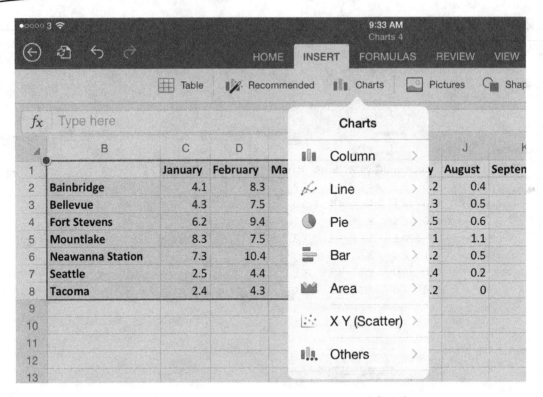

Figure 10-4. On the Charts pop-up panel, tap the chart type to use for the data you've selected

5. Tap the chart type: Column, Line, Pie, Bar, Area, X Y (Scatter), or Others (which gives you access to the Stock, Surface, and Radar chart types). The appropriate pop-up panel appears, showing the available subtypes for that chart type. For example, if you tap Column, the Column pop-up panel appears, showing the 2-D Column subtypes and the 3-D Column subtypes (see Figure 10-5).

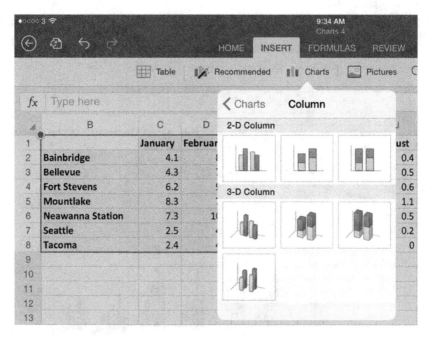

Figure 10-5. *On the pop-up panel for the chart type you selected, tap the chart subtype to use*

6. Tap the chart subtype you want to use. Excel creates the chart as an embedded object in the worksheet (see Figure 10-6).

Figure 10-6. Excel creates the chart as an embedded object on the same worksheet as its source data

You can then reposition the chart by tapping it and dragging it, and you can resize it by tapping it and dragging a resizing handle. As usual, drag a corner handle to resize the chart proportionally; drag a side handle to resize the chart only in that dimension.

Changing the Chart Type

If you find the chart type you've chosen doesn't work for your data, you can change the chart type easily. Tap the chart to select it, and then tap the Chart tab on the Ribbon to display its contents. Tap the Types button to display the Types pop-up panel, tap the chart type, and then tap the subtype.

Excel changes the chart in place. If the result is worse than before, either tap the Undo button or tap the Types button again and try a different chart type, subtype, or both.

Switching the Rows and Columns in a Chart

When Excel displays the chart, you may realize that the data series are in the wrong place; for example, the chart is displaying months by rainfall instead of rainfall by months.

When this happens, you don't need to transpose the data in the data source. Simply tap the chart in the workbook, tap the Chart tab on the Ribbon, and then tap the Switch button. Excel switches the data series in the chart, which changes accordingly.

Changing the Source Data for a Chart

Sometimes you may find that your chart doesn't work well with the source data you've chosen. For example, you may have selected so much data that the chart is crowded, or you may have missed a vital row or column.

When this happens, you don't need to delete the chart and start again from scratch. Instead, tap the chart to select it, and then drag the handles on the data source to select the data you need. Excel color-codes the data source to help you see which data you have selected. Excel changes the chart instantly, so you can see if you've got the data you need.

MANIPULATING THE DATA SERIES

In the desktop versions of Excel, you can change the order in which the data series appear in the chart from the order in which they appear in the data source. For example, if your data source includes columns B, C, and D, you can make the chart display the columns in a different order, such as C, B, D or D, B, C. You can't do this in a chart on the iPad—instead, you need to change the order of the series in the data source and then create the chart.

Another neat move you can make in the desktop versions of Excel is to add to a chart a data series from a separate set of data. For example, say your chart shows your actual sales figures, but you have a separate table or a separate worksheet that shows projected sales figures. You can use the Source Data command to add a data series from the projections to the actual sales figures in the chart without rearranging the data in your worksheet.

You can't do this either on the iPad. Instead, you need to rearrange the data so that it's in a contiguous range, and then create the chart.

Choosing the Layout and Adding Any Titles Needed

When you've got the right chart type and the source data, choose the layout for the chart. For each chart type, Excel provides various preset layouts that control whether and where the title, legend, and other elements appear. After applying a layout, you can customize it further as needed.

To choose the layout, tap the chart, tap the Chart tab, and then tap the Layout button. On the Layouts pop-up panel (see Figure 10-7), tap the layout you want to use for the chart.

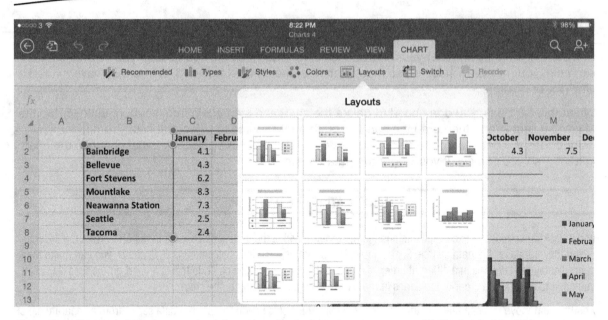

Figure 10-7. You can quickly change a chart's layout by using the Layouts pop-up pane on the Charts tab of the Ribbon

After choosing the layout, you can fill in any information the chart needs. For example, if the layout includes a chart title, tap the chart, double-tap the Chart Title placeholder, and then type the text for the title. Similarly, if the layout has axis titles, add them now.

Applying a Style and Changing the Colors

To set the overall graphical look of a chart, apply one of Excel's styles to it. To apply a style, tap the chart, tap the Chart tab on the Ribbon, tap the Styles button, and then tap the style on the Styles panel (see Figure 10-8).

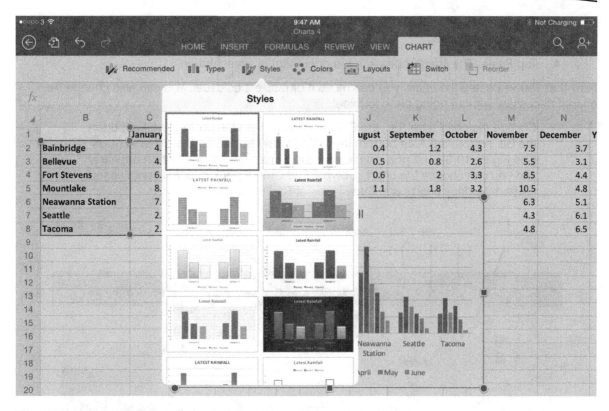

Figure 10-8. Apply a style from the Styles pop-up panel to set the overall look of a chart

After applying the style you want, you can change the colors as needed by tapping the chart, tapping the Colors button on the Chart tab of the Ribbon, and then tapping the set of colors in the Colors pane.

> **Note**   The Colors pane contains a Colorful category and a Monochromatic category. The Colorful category tends to produce charts that are easier to read, but sometimes you may need the more subdued looks that the Monochromatic category offers.

Copying and Pasting a Chart

After creating a chart in Excel, you can copy it and then paste it into a Word document or onto a PowerPoint slide by following these steps.

1.   In Excel, tap the chart, and then tap Copy on the Edit menu that appears.

2.   Switch to Word or PowerPoint, either by pressing the Home button and then tapping the app's icon on the Home screen or (if Word or PowerPoint is already running) by double-pressing the Home button and then tapping the app's preview or icon on the app-switching screen.

3. Tap at the appropriate point in the document or on the destination slide. The Edit menu appears.

4. Tap Paste. The chart appears in the document or presentation.

Now that you've pasted the chart, you can move it or resize it as usual. You can also change the chart if necessary without going back to Excel.

■ *Change the chart type*: Tap the Column button, the Line button, the Pie button, the Bar button, the Area button, the X Y (Scatter) button, or the Others button (see Figure 10-9). The pop-up panel of the same name as the button appears, and you can choose the chart subtype. The Others pop-up panel contains four types of Surface charts and three types of Radar charts.

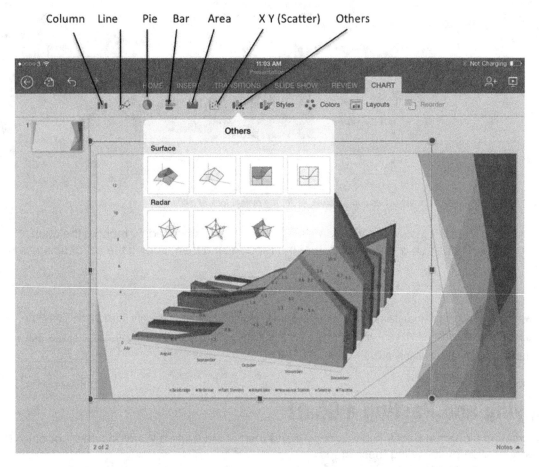

Figure 10-9. After pasting a chart from Excel, use the controls on the Chart tab of the Ribbon in PowerPoint or Word to format the chart or to change it to a different type

- *Change the chart style*: Tap the Styles button to display the Styles pop-up panel, and then tap the style you want. The styles are different visual designs for the chart type and subtype you've chosen.

- *Change the colors*: Tap the Colors button to display the Colors pop-up panel, and then tap the set of colors you want.

- *Change the Layout*: Tap the Layouts button to display the Layouts pane, and then tap the layout you want to apply.

Summary

In this chapter, you learned how to choose the right type of chart for your needs and how to create a chart from your data. You now know how to change the chart type and subtype; change the source data; and apply a suitable layout, style, and colors. And you can now take a chart you've created and paste it onto a PowerPoint slide or into a Word document so that you can use it instantly.

Becoming Expert with PowerPoint for iPad

PowerPoint for iPad brings the most widely used presentation app to your Apple tablet. At this writing, PowerPoint for iPad offers only a subset of the features in the full desktop versions for Windows and Mac, but it has enough features for you to build powerful presentations, either from scratch or by editing existing presentations, and to deliver them directly from your iPad.

Understanding PowerPoint for iPad's Features and Limitations

PowerPoint for iPad is a smaller app than the desktop versions, PowerPoint for Windows and PowerPoint for the Mac, and doesn't aim to offer all their features. In this section, you will learn about the features that PowerPoint has, about those features that are partially implemented or missing, and about what happens to content that PowerPoint for iPad doesn't support.

Which Features Does PowerPoint for iPad Have and Lack?

The following list highlights the main features that are present in PowerPoint for iPad, mentioning those areas in which they fall short:

- *Presentation themes*: PowerPoint for iPad comes with a wide selection of presentation themes in both widescreen and standard formats.

- *Slide types*: Each presentation theme contains a set of different slide types, ranging from title slides to slides with specific types of content and blank slides for you to arrange content however it is needed.

- *Slide content*: Apart from text (with your choice of formatting), PowerPoint for iPad enables you to populate your slides with tables, pictures and videos, shapes, and text boxes. You can also insert a chart by copying and pasting it from Excel.

- *Slide notes*: You can create and edit notes for each slide, and then view the notes as needed while delivering the presentation.

- *Transitions*: PowerPoint for iPad provides a good range of transitions that you can apply to animate or dramatize the changeover between slides.

- *Comments*: You can review existing comments and toggle the display of comments as a whole, but you cannot add comments, edit them, or delete them.

- *Slideshow features*: PowerPoint for iPad includes a solid basic set of features for giving a slideshow. These include Presenter view, which enables you to see the upcoming slides; the ability to display hidden slides as needed; a black screen for when you need to give the audience nothing to look at (for example, when you need to draw their attention back to yourself); and tools for drawing on the screen, plus a simulated laser pointer for highlighting key points.

> **Note**   If PowerPoint on your iPad is lacking any of the features explained here, run the App Store app and update to the latest version. Microsoft has added many features to PowerPoint since the original release. In particular, Version 1.1 was a big improvement, bringing features including Presenter View, Presenter Tools, the ability to add videos from your iPad's storage and to play media during presentation, and cropping for pictures.

These are the main items that PowerPoint for iPad is missing at this writing:

- *Views*: The desktop versions of PowerPoint include Slide Sorter view, which gives you an easy way to get an overview of a presentation and move slides to different positions, either singly or in groups.

- *Outlines*: The desktop versions also include an Outline view in the Navigation pane that helps you to create the text outline of a presentation and enables you to rearrange paragraphs or slides as needed.

- *Themes and masters*: The desktop versions enable you create themes, which PowerPoint for iPad doesn't. In the desktop versions, you can also edit the slide masters, handout masters, and notes masters.

- *Animations and transitions*: The desktop versions enable you to animate individual objects on a slide. They also provide more configuration options for transitions between slides.

- *Review tools*: The desktop versions of PowerPoint provide full commenting features, enable you to compare two versions of a presentation and integrate those changes you want to keep, and protect a presentation against changes.

- *Macros and VBA*: The desktop versions enable you to use macros written in Visual Basic for Applications (VBA) to automate tasks. You can also create user forms (custom dialog boxes) to add a user interface to your VBA macros.

What Happens to Content That PowerPoint for iPad Does Not Support?

If you open a presentation that contains content PowerPoint for iPad doesn't support, the app deals with that content as smartly as possible. Usually, you won't see a problem.

First, PowerPoint for iPad can display many content items that it cannot create or edit at this writing. For example, if you open a presentation that contains object animations, you'll find they normally play back correctly when you run the slide show, even though you cannot edit them on the iPad.

> **Tip**   PowerPoint for iPad's ability to play back content it cannot create or edit is helpful but makes it doubly important to check through a presentation before delivering it. Only by running a slide show of the presentation can you see the details of object animations that the app's user interface does not display.

Second, PowerPoint for iPad ignores any content that it truly cannot handle, such as VBA code and user forms. But it leaves these items in the file when you edit the presentation.

Creating a New Presentation on Your iPad

You can create a new presentation on your iPad quickly by following these steps.

1. Tap the New tab of the file management screen. The presentation designs appear.

2. In the upper-right corner, see if the Slide Size readout shows the size you want—either Widescreen (16:9) or Standard (4:3). If not, tap the existing size to display the Size pop-up panel (see Figure 11-1), and then tap the size you want. The screen displays the presentation designs available in that size.

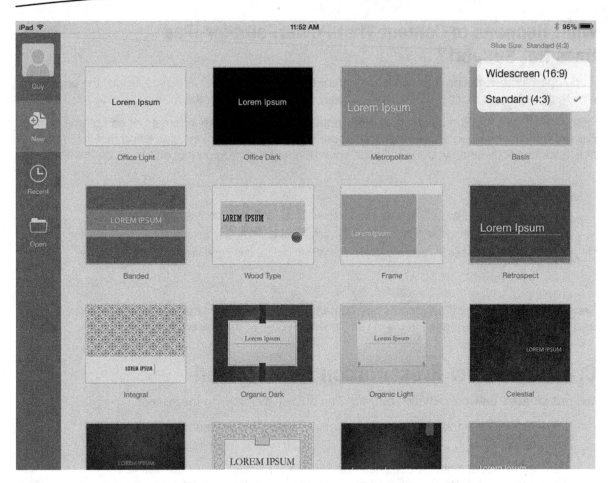

Figure 11-1. *Choose the slide size in the upper-right corner of the New screen, and then tap the design you want to use for your new presentation*

3. Tap the presentation design you want. PowerPoint opens a new presentation that uses the design.

Note   Most presentation templates for PowerPoint for iPad start you off with a single slide, leaving you to add all the rest; other templates include all the slides that form the framework for a standard presentation, which you can customize as necessary. If you need to add another slide to your presentation at this point, tap the New Slide button and then tap the slide type on the New Slide pop-up panel. You'll look at this process in more detail a little later in this chapter.

Opening a Presentation

You can open a presentation by using the file management screen as usual. The presentation can be stored either on your iPad or on an online service to which you have connected your iPad, such as your OneDrive account or a SharePoint server.

DEALING WITH THE "DOCUMENT TOO BIG" ERROR WHEN OPENING A PRESENTATION

If PowerPoint displays the Document Too Big dialog box when you try to open a presentation, you'll know that the presentation needs more memory than your iPad can provide at present. Tap the OK button—it's the only choice—to close the dialog box, and then try the following suggestions to fix the problem.

If you've opened this presentation successfully on this iPad in the past, and nothing has happened to vastly increase the presentation's file size since you last opened it, the issue is most likely that your iPad is low on memory. Double-press the Home button to bring up the app-switching screen, and then close as many apps as possible by dragging or swiping them upward off the screen. You can swipe three at once if you're handy with your fingers.

After closing all the apps you don't need, power your iPad down by pressing and holding the Sleep/Wake button until the Slide to Power Down slider appears, and then sliding that slider. After your iPad shuts down, give it 10 seconds to contemplate nothingness, and then press and hold the Sleep/Wake button until the Apple logo appears on the screen. When the lock screen appears, unlock the iPad, launch PowerPoint, and then try opening the presentation. It should be okay this time.

If not, chances are that the presentation has become bloated. Perhaps one of your colleagues has edited it and inserted a video file of an unwise length. In this case, you'll need to get the presentation back down to a size that your iPad can handle. Open the presentation in a desktop version of PowerPoint, identify the bloat, and remove it. Use the Save As command to save the presentation under a new file name if your colleague will still need the full-fat version. Then try opening the slimmed-down presentation on your iPad.

In passing, if the iPad you have is an older one, but you have access to a newer iPad, you could try using the newer one to open a presentation that produces the "Document Too Big" dialog box. Newer iPads have more RAM than older ones, so (all other things being equal) they can open larger documents. The original iPad has 256MB RAM; the second-generation iPad and first-generation iPad mini have 512MB; and the third-generation and fourth-generation iPad, the iPad Air, and the second-generation iPad mini have 1GB.

Navigating the PowerPoint Interface

The PowerPoint interface is easy to navigate. Figure 11-2 shows PowerPoint with a presentation open that contains several slides.

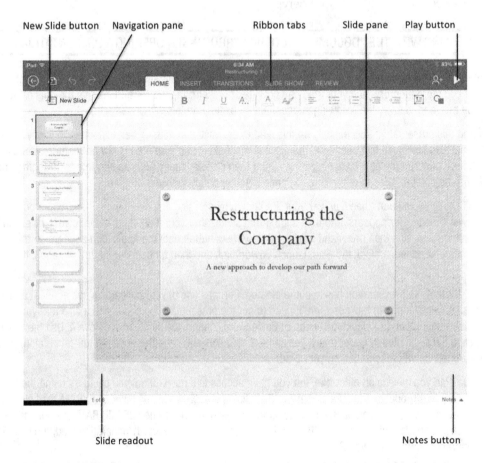

Figure 11-2. The PowerPoint interface

The PowerPoint interface has these seven main components:

- *Ribbon*: PowerPoint's Ribbon contains five static tabs—Home, Insert, Transitions, Slide Show, and Review—plus various contextual tabs that appear when you are working with an object that requires a contextual tab. For example, when you select a picture, the Picture tab appears; and when you select a table, the Table tab appears.

- *New Slide button*: Tap this button to display the New Slide pop-up panel, which contains the slide types available in the presentation design.

- *Navigation pane*: This pane on the left side of the screen shows a thumbnail for each slide in the presentation in their start-to-finish order. You tap a slide in the Navigation pane to display it for editing in the Slide pane.

- *Slide pane*: This pane is where you edit your slides or admire their brilliance. This pane takes up most of the user interface.

- *Play button*: Tap this button to start playing the presentation from the current slide.

- *Slide number*: This readout in the lower-left corner of the Slide pane shows the number and position of the slide displayed—for example, 1 of 6.

- *Notes button*: Tap this button in the lower-right corner of the PowerPoint interface to display the Notes pane for the current slide. You can then add notes to the slide to help you or whoever delivers the presentation.

Adding, Deleting, and Rearranging Slides

To get your presentation into shape, you'll need to add new slides, delete existing slides, and rearrange the remaining slides into the right order for the presentation.

Adding a Slide

Here's how to add a slide to a presentation.

1. In the Navigation pane, tap the existing slide after which you want to add the new slide. If the right slide is already displayed in the Slide pane, you're all set.

2. Tap the New Slide button to display the New Slide pop-up panel (see Figure 11-3). The selection of slide types varies depending on the template on which you based the presentation. Table 11-1 explains some of the widely used slide types.

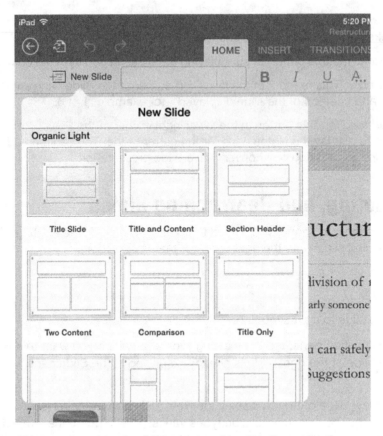

Figure 11-3. In the New Slide pop-up panel, tap the slide type you want to add to the presentation

    3.   Tap the slide design you want to use for the new slide.

Table 11-1. Widely Used Slide Types in PowerPoint Presentations

Slide Type	Contents and Usage Notes
Title Slide	A title placeholder on a theme background.
Title and Content	A title placeholder, usually at the top of the page, with a content placeholder below it.
Section Header	Two text placeholders, designed to contain the section heading of the upcoming section and text briefly explaining its contents.
Two Content	A title placeholder across the top, with side-by-side portrait-shape placeholders below it, for positioning two types of content side by side.
Comparison	A title placeholder across the top, with side-by-side portrait-shape placeholders below it, for positioning content you intend the audience to compare directly.

(continued)

Table 11-1. (*continued*)

Slide Type	Contents and Usage Notes
Title Only	A title placeholder only, with no other content.
Blank	Nothing—a blank canvas for whatever you need to add.
Content with Caption	A placeholder for content of your choice (such as text or a table) with a text placeholder beside it.
Picture with Caption	A placeholder for a portrait-format picture with a text placeholder beside it.
Panorama Picture with Caption	A placeholder for a wide-format picture, such as a panorama or a photo cropped to a shallow depth, with a text placeholder beneath it. Some templates contain multiple versions of this slide type with different layouts.
Title and Caption	A title placeholder and a caption placeholder
Quote with Caption	A title placeholder with double quotation marks around it, for entering a motivational quote, with a text placeholder below it for entering an explanation, follow-up, or the like.
Name Card	A title placeholder for the person's name and a text placeholder for the person's position or description.
Quote Name Card	A title placeholder with double quotation marks around it, for entering an inspiring quote, with two text placeholders below it, the first for the name of the person you're quoting and the second for the person's title or description.
Title and Vertical Text	A horizontal title placeholder across the top of the slide with a text placeholder under it in which the text runs vertically, as if the text placeholder has been rotated 90 degrees clockwise.
Vertical Title and Text	A vertical title placeholder and a vertical text placeholder—the text runs vertically in both placeholders. This slide type is mostly useful for delivering in portrait orientation rather than landscape orientation.

The new slide appears in the presentation, and you can add content to it as discussed in the section "Adding Content to a Slide," earlier in this chapter.

Deleting a Slide

To delete a slide, double-tap it in the Navigation pane, and then tap Delete on the Edit menu. There's no confirmation of the deletion.

Tip   If you need to recover a slide you've deleted, you can tap the Undo button on the Ribbon one or more times to get the slide back. If you've gone too far to retrieve the slide by using Undo, and you're prepared to lose the changes you've made since deleting the slide, tap the File button to display the File pop-up panel, tap Restore, and then tap the latest version available. If that version doesn't contain the deleted slide, restore the second latest version, and so on until you find the slide.

If you have made extensive changes since deleting the slide, use the Duplicate command on the File menu to duplicate the new version of the presentation, saving your changes in it. Then restore the latest version of the old file so that you can retrieve the deleted slide from it and paste it into the new version.

Rearranging Slides

To rearrange the slides in a presentation, go to the Navigation pane and double-tap the slide you want to move. When the slide becomes mobile, drag it to its destination and drop it there.

Duplicating a Slide

When you've created a slide that looks exactly the way you want it to, you may want to base other slides on that slide rather than creating them from scratch using the New Slide pane. You can duplicate a slide easily by tapping and holding it and then tapping Duplicate on the Edit menu.

PowerPoint adds the duplicate slide directly after the original slide in the presentation. PowerPoint selects the duplicate slide automatically, so you can start editing it immediately in the Slide pane.

Cutting and Copying Slides

PowerPoint enables you to cut and copy slides in a presentation. By cutting a slide, you can easily move it either to another presentation or simply to another point in the same presentation. By copying a slide, you can paste a copy in either another presentation or the same presentation.

To cut or copy a slide, double-tap the slide to display the Edit menu, and then tap Cut or Copy, as needed. You can then move to the destination, either in another presentation or the same presentation, double-tap a slide, and tap Paste on the Edit menu.

Hiding a Slide

When you need to keep a slide in reserve, you can hide it so that it doesn't appear in the slide show. Double-tap the slide in the Navigation pane, and then tap Hide on the Edit menu.

PowerPoint displays an icon showing a circle with a diagonal line across it to indicate a hidden slide, as you can see in the second slide in Figure 11-4.

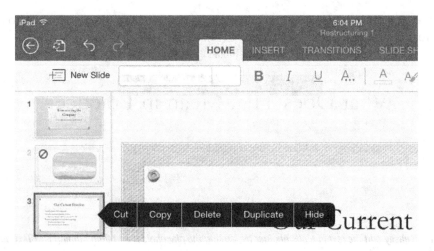

Figure 11-4. *To hide a slide, double-tap it in the Navigation pane and then tap Hide on the Edit menu. A hidden slide bears a gray circle with a diagonal line across it, as you can see in the second slide here*

As you'd imagine, you unhide a slide by tapping it in the Navigation pane and then tapping Unhide on the Edit menu.

Adding Content to a Slide

You can quickly build your slides by adding text, pictures, and tables to it. You can also add other objects such as shapes, text boxes, and even charts from Excel.

Adding Text

Many slide types contain text placeholders positioned and formatted so that you can add text easily. A text placeholder displays the prompt "Double tap to add *text*," where *text* is the text type, such as "title," "subtitle," or "text." When you double-tap the placeholder, the prompt disappears and the insertion point appears. You can then type the text for the placeholder.

Note   If you've cut or copied text to the Clipboard, you can paste it by double-tapping at the appropriate place in the placeholder and then tapping Paste on the Edit menu.

After adding text to a placeholder, you can change it as needed. Tap the placeholder to select it, and then tap Edit Text on the Edit menu (see Figure 11-5).

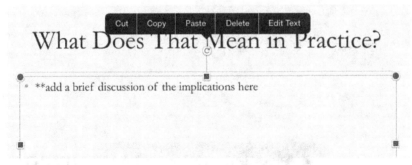

Figure 11-5. You can easily edit the text in a placeholder by tapping the placeholder and then tapping Edit Text on the Edit menu

Tip   You can also double-tap in a placeholder to open it for editing. Double-tap after the end of the existing text to place the insertion point at the end of the text. Double-tap a word to select it.

The quick way to format the text in a placeholder is to format the entire placeholder. Tap the placeholder to select it, and then tap the appropriate controls on the Home tab of the Ribbon. For example, tap the Font box and then tap the font you want to apply to all the text in the placeholder.

Tip   Triple-tap to select an existing paragraph of text in a placeholder.

To format just some of the text in the placeholder, open the placeholder for editing, select the text, and then apply the formatting. For example, double-tap a word to select it, tap the Home tab of the Ribbon (if it isn't already displayed), and then tap the Underline button to apply underline to the word.

Adding Text Boxes to Slides

When you need to add text to part of a slide that doesn't contain a suitable placeholder, you have two choices:

- *Insert a text box*: Tap the Home tab on the Ribbon, and then tap the Text Box button near the right end (see Figure 11-6); alternatively, tap the Insert tab on the Ribbon, and then tap Text Box. Either way, PowerPoint inserts a standard-size text box bang in the middle of the slide. You can then drag the text box to where you need it and drag its handles to resize it. To enter text in the text box, open it for editing either by double-tapping it or by tapping it and then tapping Edit Text on the Edit menu. After entering the text, you can select the text box and format it as needed.

Text Box button

Figure 11-6. You can insert a text box by tapping the Text Box button on the Home tab of the Ribbon

■ *Copy a text placeholder and paste it*: The advantage to this method is that you can pick up the contents and formatting of the placeholder, so you don't need to duplicate the formatting if the new text needs the same look as the existing text. Copying and pasting a text placeholder sometimes fails if the placeholder is empty, so either copy a placeholder that already contains "real" text or add some dummy text to the placeholder, copy and paste it, and then replace the dummy text.

Adding Pictures to Slides

You can add pictures to slides by displaying the Insert tab of the Ribbon and using the Pictures command as usual. You use this command even when you've selected a picture placeholder—the picture placeholder doesn't have a shortcut for invoking the Insert ➤ Pictures command.

After inserting a picture, you can resize it proportionally by dragging a round corner handle, stretch or shrink the picture by dragging a square side handle, or rotate the picture by dragging the rotation handle at the top. But PowerPoint also enables you to reshape the corners of a picture you insert in a picture placeholder. To reshape the picture corners, drag the yellow handle that appears (see Figure 11-7).

Figure 11-7. Drag the yellow handle on a picture placeholder to reshape the corners

Adding Videos to Slides

PowerPoint enables you to add videos to your slides. Video can be a great way to enliven a presentation, but you need to be careful not to overuse it.

Note   At this writing, you can insert only those videos that are stored in the Photos app—you can't reach across your iPad's file system and insert videos from elsewhere. Any videos you shoot using the Camera app go into the Photos app automatically, as do any videos you save from e-mail messages, instant messages, web pages, or social-media apps. From your computer, you can sync videos by connecting your iPad and using the Photos category in iTunes. If you are using automatic syncing, make sure you select the Include Videos check box on the Photos screen.

To insert a video on the current slide, display the Insert tab of the Ribbon, and then tap Videos. In the Videos pop-up panel, tap the appropriate photography source. For example, to add a video you've just taken using your iPad's camera, tap Videos. In the pop-up panel that opens, tap the video and then tap the Use button.

The video appears on the slide, showing the first frame as a still photo. To reposition the video, tap it and drag it to where you need it. To resize the video, tap it and then drag a corner handle or a side handle, just as for a picture. To view the video, tap the Play button at the right end of the Ribbon to launch the slide show, and then tap the Play button for the video to set it playing.

> **Tip**   PowerPoint automatically compresses videos you insert in your presentations. But even so, adding long videos can greatly increase the size of a presentation. When working on a presentation that uses a lot of video, save it on your iPad rather than on OneDrive or SharePoint to minimize the amount of data PowerPoint needs to transfer across the Internet connection.

Adding Tables, Shapes, and Text Boxes to Slides

You can add tables, shapes, and text boxes to slides by using the standard techniques you learned in Chapter 2. After adding the objects, you can reposition, resize, and arrange them as usual.

Here are three suggestions for using these objects effectively in PowerPoint:

- *Tables*: When you use tables on slides, make them large and easy to read— otherwise, your audience may struggle to read the table's contents during the presentation or to process the information.

> **Tip**   Be careful when copying tables from Word and pasting them into PowerPoint. Technically, the copy-and-paste process could hardly be easier, but often the result doesn't deliver information effectively, because tables in Word are often complex and contain large amounts of information. Often, it's better to take your existing tabular information and break it down into multiple tables for your slides, so that each table makes a single point.

- *Shapes*: Callout shapes can be a good way to draw attention to particular points on your slides. Similarly, you may sometimes need to use shapes to create objects that contain text.
- *Text boxes*: Use text boxes when you need to create complex layouts or intricate arrangements of text. As mentioned earlier, you can rotate a text box to display its contents at an angle or upside down. For regular text, you're usually better off using text placeholders.

Adding a Chart from Excel to a Slide

If your presentation needs a chart on a slide, you can create the chart in Excel, copy it, and then paste it onto the slide. You can then resize the chart object on the slide as needed.

When you select the chart on the slide, PowerPoint displays the Chart tab of the Ribbon. You can then format the chart as explained in the "Copying and Pasting a Chart" section in Chapter 10.

Adding Notes to Slides

To add notes to a slide, tap the slide in the Navigation pane to display it, and then tap the Notes button in the lower-right corner of the screen. The Notes pane appears (see Figure 11-8), and you can type or paste the notes for the slide.

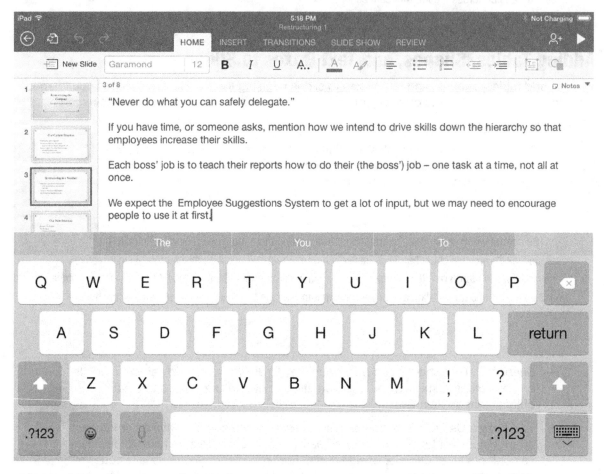

Figure 11-8. *Type or paste the notes for a slide into the Notes pane. Tap the Notes button in the upper-right corner when you're ready to return to the slide's content*

When you finish the notes for this slide, you can tap another slide to display its notes. When you're done with notes for now, tap the Notes button at the upper-right corner of the Slide pane to return to the slide's content.

Adding Transition Effects Between Slides

To smooth—or enliven—the changeover from one slide to another, you can add a transition effect. PowerPoint provides a wide variety of transition effects that it breaks up into three categories: Subtle, Exciting, and Dynamic Content.

PowerPoint considers the transition to belong to the incoming slide rather than the outgoing slide, so to get a transition effect between the first and second slides, you apply the transition effect to the second slide.

Here's how to apply a transition.

1. Tap the slide to which you want to apply the transition—the second slide in the pair, as it were.

2. Tap the Transitions tab of the Ribbon to display its controls.

3. Tap the Transition Effect button to display the Transition To This Slide pop-up panel (see Figure 11-9).

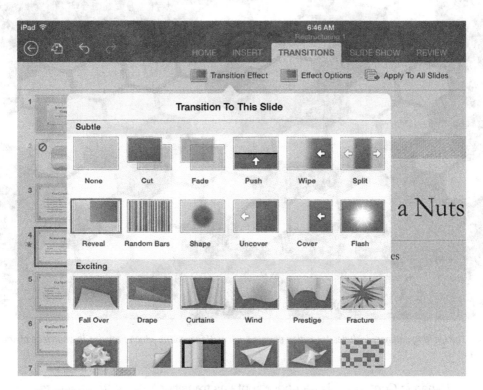

Figure 11-9. *Tap the slide in the Navigation pane, tap Transition ➤ Transition Effect, and then tap the transition you want to apply*

4. Scroll up or down as necessary to locate the transition effects category you want:

   a. *Subtle*: This category includes transitions such as Fade, which fades the incoming slide in as the outgoing slide fades out; Push, in which the incoming slide pushes the outgoing slide off the screen in the direction you choose; and Split; which splits the outgoing slide in the middle to reveal the incoming slide underneath it, and then moves the halves of the outgoing slide off the screen.

b. *Exciting*: This category includes transitions such as Honeycomb, which displays a honeycomb lattice that it turns and zooms toward the viewer to enliven the changeover between slides (see Figure 11-10); and Origami, which folds up the current slide into an origami bird and then flutters it away.

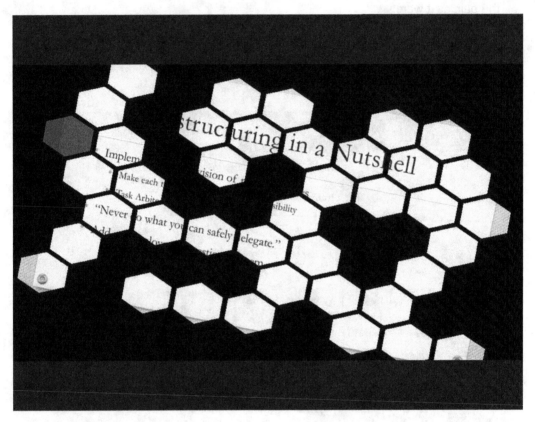

Figure 11-10. The Exciting category includes transition effects such as Honeycomb, which provides in-your-face changeovers between slides

c. *Dynamic Content*: This category contains transition effects that animate the slides' content rather than simply animating the slide as a whole. For example, the Rotate transition effect rotates away the content of the outgoing slide, replacing it with the content of the incoming slide.

5. Tap the transition you want to apply. PowerPoint displays a star to the left of the slide's thumbnail in the Navigation pane to indicate that the slide has a transition applied.

6. If the Effect Options button on the Ribbon is available, tap it to display the Effect Options pane (see Figure 11-11), and then tap the option you want to use. The options available depend on the transition effect, but many transition effects let you choose the direction in which they work. Some transition effects have no options; in this case, the Effect Options button is dimmed to indicate it's not available.

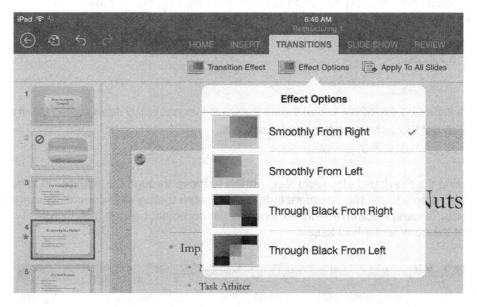

Figure 11-11. Tap the Effect Options button and then tap the appropriate option on the Effect Options panel

After applying a transition effect, review it and see how well it works. Tap the slide before the slide to which you've applied the transition effect, and then tap the Play button at the right end of the Ribbon to start the presentation playing from that slide. Swipe left to advance the presentation, and the transition effect will play.

> **Tip**   For some presentations, you may want to use the same transition effect for most of the slides. The quick way to do this is to apply the transition effect, and the effect option if appropriate, to one of the slides and then tap the Apply To All Slides button on the Transitions tab of the Ribbon. PowerPoint briefly displays a readout saying that the effect has been applied to all the slides. You can then apply another transition effect to any slide that needs different treatment.

To remove the existing transition, tap the slide, tap the Transitions tab, tap Transition Effect, and then tap the None "effect" in the Subtle category on the Transition To This Slide pane.

Reviewing Comments

If a presentation contains comments (for example, ones added using a desktop version of PowerPoint), you can review them by tapping the Review tab of the Ribbon and using its controls:

- *Show Comments switch*: Set this switch to On to display any comments on the slides. Set the switch to Off when you don't need to see the comments.

- *Previous button*: Tap this button to go back to the previous comment and display its contents in a balloon.

- *Next button*: Tap this button to go to the next comment and display its contents in a balloon.

> **Note**   At this writing, PowerPoint for iPad doesn't enable you to create, edit, or delete comments, but it seems likely that Microsoft will add these capabilities soon.

Instead of using the Previous button and Next button to move through the comments in sequence, you may prefer simply to tap the comment indicators to work through the comments in whichever order suits you. Tapping a comment indicator opens the comment balloon (see Figure 11-12) so you can see what the commenter had to say.

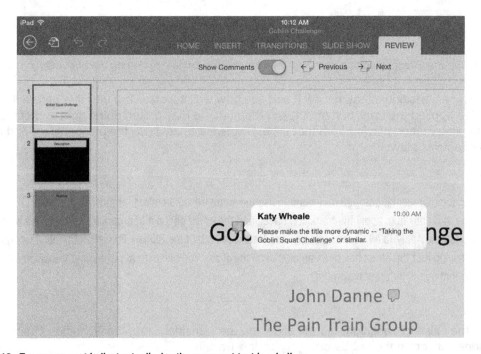

Figure 11-12. Tap a comment indicator to display the comment text in a balloon

Giving a Presentation from Your iPad

Your iPad is a great tool not only for creating and editing presentations but also for delivering them. PowerPoint for iPad enables you to deliver a slide show either on your iPad's screen or on a connected screen. You can pause the presentation as needed, draw on your slides or display a black screen, and display hidden slides if the audience requires them.

Ways of Giving a Presentation from Your iPad

You can deliver a presentation from your iPad in three main ways:

- *Deliver the presentation on your iPad's screen*: This is the most straightforward way to give the presentation, but it works only for the smallest of audiences. It's great for giving the presentation one on one—for example, on a sales call—because you can stop and start the presentation as needed. You can also jump easily from slide to slide, or summon up hidden slides, to tailor the presentation to the audience.

- *Connect the iPad to a projector or display*: By connecting your iPad to a project or a display, you can give the presentation much as you would using a laptop or desktop computer, except that PowerPoint for iPad offers fewer presentation features. You'll look at the details of making the connection a little later in this chapter.

- *Use AirPlay to send the presentation output to a display connected to an AirPlay receiver*: AirPlay is Apple's technology for streaming content wirelessly from a device to a receiver—in this case, streaming the PowerPoint slide show from your iPad to an AirPlay receiver connected to a device that can display it. You'll look at the details of this too shortly.

Setting Up the Presentation

If you're going to give the presentation from your iPad, you should set it up with the presentation hardware beforehand. That means connecting to any external screen or projector you'll be using, either via a cable or via AirPlay, and making sure that all looks well both on the screen and in Presenter view on your iPad.

Let's dig into each step.

Connecting Your iPad to a Monitor or Projector with a Cable

To connect your iPad directly to a monitor or a projector, you'll need a cable with a suitable connection at one end for the iPad and at the other end for the monitor or projector.

For all recent iPads, such as the iPad Air or the iPad mini, you'll need a Lightning connector at the iPad's end of the cable. The Lightning connector is the little connector smaller than the nail on a typical little finger. For older iPads, such as the iPad 2 or iPad 3, you'll need a Dock Connector, the wider, flat connector.

For the monitor or projector, you'll typically need an HDMI connector, a DVI connector, or a VGA connector.

> **Tip** If the monitor or projector gives you a choice of ports for connecting your iPad, choose HDMI first, DVI second, and VGA last. HDMI and DVI are digital ports, so the signal stays digital all the way, maintaining quality. By contrast, VGA is an analog port, so your iPad's digital output needs to be converted to analog for the VGA port, losing quality.

Connecting Your iPad to a Monitor or Projector via AirPlay

Apple's AirPlay feature enables you to stream a presentation from your iPad to an AirPlay receiver device connected to a project or display. This is a great way to give a presentation because your iPad isn't tethered to the display device via a cable, so you can move freely around the room as needed carrying the iPad.

These are your choices of AirPlay device:

- *Apple TV*: Apple's Apple TV streaming device connects to a TV or display via an HDMI cable. If the TV or display has a different type of input, you'll need an adapter or cable to convert HDMI to that input.

- *AirPlay adapter*: You can buy various adapters that receive an AirPlay stream and output it to a suitable port. For example, you can get an AirPlay-to-VGA adapter for converting an AirPlay stream to VGA output suitable for a projector or monitor.

- *Projector with built-in AirPlay*: Some projectors have a built-in AirPlay feature. If you're using such a projector, AirPlay is an easy choice.

- *Mac or PC running the Reflector app*: If you don't have an Apple TV to use for AirPlay, but you have a Mac or PC, consider using the Reflector app from Squirrels (www.airsquirrels.com; $12.99, but give the trial version a spin before buying). This app enables your Mac or PC to act as an AirPlay receiver. On your iPad, open the Control Center, tap the computer's entry in the AirPlay list, and set the Mirroring switch to On. Your iPad's screen then appears mirrored in the Reflector window.

Here's how to connect to the presentation device using AirPlay:

1. Connect your iPad to the same network that the AirPlay device is on. Your iPad must connect to the network via Wi-Fi, but the AirPlay device can connect either via Wi-Fi or via Ethernet.

2. Swipe up from the bottom of the screen to open Control Center.

3. Tap the AirPlay button to display the AirPlay dialog (see Figure 11-13).

Figure 11-13. Tap the AirPlay button in Control Center and then tap the appropriate button in the AirPlay dialog box

4. Tap the button for the AirPlay device, placing a check mark on the right of the button.

5. Set the Mirroring switch to On. This switch appears in the AirPlay dialog only when you've selected a device that supports mirroring. (Devices such as the AirPort Express don't support mirroring because they stream only audio, not video.)

6. Tap outside the AirPlay dialog to close the dialog.

Note When you want to stop using AirPlay, open Control Center again, tap the AirPlay button, and then tap the iPad button in the AirPlay dialog.

TROUBLESHOOTING AIRPLAY

AirPlay is great when it works, but it can give you a headache when it doesn't. If you're having trouble with AirPlay, try the following moves, stopping as soon as AirPlay is working:

- *Connect to the right wireless network*: If the AirPlay icon doesn't appear in Control Center, press the Home button, tap Settings, and check the Wi-Fi readout to see which network your iPad has connected to. Change the network if necessary.

- *Make sure that AirPlay is enabled on an Apple TV*: If you're using an Apple TV, you may need to turn on AirPlay. Display the Home screen, open the Settings app, and select AirPlay. On the AirPlay screen, make sure the AirPlay button says On; if not, highlight the AirPlay button and press the Select button to toggle AirPlay's status. While you're in the Settings app, you may want to make sure the Apple TV is connected to the right network. To do so, select the General button on the Settings screen, and then look at the Network readout.

- *Restart the AirPlay device*: If your iPad is connected to the right Wi-Fi network, but either the AirPlay button doesn't appear in Control Center or the AirPlay button appears but the AirPlay dialog doesn't list the device, restart the AirPlay device. How you do this depends on the device. For example, on an Apple TV, display the Home screen, open the Settings app, and select General. On the General screen, scroll all the way down to the bottom and select Restart.

- *Turn Wi-Fi off and on:* If your iPad still can't see the AirPlay device, try turning Wi-Fi off and then back on again. You can do this directly from Control Center, but you may need to make sure that your iPad connects to the right network after you restart Wi-Fi. To check which network it's using, and to change the network if necessary, look in the Settings app.

- *Update iOS to the latest version:* Press the Home button to display the Home screen and tap the Settings icon to open the Settings app. Tap General in the left column, and then tap the Software Update button. If the Software Update screen shows an update, tap the Download and Install button.

- *Update Apple TV's firmware:* If you're using an Apple TV, it's a good idea to update its firmware to the latest version too. Display the Home screen, open the Settings app, and select General. On the General screen, select Software Updates to display the Software Updates screen. On the Software Updates screen, select the Update Software button.

One word of warning—updating iOS or the Apple TV firmware can take a while, so it's best to avoid these moves if you must deliver the presentation soon.

Testing Presenter View and Your Presentation

Once you've connected your iPad to the projector or monitor via either a cable or AirPlay, go into Presenter view and test that all is working as it should. Tap the Slide Show tab on the Ribbon to display its contents, and then tap the Presenter View button.

Presenter view (see Figure 11-14) has the following components and controls:

- *Current slide*: Use this slide to present the information.

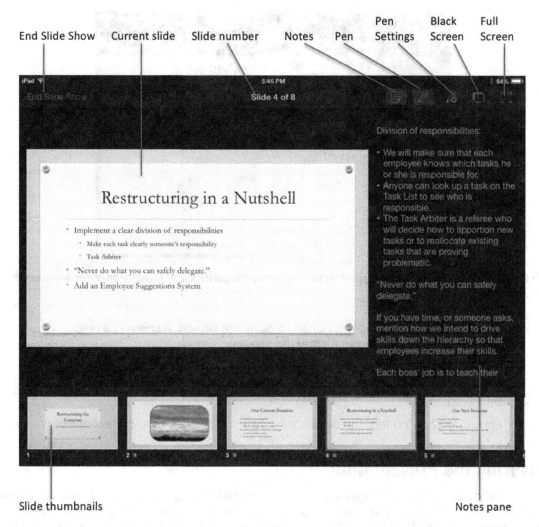

Figure 11-14. Presenter view includes thumbnails for easy navigation and the Notes pane for reference

- *Slide thumbnails*: Tap a thumbnail to display the slide.

- *Notes button*: Tap this button to toggle the display of the Notes pane.

- *Pen button*: Tap this button to toggle the pen on and off. With the pen turned on, you can draw on the screen with your fingertip or a stylus.

- *Pen Settings button*: Tap this button to display the Pen Settings pop-up panel (see Figure 11-15). You can then tap the pen color and thickness you want, or tap an eraser thickness to erase some of the pen markings. Tap the Clear Pen Markings button if you want to get rid of all the pen markings in the presentation (not just on the current slide).

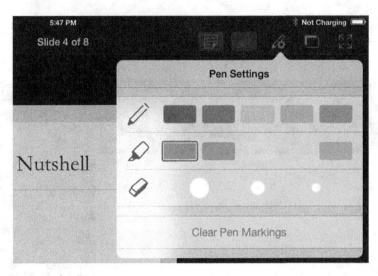

Figure 11-15. Use the Pen Settings pop-up panel to select your pen color and thickness, to choose an eraser, or to clear all pen markings from the presentation

- *Black Screen button*: Tap this button to blank the screen, displaying a black screen instead. Tap again to display the slide once more.

- *Full Screen button*: Tap this button to display the current slide as large as it will go, hiding the slide thumbnails and the Notes pane (if it's displayed). Tap this button again to go back to your previous display.

- *End Slide Show button*: Tap this button when you're ready to end the slide show.

Delivering the Presentation

To start the slide show from the beginning, tap the From Start button on the Slide Show tab of the Ribbon. If you want to start the slide show from a particular slide other than the first, tap that slide in the Navigation pane, and then tap the From Current button on the Slide Show tab or the Play button at the right end of the Ribbon.

Whichever way you start the slide show, PowerPoint switches to full-screen slide-show view and displays the first slide (or the slide you chose). You can then move through the presentation easily via these motions:

- *Next slide*: Swipe left.

- *Previous slide*: Swipe right.

- *End the slide show*: Swipe left on the last slide, and PowerPoint displays a slide saying "End of slide show." Swipe left to exit the full-screen view and return to editing the presentation. (You can also swipe to the right to go back to the previous slide if you want.)

Using the Slide Show Control

If you're not using Presenter view, your slides appear full-screen on your iPad and on any connected presentation device. When you start the presentation, PowerPoint displays the slide show controls at the top of the screen for a moment and then hides them if you don't use them for a few seconds. You can display these controls at any point by tapping near the top of the screen.

The slide show controls bar has the End Slide Show button at its left end, the slide number readout in the middle, and the Pen button, Pen Settings button, Black Screen button, and Full Screen button at its right end—in other words, all the controls from Presenter view except for the Notes pane, which you don't get to use.

Working with Hidden Slides

Any slides you've hidden in your presentation appear in the slide thumbnails pane in Presenter view grayed out, as you see for the third slide in Figure 11-16. If you advance through the presentation by swiping, you pass over the hidden slides, but you can display a hidden slide by tapping it.

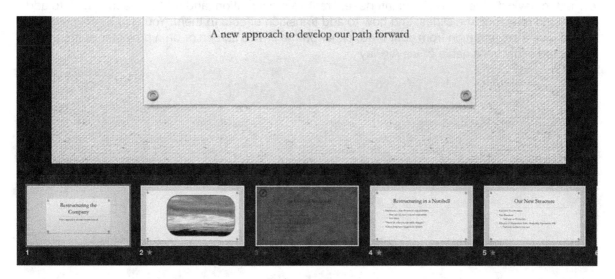

Figure 11-16. Presenter view displays hidden slides as grayed out, like Slide 3 here, but you can tap a hidden slide to display it on screen

Using the Laser Pointer

When you need to draw your audience's attention to a particular point on the screen, use the laser pointer. Tap and hold the screen until the red circle appears. You can then move your finger around the screen to highlight the points that need the audience's attention.

Ending the Slide Show Short of the End

To end the slide show before the end, swipe down from the top of the screen to display the control bar if you're not in Presenter view, and then tap End Slide Show.

Caution   While the slide show is running, you can display the Home screen by pressing the Home button or (if you have Multitasking Gestures enabled) by pinching inward with four or five fingers. You can also display the app-switching screen by double-pressing the Home button or swiping upward with four or five fingers, and then tap another app to display it. The problem with doing this is that when you return to PowerPoint, the app may go back to the file management screen and re-download the presentation before displaying it again. You'll then need to restart the slide show at the slide where you want to resume. This means that you can't switch away from the slide show and go back to it seamlessly—even for a presentation stored on your iPad rather than online.

Summary

In this chapter, you learned how to make the most of PowerPoint for iPad. You now know the app's features and limitations, so you're in a good position to judge how to use it most effectively. You learned to navigate the PowerPoint interface, create a presentation, and add slides to it; how to add, delete, and rearrange the slides; and how to add transition effects to them. You also discovered how to give a presentation from your iPad, either on the iPad's screen or on a projector or monitor connected either via a cable or via AirPlay.

Chapter 12

Taking Notes in OneNote

OneNote is a powerful app for recording, storing, and manipulating information. OneNote enables you to collect many different types of data, organize it to suit your needs, and share it with your other devices. OneNote runs on Windows, on the Mac, and on various devices including Windows Phone, Android devices, the iPhone, and the iPad. OneNote syncs with your account on OneDrive or on a SharePoint server, making it easy to sync your notebooks between your computers and devices.

Understanding How OneNote for iPad Works and What It Can and Cannot Do

The OneNote app for iPad brings OneNote's powerful note-taking capabilities to the iPad. This is great news if you have an iPad, because you can use your iPad to browse your notes and update them. What's not so good is that—at this writing, at least—OneNote for iPad has only a subset of the features that the Windows and Mac versions have.

> **Note**   If you're just getting started with OneNote, you may want to look ahead to the section "Working with Notebooks, Sections, and Pages," which explains terms such as "notebook," "section," and "section group."

OneNote for iPad has several major limitations at this writing:

- *Section groups*: You cannot create or manage section groups on the iPad. You must use a desktop or web version of OneNote instead.

- *Moving section groups between notebooks*: You cannot move a section group from one notebook to another notebook. For this, you must use a desktop or web version of OneNote.

- *Notebook storage*: You must store all your OneNote notebooks in your OneDrive or SharePoint accounts. You cannot store notebooks directly on your iPad.

Because of these limitations, if you use OneNote on your PC or Mac, there's a strong argument for using the computer to create the structure of your notebooks—especially the section groups, assuming you use them. Once a notebook's basic structure is in place, you can use OneNote for iPad to enter information in the notebook, creating new sections and pages as needed. If you need to reorganize material in the notebook, such as moving pages from one section to another or creating a new section group, you'll need to make that change on your computer and sync it back to your iPad.

That said, using OneNote only on your iPad is perfectly viable—but you'll want to plan your notebooks carefully so that you don't need to rearrange them.

Setting Up Your Notebooks

OneNote is essentially a database, but the interface looks like a physical notebook, the ring-binder kind of notebook to which you can add sections and pages wherever you need them.

Launching OneNote and Opening a Notebook

To launch OneNote, press the Home button and then tap the OneNote icon on the Home screen. The OneNote document management screen appears, and you can either create a new notebook or open an existing notebook.

To create a new notebook, follow these steps.

1. Tap the Notebooks tab in the left column (see Figure 12-1).

Figure 12-1. To create a new notebook, tap the Notebooks button in the left column of the file management screen, and then tap the Create Notebook button

2. Tap the Create Notebook button to display the Create Notebook dialog box (see Figure 12-2).

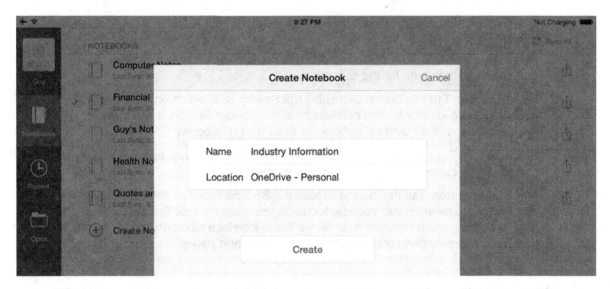

Figure 12-2. Type the name for the new notebook in the Create Notebook dialog box, and then tap the Create button

3. Type the name for the notebook in the Name box.

4. Tap the Create button.

To open an existing notebook, tap the Notebooks tab button, the Recent tab button, or the Open tab button, depending on how you want to navigate to the notebook. Then tap the notebook's button.

Note   If you get the message "Sync Error: Sign in to sync this notebook," tap the Sign In button. The OneDrive dialog box opens. Type your Microsoft account name and password, and then tap the Sign In button.

Exploring the OneNote Interface

With a notebook open, you can explore the OneNote interface. If you've used OneNote on a desktop computer, you'll no doubt get the hang of it quickly. Figure 12-3 shows the main elements of the OneNote interface:

- *Ribbon tabs*: Tap the Home tab button, the Insert tab button, or the View tab button to switch among the Ribbon tabs.

- *Notebooks button*: Tap this button to display the Notebooks pop-up menu, which gives you a quick way to switch among your notebooks.

- *Section tabs*: Tap the section tab for the section you want to see.

- *Create a New Section button*: Tap this button to create a new section after the last section in the current section group. (More on section groups in a minute.) You can then type the name for the new section.

- *Pages pane*: This pane displays the list of pages in the current section. You can tap a page to display it.

- *Add Page button*: Tap this button to add a new page in the current section. You can then type the name for the new page.

- *Search button*: Tap this button to display the Search box, which enables you to search using keywords. You can search in the current section, in the current section group, in the current notebook, or in all your notebooks.

- *Share button*: Tap this button to display the Share pop-up panel, from which you can share the current notebook or the current page.

- *Full-Screen button*: Tap this button to hide the Section Tabs bar, the Ribbon, and the Pages pane so that you can focus on the current page. Tap the Exit Full Screen button, which replaces it, to reveal these interface elements again so that you can navigate among your notebooks, sections, and pages.

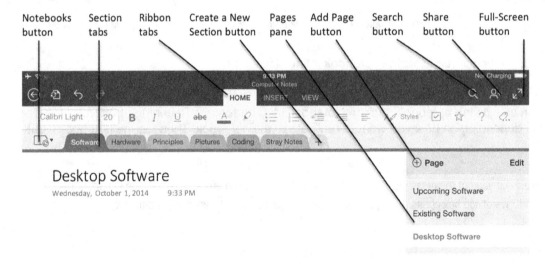

Figure 12-3. OneNote has a straightforward interface that enables you to navigate your notebooks quickly

Working with Notebooks, Sections, and Pages

To get the most out of OneNote, you'll need to organize your notes effectively into notebooks, sections and section groups, and pages. The following list explains these items:

- *Notebook*: A notebook is a file that contains whatever data you want to keep together. Typically, you'll want to populate each notebook with related data. For example, you might create a Work notebook, a Family notebook, and a Personal notebook.

- *Sections*: A section is a container within a notebook. For example, in your Work notebook, you might create sections such as Projects, Research, and Blue Sky. A section contains one or more pages (you'll learn about pages in a moment).

- *Section group*: A section group is a container for organizing sections. For example, if your Work notebook contains many sections in the Projects section, you could divide them into section groups such as Active, On Hold, and Old.

> **Note**   You can create section groups only in the desktop and web versions of OneNote, not in OneNote for iPad.

- *Page*: A page is the item on which you put information, much like a physical page in a real notebook. But unlike a physical page, a page in OneNote can be as long as you need it to be, so you can take notes freely.

Looking Around in the Personal Notebook

If you've just launched OneNote for the first time, OneNote will have opened the Personal notebook that it creates for you. The Personal notebook is named using your first name and "Notebook"—for example, Jane's Notebook—and contains a single tab called Quick Notes, which in turn contains a single page called Welcome to OneNote for iPad.

Read the Welcome to OneNote for iPad page, and then decide whether to keep it. If not, delete the page by sliding its button in the Pages pane to the left and then tapping the Delete button that appears. You can then use the Personal notebook for your notes.

Adding a Section to a Notebook

Sections are the tool you use to organize the pages in a notebook. You can create as many sections as you need, assign them easily identifiable names, and create pages within them.

To create a section, follow these steps.

1. Click the Create New Section button, the + button that appears to the right of the last section tab. OneNote adds a section after the last section, gives it a default name such as New Section 1, and adds an untitled page (a page with the default name Untitled Page) to it. OneNote selects the default section name so that you can change it (see Figure 12-4).

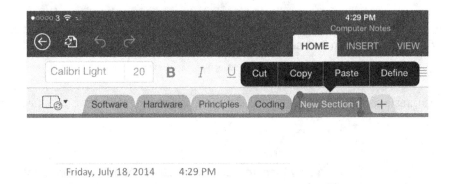

Figure 12-4. To create a new section, tap the + button after the last section tab, and then type the name

2. Type the name for the section, and then tap the Done button on the keyboard. OneNote selects the page title on the page so that you can enter that too.

3. Type the title for the page and then tap the Return button. OneNote places the insertion point in the default text container in the page so that you can start taking notes on the page.

Deleting a Section

To delete a section, follow these steps.

1. Tap the section's tab to bring it to the front.

2. Tap the section's tab to display the Edit menu.

3. Tap the Delete button on the Edit menu. A confirmation dialog box opens.

4. Tap the Delete button in the confirmation dialog box. OneNote deletes the section.

Renaming and Reorganizing Sections

To rename a section, double-tap its tab button, making OneNote select the current name. Alternatively, tap the sections tab to bring it to the front, tap again to display the Edit menu, and then tap the Rename button. You can then type the new name and tap the Done button on the keyboard to apply the name.

To move a section, follow these steps.

1. Tap the section's tab to bring it to the front.

2. Tap the section's tab again to display the Edit menu.

3. Tap the Move button on the Edit menu. The Move this section to a new notebook dialog box opens (see Figure 12-5).

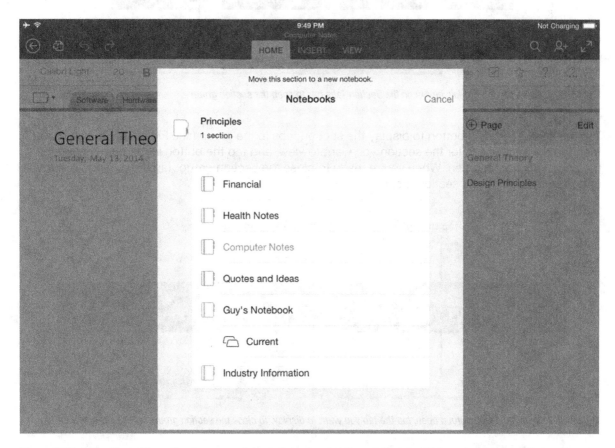

Figure 12-5. *In the Move this section to a new notebook dialog box, tap the notebook to which you want to move the section*

4. Tap the notebook to which you want to move the section.

Working with Section Groups

If you use OneNote for Windows, OneNote for Mac, or the web version of OneNote, you can create section group to organize the sections in your notebooks. A section group appears as a button on the Section Tabs bar bearing a symbol showing two tabs, as for the Current section group you can see in Figure 12-6.

A section group button

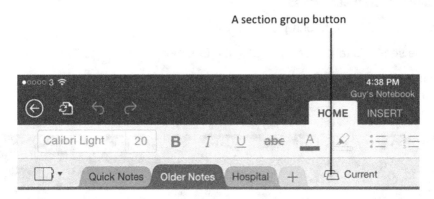

Figure 12-6. Tap a section group's button on the Section Tabs bar to open the section group

Tap the section group's button to display the section tabs in the group (see Figure 12-7). You can then tap the section tab for the section you want to view, and tap the button in the pages pane for the page you want to open. When you're ready to close the section group, tap the curling up-arrow button to the right of the section group's name.

Tap the up-arrow button to close a section group

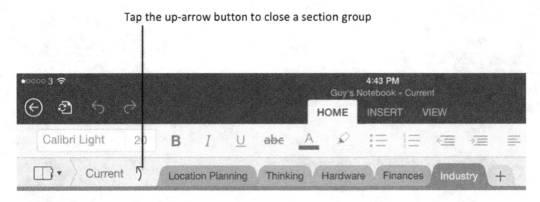

Figure 12-7. With the section group open, tap the tab you want to display. To close the section group, tap the up-arrow button

Adding Pages

Inside a section, you can add the pages you need and create notes on them. This section shows you the main moves for working with pages.

Creating a New Blank Page

To create a new blank page, follow these steps.

1. On the Section Bar, tap the section tab for the section in which you want to create the page.

2. Tap the Add Page button at the top of the Pages pane. OneNote adds a new page, gives it the default name Untitled Page, and places the insertion point in the page's title area so that you can rename it.

3. Type the title for the page and then tap the Return button. OneNote places the insertion point in the default text container in the page so that you can start taking notes on the page. The text container appears only when you start entering content in it.

Renaming a Page

To rename a page, first tap its button in the Pages pane to display it. Then tap the title at the top of the open page and either edit the exiting name or simply delete the existing name and type the new name.

Moving a Page

Often, you'll need to move a page to a different position in a notebook. To do so, follow these steps.

1. On the Section Bar, tap the tab for the section that contains the page you want to move.

2. In the Pages pane, tap the Edit button to switch to Edit mode.

3. Tap the radio button for the page you want to move. The buttons on the bar at the top of the Pages pane become enabled (see Figure 12-8).

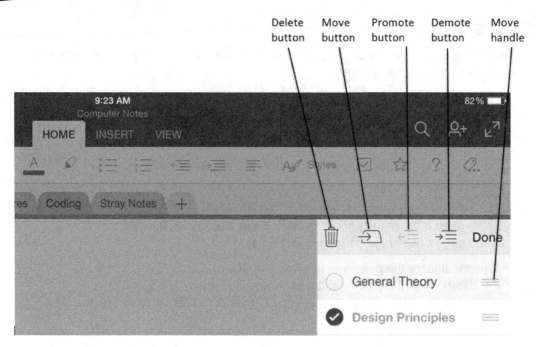

Figure 12-8. With the Pages pane in Edit mode, select the page you want to move, and then tap the Move button

4.   Tap the Move button to display the Move this page to a new section dialog box (see Figure 12-9).

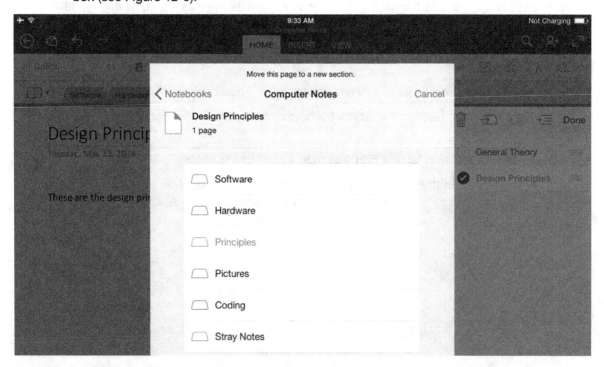

Figure 12-9. In the Move this page to a new section dialog box, tap the section where you want the page to go

5. Tap the section where you want the page to go.

> **Note**   To move the page up or down the list of pages, drag it by the drag handle on the right of it button in Edit mode. You can also delete the page by tapping the Delete button, make it a subpage by tapping the Demote button, or (if it is a subpage) promote it to a page by tapping the Promote button.

Working with Subpages

OneNote enables you to add one or more subpages to a page. Subpages are useful when a page grows so long that it becomes hard to navigate. You can make the page shorter by moving some of the information into one or more subpages attached to the page.

To create a subpage, follow these steps.

1. On the Section Bar, tap the tab for the section you want to create the new page in.

2. In the Pages pane, tap the page you want to add the subpage to.

3. Tap the Add Page button to create a new page.

4. Type the name for the new page.

5. Tap the Edit button in the Pages pane to switch to Edit mode.

6. Tap the radio button for the page you want to turn into a subpage.

7. Tap the Demote button on the bar at the top of the Pages pane.

8. Tap the Done button.

A subpage appears as a button with an indented name in the Pages pane. To display the subpage, simply tap its button.

Navigating from Page to Page

You can quickly navigate from page to page by tapping the appropriate page button in the Pages pane. You can reach any page quickly and easily by opening the notebook, opening the section group (if there is one), opening the section, and then opening the page.

1. Tap the Notebooks button on the Section Tabs bar to display the Notebooks pane, and then tap the notebook.

2. If the section is in a section group, tap the section group's name to display the section tabs that the group contains.

3. Tap the section tab to open the section.

4. In the Pages pane, tap the page to display it.

Entering Notes on a Page

On the pages you create in your notebooks, you can store a wide variety of information. Let's start with a quick overview of all the types of information that you can enter. You'll then dig into how to work with each type of information.

Understanding Which Types of Information You Can Save in OneNote

The following list explains the types of information you can save in a OneNote notebook:

- *Text*: You can store any amount of text, either leaving it plain or formatting it using styles or direct formatting.

- *Tables*: You can create either simple tables (ones with a regular structure) or complex tables (ones that include other tables nested inside cells). Your tables can include text, pictures, and other objects.

> **Note**   Using the Windows version of OneNote, you can also insert several other types of information. These include: screen clippings (which are useful for quickly capturing information from sources such as web pages as well as for documenting computer procedures); document printouts from Office apps; scanner printouts; video from your PC's video camera; and equations including binomials, Fourier series equations, and quadratic equations. You can also attach many types of files to a OneNote notebook to make that file available with the notebook. The Mac version of OneNote also enables you to enter equations.

- *Pictures*: You can add pictures to your notebooks and position them as needed.

- *Photos*: You can take photos with your iPad's camera and insert them directly into your notebooks.

- *Hyperlinks*: You can insert a hyperlink to a web page or another URL, such as a hyperlink to start an e-mail message to a specific address.

Adding Text to a Page

To add text to a page, simply tap the point on the page where you want to start entering the text. OneNote adds a container for the text where you tap. When you start entering the text, the container appears, and the text appears inside it.

You can enter text by typing it or by pasting it from the clipboard. To paste text, tap and hold the appropriate point in the container or on the page until the Edit menu appears, and then tap the Paste button.

Each container works like a mini document, and you can format the text much as you would in Word:

- *Apply a style*: The quick way to apply formatting consistently is to use the styles in the Styles pop-up menu on the Home tab of the Ribbon. Figure 12-10 shows the Styles pop-up menu open for applying a style. OneNote gives you a Page Title style for the page title, Heading 1 through Heading 6 styles for headings, a Citation style, a Quote style, a Code style, and a Normal style for everything else.

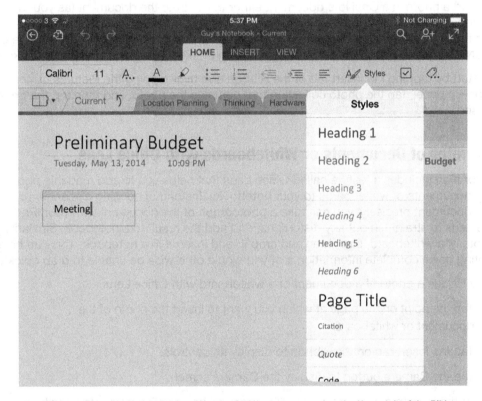

Figure 12-10. The quick way to apply formatting is to use the Styles pop-up menu on the Home tab of the Ribbon

Tip   Use styles wherever possible when formatting text-based notes. When you export notes to Word, the text keeps the styles, and you can snap in a different set of formatting in moments by attaching a different template to the resulting Word document.

- *Apply direct formatting*: You can apply direct formatting (such as bold, italic, or highlighting) by using the controls at the left end of the Home tab of the Ribbon. For example, to change the font, select the text, tap the Fonts button, and then tap the font on the Fonts pop-up menu.

Adding Graphics to a Page

To illustrate your notes, you can quickly add one or more graphics to a page. You can either insert a graphic using the technique explained in Chapter 2 or insert a photo that you take with one of the iPad's cameras.

Inserting a Photo

You can insert a photo in a OneNote document either to illustrate the document (as you might do in the other apps) or as a way of capturing information quickly and effortlessly. Because photos can play these two roles, inserting a photo in a OneNote document works differently than in the other apps. OneNote enables you to crop a photo, straighten or skew it, and manipulate its background.

As usual, start by tapping the Insert tab of the Ribbon and then tapping the Pictures button. On the Photos pop-up panel, tap the photo collection that contains the photo, and then tap the photo you want to insert.

Taking Photos of Documents or Whiteboards with Office Lens

OneNote for iPad includes a feature called Office Lens that helps you to add readable photos of hard-copy documents or whiteboards to your notebooks. Instead of needing a scanner to capture a hard-copy document precisely, you can take a photograph of the document with your iPad's camera, use Office Lens to straighten out any distortions, and add the result to a notebook. Similarly, you can take a photo of a whiteboard, straighten and crop it, and insert it in a notebook. This can be a great way of noting down complete information that you would otherwise be unable to grab quickly.

Here's how to take a photo of a document or a whiteboard with Office Lens.

1. Tap the point on the page at which you want to insert the photo of the document or whiteboard.

2. Tap the Insert tab on the Ribbon to display its controls.

3. Tap the Camera button to display the Camera screen.

4. At the bottom of the screen, tap Whiteboard, Photo, or Document to specify how you want Office Lens to process what you're photographing.

> **Note**   Tap Whiteboard on the Camera screen to reduce glare and shadows. Tap Document to optimize the color balance for a grayscale document. Tap Photo if you're taking a photo of graphical subjects or a graphical document.

5. Line up the photo as best you can (see Figure 12-11) and tap the shutter release.

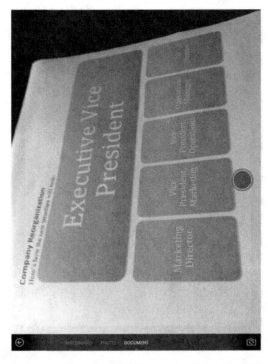

Figure 12-11. *To photograph a whiteboard or a document, tap Whiteboard or Document at the bottom of the screen, and then tap the shutter release*

6. In the preview that appears (see Figure 12-12), you can tap the Crop button and adjust the cropping by dragging the handles.

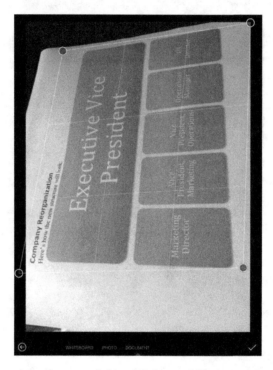

Figure 12-12. *Adjust the cropping and skewing as needed to produce a readable document, and then tap the check mark to insert the result in your notebook*

7. Tap the check mark to insert the photo in your notebook.

SWITCHING BETWEEN OFFICE LENS AND THE CAMERA APP

If you want to use the iPad's Camera app to insert pictures in your OneNote notebooks instead of using Office Lens, you must turn off the Office Lens feature in the Settings app. You then need to restart OneNote to make it notice the change. Follow these steps.

1. In OneNote, tap the Back button at the left end of the Ribbon to display the Notebooks list.

2. Tap the Sync All button in the upper-right corner to sync all your changes.

3. Double-press the Home button to display the app-switching screen.

4. Drag or swipe the OneNote thumbnail up off the list of apps to close OneNote.

5. Press the Home button to display the Home screen.

6. Tap the Settings icon to open the Settings app.

7. In the left column, tap the OneNote icon to display the OneNote screen.

8. Tap the Camera Setting button to display the Camera Setting screen.

9. Set the Use Office Lens switch to the Off position.

10. Press the Home button to display the Home screen.

11. Tap the OneNote icon to launch OneNote again.

Creating Tables

A table is often an easy way to record information in an organized fashion. OneNote makes it easy to create tables on the pages of your notebooks.

To create a table, you use the Insert tab of the Ribbon as usual. The process is a little different from that in the other Office apps.

1. Tap the place on the page where you want to insert the table.

2. Tap the Insert button on the Ribbon to display the Insert tab.

3. Tap the Table button. OneNote inserts a two-row-by-two-column table in the container where you tapped. The Table tab appears on the Ribbon, displaying controls for manipulating tables (see Figure 12-13).

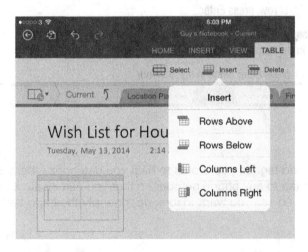

Figure 12-13. After using the Insert ➤ Table command on the Ribbon to insert a two-row-by-two-column table, open the Insert pop-up panel and add extra rows or columns as needed

4. Change the table as needed by tapping the Insert button and then tapping the appropriate button on the Insert pop-up panel: Rows Above, Rows Below, Columns Left, or Columns Right.

> **Note**   You can also delete rows or columns from the table by tapping in your target row or column, tapping the Delete button on the Table tab of the Ribbon to display the Delete pop-up panel, and then tapping the Rows button or the Columns button, as needed. To delete the whole table, tap the Delete button and then tap the Table button on the Delete pop-up panel.

CREATING A TABLE QUICKLY USING A HARDWARE KEYBOARD

If you're using a hardware keyboard connected to your iPad, you can also create a table quickly by simply typing in a container. Follow these steps.

1. Tap the appropriate point on the page to place the insertion point.

2. Type the text for the first cell as regular text within the container.

3. Press Tab. OneNote automatically inserts the table with two cells, positioning the insertion point so that you can type the second cell.

4. Type the second cell's contents.

5. Press Tab again to create another cell.

6. When you end the first row, press Enter.

7. You can then press Tab to move from cell to cell. Also press Tab to move to the next row when the insertion point is in the last cell in a row.

When you want to end the table, press Enter twice in succession.

Applying Tags

OneNote enables you to add tags to your notes to help you categorize them. For example, you can apply the Phone Number tag to any phone number so that you can locate it more easily, apply the Web Site to Visit tag to a web site you want to look up, or apply the Important tag or the Critical tag to vital information.

> **Note**   At this writing, OneNote for iPad provides a list of preset tags but doesn't let you create custom tags. In OneNote for Windows, however, you can create custom tags, which enables you to tag your notes exactly the way you need them.

To apply a tag, follow these steps.

1. Tap the item you want to tag. For example, tap the page title to apply the tag to the page as a whole, or tap a text container or a photo.

2. If the Home tab of the Ribbon isn't displayed, tap the Home tab to display it.

3. Tap the Tags button to display the Tag pop-up panel (see Figure 12-14).

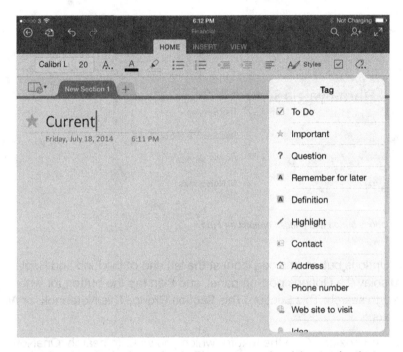

Figure 12-14. You can tag an item by selecting it, opening the Tag pop-up panel, and then tapping the tag you want to apply

4. Tap the tag you want to apply. The tag's symbol appears to the left of the item.

Using the Find Feature

OneNote includes a Find feature that enables you to search your notebooks for specific text. You can search the current section, the current section group, the current notebook, or all your notebooks. Unlike the Find features in Word and Excel, the Find feature in OneNote does not include Replace functionality.

Follow these steps to use Find.

1. If you want to restrict the search to a particular notebook, section, or section group, open that notebook and make the appropriate section or section group active.

2. Tap the Search icon (the magnifying glass) near the right end of the Ribbon to display the Find bar (see Figure 12-15).

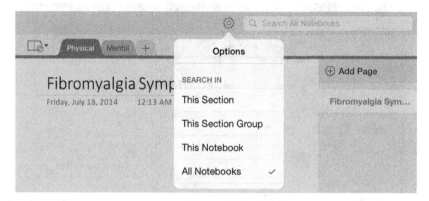

Figure 12-15. Tap the Options button and choose options for Find

3. Tap the Options button (the cog icon) at the left end of the Find and Replace bar to display the Options pop-up panel, and then tap the button for where you want to search: This Section, This Section Group, This Notebook, or All Notebooks.

4. Tap the Find box and type the text for which you want to search. OneNote searches automatically as you type the search text and displays the Search Results pop-up panel (see Figure 12-16).

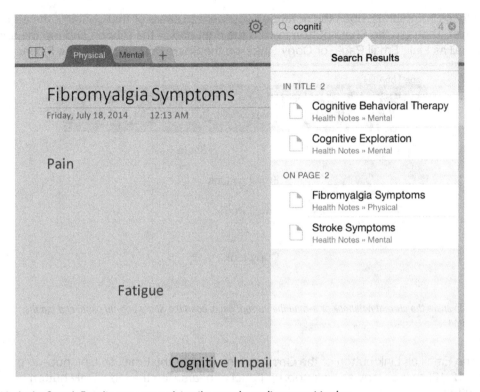

Figure 12-16. *In the Search Results pop-up panel, tap the search result you want to view*

5. Tap the search result you want to view. OneNote displays that page. The
    Search Results pop-up panel remains open, so you can tap another result if
    need be.

6. When you find what you are searching for, tap the page to hide the Find
    bar again.

Sharing Your Notes with Others

OneNote enables you to share your notes with other people in three ways:

■ *E-mail a link to a notebook*: You can choose whether the recipient can view and
   edit the shared notebook or just view it without being able to edit it.

■ *E-mail a page from the notebook*: This capability is great when you need to
   share one page of notes. You don't need to export the page to a separate
   document first—you can send it directly from the OneNote interface.

■ *Copy the link to a notebook*: You can create a link that enables the recipient to
   view and edit the shared notebook or just view it but not edit it. Copying the
   link works in a similar way to e-mailing a link, but you can send the link in other
   ways, such as via Messages or via Skype.

To access these commands, open the notebook you want to share or that contains the page you want to e-mail. Then tap the Share button toward the right end of the Ribbon and tap the appropriate button—Email as Link, Email Page, or Copy Link—on the Share pop-up panel (see Figure 12-17).

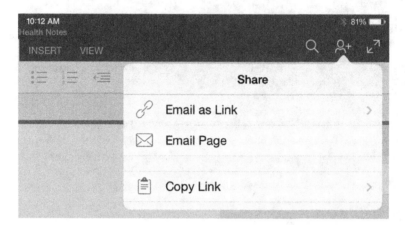

Figure 12-17. *To share the current notebook or e-mail the current page, open the Share pop-up panel and tap the appropriate button*

If you tap the Email as Link button or the Copy as Link button, the Email as Link pop-up panel (see Figure 12-18) or the Copy as Link pop-up panel appears. Tap the View Only button or the View and Edit button, as needed.

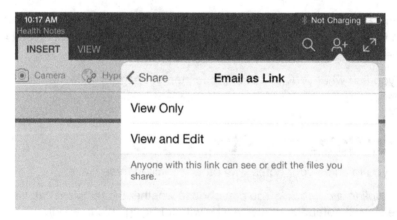

Figure 12-18. *To share the current notebook or e-mail the current page, open the Share pop-up panel and tap the appropriate button*

After you tap the View Only button or the View and Edit button on the Email as Link pop-up panel, Mail opens with the skeleton of an e-mail message created. Similarly, when you tap the Email Page button, Mail creates a new message with the page attached. Fill in the recipient, add any text needed, and then tap

Summary

In this chapter, you learned how to use OneNote on the iPad to collect data, organize it in the way you prefer, and share it among your computers and devices. You now know your way around OneNote's notebooks, sections, and pages; you know how to add pages and enter notes on them; and you can share your note pages and notebooks with others.

This is the end of the book. I hope it has helped you to get your work—or play—done with the Office for iPad apps. If you have suggestions for improving the book in future editions, do send them to the publisher.

Index

R

S

Get the eBook for only $10!

> Now you can take the weightless companion with you anywhere, anytime. Your purchase of this book entitles you to 3 electronic versions for only $10.

This Apress title will prove so indispensible that you'll want to carry it with you everywhere, which is why we are offering the eBook in 3 formats for only $10 if you have already purchased the print book.

Convenient and fully searchable, the PDF version enables you to easily find and copy code—or perform examples by quickly toggling between instructions and applications. The MOBI format is ideal for your Kindle, while the ePUB can be utilized on a variety of mobile devices.

Go to www.apress.com/promo/tendollars to purchase your companion eBook.